TRAVELERS' TALES

THE
ADVENTURE
OF FOOD

TRUE STORIES OF EATING EVERYTHING

TRAVELERS' TALES

THE
ADVENTURE
OF FOOD

TRUE STORIES OF EATING EVERYTHING

Edited by

RICHARD STERLING

Series Editors
JAMES O'REILLY AND LARRY HABEGGER

TRAVELERS' TALES
SAN FRANCISCO

The Adventure of Food: True Stories of Eating Everything
Edited by Richard Sterling

Copyright © 1999 Travelers' Tales, Inc. All rights reserved.

Travelers' Tales and *Travelers' Tales Guides* are trademarks of Travelers' Tales, Inc.

Credits and copyright notices for the individual articles in this collection are given starting on page 307.

We have made every effort to trace the ownership of all copyrighted material and to secure permission from copyright holders. In the event of any question arising as to the ownership of any material, we will be pleased to make the necessary correction in future printings. Contact Travelers' Tales Inc., 330 Townsend Street, Suite 208, San Francisco, California 94107.

Cover and interior design by Judy Anderson, Susan Bailey, and Kathryn Heflin
Cover photograph: Copyright © WORKBOOK CO/OP STOCK/Dorit Lombroso
Page Layout by Cynthia Lamb, using the fonts Bembo and Boulevard

Library of Congress Cataloging-in-Publication Data

The adventure of food: true stories of eating everything / edited by Richard
    Sterling. —1st ed.
        p.   cm. — (Travelers' Tales)
    Includes index.
    ISBN 1-885211-37-6
    1. Food—Anecdotes. 2. Travel—Anecdotes.   I. Sterling, Richard.
II. Series.
TX357.A38   1999
641.3—dc21   99-33282
                                                                        CIP

First Edition
Printed in the United States
10 9 8 7 6 5 4 3 2 1

In darkness, crocodiles offer us benedictions:
We have eaten of the world.
Molecules of chaos and chance
reign in our bodies.
You are cast in the river
to dwell in the transformation.

—HOLLY ST. JOHN BERGON

Table of Contents

Part Two
SOME THINGS TO DO

Part Three
GOING YOUR OWN WAY

Part Four
IN THE SHADOWS

Part Five
LAST WORD

The Adventure of Food: An Introduction

The great adventure of food begins in utero in the warm wash of maternal nourishment and ends with a last meal, a final sip of water, an ultimate taste on the tongue of the waning body. It's an adventure lived every waking moment whether we are aware of it or not, whether we care much for its implications or search out its delights, as do the writers and travelers in this collection.

The journey begun in *Travelers' Tales: Food* continues here: roving gastronomes and voracious travelers discover the world and its people through the medium of its universal constant: food (and other consumables). While on the great open road to Anywhere, all but the dullest palate can experience the fearsome need, the roaring passion, the lust, to consume the world. And in consuming it, to make it our own. To consume and assimilate the physical world is, of course, to make us one with it.

But in the thoughtful, curious and delightful pursuit of suste nance we are nourished spiritually as well. Witness Robert L. Strauss's "The Ceremony of One Chip," in which nibbling on one potato chip becomes an exercise in Zen meditation. And yes, as you will see, you can eat just one. In "The Last Meal," Michael Paterniti relives not only part of the life, but the death as well, of François Mitterand of France by recreating the president's last, gargantuan, and illegal feast of farewell to life. In "Eat, Drink, Man, Woman," Heather Corinna eats and drinks her way not to an end, but to a beginning, of an erotic tryst that we can fairly taste as we read. In other stories, such as Lisa Kremer's "Tibetan Cravings," vegetarians and people with a deep concern for the welfare of animals find that the feast of the road requires them to look at themselves in a larger context of human and animal experience and thus realign or reaffirm their precepts.

These, you see, are not just stories of eating, or drinking, or getting full, or getting high. These are stories of living, and loving, and dying, and of being renewed and restored. These are stories of those epiphanies great and small that occur when we venture out into the wide world, are introduced to the unexpected and forced to accommodate it. We are made to eat it. In the process, by the special alchemy of the road, we are returned as not quite the same traveler who erstwhile sallied forth. Jeffrey Tayler encounters the pain of post-Soviet Russia in a humble sausage. Jeffrey Steingarten learns that dieting is not in his karma. Taras Grescoe, in Spain, looks into the appeal and the darkness of absinthe. And Jennifer L. Leo, sans ruby slippers, finds that, maddeningly, there's no place like home.

Sometimes it's difficult to travel. You don't speak the language; the art museum leaves you confused; the popular resorts shouldn't be; the natives are restless. But gastronomic travel is accessible and satisfying to all who are willing to taste not only food and drink, but life as well. Renée Restivo will show you that the table is friendly territory, and Joseph Diedrich can humanize even a French waiter. Jack Lamb will show you that you don't even have to leave your own bailiwick to go on a culinary odyssey. Follow Frances Mayes on a perfectly delightful afternoon of simple grocery shopping in Tuscany, get high with Derek Peck on a mountain in Mexico, and contemplate it all with Jim Harrison in Paris. I urge you to use these writers as examples for your own travels. You'll find that, though the world continues to shrink, it's only in the dimensions of miles and hours. These stories will reveal to you a whole other dimension. A dimension limited only by the people in it, and their hungers.

—RICHARD STERLING

PART ONE

THE ESSENCE OF FOOD

LAURIE GOUGH

Breakfast in Fiji

Maybe civilization isn't all it's cracked up to be.

WHEN I WAKE TODAY THE SKY IS A BRIGHT ACHING BLUE, BLUE enough to stab through light. Clouds collect in wisps but don't mean anything. They swirl through the sky like thoughts through the mind, leaving nothing in their wake but memories of childhood days at the beach with sand castles and suntan lotion.

This morning, Laudi and I climb into the hills to what they call the plantation to collect the day's fruit for the family. Fruit falls all over the place. I trip over what I pay a lot of money for at home. The soil is rich; it's a volcanic island. By the time we get up to the plantation we're so baked by the heat we drink the water inside three whole green coconuts. Laudi chops the top off the coconut with his machete and we guzzle the liquid almost desperately. It slides down my throat like sweet wine until it spreads through every vein. After we're surging with liquid, Laudi carves a spoon from the coconut's top to be used for eating the soft white flesh inside. Eating the flesh is like biting into the solid life of the coconut water, slippery and sweet and sure of itself. This feast wouldn't be the same anywhere else. Only on a green island this saturated, in a forest where sweet decadence is deeply hidden, could this occur, this delicate ancient feast.

3

Laudi climbs the tallest coconut tree like a monkey. Every Fijian man can do this. Even Fijians with Ph.D.'s who dress in business suits and live in Suva can climb coconut trees. I can't think of a North American equivalent. Not every man in North American can fix an engine, nor can every woman make chocolate brownies. In Fiji, as in most of the non-Western world, gender roles are clearly defined. A man wouldn't be caught dead washing clothes, or chopping an onion, nor would a woman hunt wild boar or pound kava.

In the hills we collect basketfuls of juicy mandarins the size of grapefruit by climbing the trees to get them. Half of them we eat right there. To collect avocados we throw rocks at the tree until they fall down. We gather mini bananas, guavas, jackfruit, and cassava and find a luscious vine of passion fruit. It's too early for mango season. Inside this forest of fruit I start to feel like a ripe melon on a vine gushing and dripping heavy with sun. Laudi walks ahead of me. I love watching his calves, strong and warm brown in the sunlight. He's bushwhacking our way through this thick rain forest with his razor-edged long machete. All Fijians, even children, can swing a machete as if it were an extension of their arms. They walk barefoot almost everywhere, especially in the bush. Every day in countless ways they make use of the bush's virtues. We run out of baskets to carry the food back, so Laudi hacks off long reeds from a plant and weaves a new basket in two minutes. I feel so useless and ignorant of everything here. Too cerebral. They have control over their immediate world, know it intimately. When we walk back down to the beach, he asks about finding food in Canada. Where do I begin?

Laurie Gough is a writer, teacher, and traveler whose work has appeared in national newspapers, magazines, and in Travelers' Tales: A Woman's World. *She lives in Guelph, Ontario, but plans to move to northern California, where nature is big, majestic, and doesn't include winter. This story was excerpted from her book,* Kite Strings of the Southern Cross: A Woman's Travel Odyssey.

THOM ELKJER

✴

Seduction à la Carte

She was reading from a different menu.

I HAD FINISHED AN INTERVIEW IN THE BELGIAN CITY OF GENT, and was staying the night at a small hotel in the center of town. It was nearly nine o'clock when I checked in, and the friendly young woman at the front dusk asked if I was in town on business. When I told her my business was finished for the day she frowned at the clock. "Not until ten-thirty for me," she said. We chatted a while and she seemed very nice, so I asked her where I might get a bite to eat. She thought for a minute, then directed me to a place within walking distance. I dropped my suitcase in my room and headed out for dinner.

Half an hour later, I was back at the hotel desk. I explained to the woman that the restaurant was fully booked and asked for another recommendation. She apologized, pulled the combs from her auburn hair, and swept it over her shoulder as she explained the route to another nearby café. "Tell them Marianne sent you," she told me. Twenty minutes later, I was back in the hotel again. The owners of the café, it appeared, had gone away on vacation the day before.

Marianne put her hand on my arm and apologized even more warmly. "Usually I can find a man his dinner the first time," she said in her charmingly accented English. Her eyes, I noticed, were a lovely shade of golden green. The third place she recommended was closing its doors as I arrived. My stomach growled angrily, and I feared I would never get dinner at all. Then it dawned on me that I had been sent on a wild goose chase for more than an hour. By the time I got back to the hotel, it would be…ten-thirty. When I walked in the door, Marianne was waiting for me in the lobby. Her lipstick was fresh, her hair was brushed, and her purse was tucked under her arm. "I just finished work," she said, "but I cannot allow a guest of the hotel to go without his dinner. You will come home with me and I will give you the finest meal you will get in Gent."

We never did eat, unless you count the croissant and coffee she brought me before taking me to my train the next morning. Food is a powerful aphrodisiac, whether you get around to eating it or not.

Thom Elkjer is a novelist and freelance journalist. He and his suitcase live in San Rafael, California.

LARA NAAMAN

Cat Fight *Cachapas*

Think twice before you insult the cook.

LATINS ARE REPUTED TO BE A HOT-TEMPERED PEOPLE. MAYBE Hollywood created the stereotype with all those frontier cantina brawl scenes. Maybe the Colombians added to it by killing the soccer player who cost them the World Cup one year. Add to the list traditions like bullfighting and movies like *Scarface*.

"It's the chile peppers," Rogelio, the owner of my favorite Mexican restaurant, once explained, "They put hair on your chest and heat in your blood." But the most brutal fight I ever saw in South America involved a very un-spicy food called *cachapa* and two un-hairy-chested women.

I was spending the night in Cumana, Venezuela. I had checked myself into a bottom-end hotel and headed out to the street for dinner. As luck would have it, there was a *cachapa* stand right outside. *Cachapas* are large, sweet, corn pancakes wrapped around a mild, salty, white cheese. They are plain, but make a tasty and filling meal.

I ordered one from the lady at the stand. She ladled the bubbling corn mixture from a large vat onto the griddle to fry and began slicing pieces of cheese with a large knife. I was sitting there in happy anticipation of dinner when the *cachapa* lady suddenly raised the cheese knife above her head and hurled it towards the door of my hotel. *"Tu! Puta! Sal de aqui!"* she yelled. Get out of here you whore!

My gaze followed the flight of the cheese machete to see who might be the object of this invective. Crouched in the doorway, with her arms raised as a shield against flying cutlery, was a young woman in a tight white skirt and matching tube top. The black thong underwear showing through the skirt indicated that *"Puta"* was more than just an insult, it was probably her profession. She stood up and retorted, in a less-than-masterful display of argumentative rhetoric, "You're the whore!"

My *cachapa* lady, somewhat saggy and wrinkled in a pink teddy-bear t-shirt, looked more grandmotherly than whorish. Her response was to grab the next available weapon—a rolling pin—and yell, "How dare you show your face here after you slept with my husband!" It was turning into dinner theater. And I figured it was the wrong point in the plot to point out that my *cachapa* was burning.

The prostitute had recovered enough from the surprise attack to deliver her own verbal onslaught. "You're an old whore and a terrible cook!"

This was the equivalent of insulting someone's mother in all those L.A. gang movies. A sudden tense hush fell over the small crowd of onlookers.

"I'll show you cooking you little slut!" yelled Grandma Cachapa. She grabbed my burned food straight off the grill and pelted the prostitute with chunks of the charred corn patty, reloading with raw ammunition from the vat when that ran out.

Now, it was all fun and games until my dinner got involved. I was about to say so until the prostitute came running at Granny with the cheese knife in her hand. Three of the men at the food stall sprung into action at this point, figuring blood doesn't do much for the flavor of *cachapas*.

There were a few moments of scuffling while two men restrained the combatants and the third pried loose all the battle weapons. "For the love of God!" cried the disarmament specialist, wielding the recovered rolling pin and cheese knife exasperatedly. "People are trying to eat in peace!"

Grandma Cachapa took a deep breath and freed one hand to cross herself. The prostitute broke down into sobs. Both were coated with gloppy *cachapa* batter.

"But she attacked me," the prostitute protested tearfully to her captor. His grip of restraint turned into a consoling embrace. "There, there," he comforted her, picking pieces of my meal out of her hair. "You just shouldn't have said she was a bad cook. That was very disrespectful."

Nobody mentioned the disrespect involved with the prostitute's adultery or, more importantly, the mutilation of my dinner-to-be.

The prostitute then picked herself up and went back inside the hotel to clean up for work. Grandma Cachapa fumed in hushed tones with one of the other onlookers. I went to look for a nice boring restaurant with male waiters and dull cutlery.

After studying the street food of South America for a year, Lara Naaman returned to Houston, Texas, with 100 recipes, a case of tapeworm, and a well-cultivated Latin temper. If you know what's good for you, you won't mess with her mother, her man, or her lunch.

DAVID ROBINSON

The First Supper

The "dark continent" is filled with light.

WHEN THE GAS STATION ATTENDANT WIPED MY FORK ON HIS greasy rag, I realized I had crossed an invisible boundary. This was my first day in Nigeria, and my friend and I were looking for some place to eat. We had just come from Ghana on a minibus full of African students and had been forced to sleep on the ground at the Benin border because the guard had gone home for the night. In the morning, after we were let in to Nigeria, the bus dropped us in the center of Lagos, and we began to explore the city on foot.

Lagos is a cauldron, a steamy, smelly, hot stew. People fill the crowded streets, moving much faster than the cars that are stuck in irregular lanes each jousting for some advantage where none is to be had. Car horns and radios blare constantly, people shout to be heard. Almost everyone is carrying something, usually on their heads, kicking up dust as they move along. The paved streets are flanked by dirt paths and lined with open sewers covered only with slotted slabs which do not pretend to contain the odor of waste and rotting garbage. Our eyes sting, and we are the object of curiosity and comment to everyone. Two Europeans walking through Lagos is not a common sight. Children shout and sometimes dare to run up to us. Adults stop whatever they are doing to stare. But no one in Lagos seems to stop for very long; we are small pebbles making tiny ripples in their big pond.

The heat and smell and noise begin to wear on us, especially after our bad night at the border. We have been given the address of a small, inexpensive hotel of a class somewhere in the divide between African and European styles of lodging. But we are getting hungry and decide we should eat before confronting what promises to be another night of dubious comfort.

We carry provisions with us. We have for tonight's menu tins of corned beef and applesauce, not as bad as it sounds, a tasteful and safe combination but one that is much better if mixed with rice. So, the task is to find some rice, something we are confident will be possible. But we see no restaurants, and it's hard to recognize the local places that prepare and sell food. So, we do what is natural for Americans to do; we go into a gas station to enquire where we might find some cooked rice.

"Wait," says the attendant, a young boy, who immediately disappears. He returns quickly and repeats the same caution to us: "Wait." A car pulls in, and he rushes over to pump a couple of liters for which he accepts a single folded note. Afterward, he takes the rag hanging from his pocket, lifts the hood to check the oil and then washes the windshield. Although the operation is entirely familiar, the local idiosyncrasies of the performance fascinate us. While we watch them, the people in the car blankly stare back at us.

After the car pulls out, the attendant brings out from behind the station house one chair and one stool and says simply, "Sit." Obedient, we now both sit and wait on the station tarmac not far from the gas pumps. As we look around, we can see that the gas station is gleaming white in contrast to the dull mud walls and rusting tin roofs of the surrounding buildings. It is brightly lit by long fluorescent lights whereas the other buildings have single bare bulbs if any light at all. The gas station, for us, is an oasis.

From inside the station, the attendant produces a rickety wooden table stained with grease and seriously off kilter. "Wait," he says again. By now, it is dawning on us that it is his intention to serve us, and sure enough, in a minute or two he returns with two bowls of steaming rice and puts them on the table for us. At that moment, another car pulls in for gas, and he hurries over to it to perform the usual ablutions. In the meantime, we open our tins but realize we have brought no utensils or glasses with us. In an instant, our host sees our predicament and runs into the station house to forage.

To our amazement, he returns with forks, knives and glasses. He is as efficient and solicitous with us as he would be with any car that pulled into his station. In order to do things properly for us, he takes the rag from his pocket and vigorously wipes both the utensils and glasses. He brings us two orange Fantas, and we pour.

The gas station is getting busier now, and more cars pull in past us to the pumps. All heads are turned in our direction, and there now is much comment about two white men sitting on the gas station tarmac eating.

But the rice is good and the meal is satisfying. Who needs snotty elegance anyhow?

Any concerns I might have had about germs, cleanliness, propriety and whatever else had been drummed into me as an American have slipped far behind me. I am in a new territory now, living a new life and developing new repertoires. Although I am conscious of being an actor on an impromptu stage, I am totally relaxed in this bright oasis right in the middle of Lagos. After we are done eating, we try to pay for the rice and the Fanta if not for the table and service, but the attendant will have none of it. We are guests in his country, and I know I have arrived.

David Robinson is a photographer who spent four years in West Africa, first as a student at the University of Ghana and then as a teacher in Nigeria. He began photographing in Africa and since has published six books of his photographs plus numerous articles on photography and travel. His two most recent books are on European cemeteries: Saving Graces *and* Beautiful Death. *He and his wife live in Mill Valley, California.*

FREDDA ROSEN

Pizza Love

When the moon hits your eye like
a big pizza pie that's amore!

WHEN IT COMES TO TRAVEL, I LONG FOR ROMANCE. I DREAM OF
evenings in Paris and the Marrakech Express. I always thought I'd
take a Roman holiday…but I never figured on a weekend in
Dubuque, Iowa.

A small Midwestern city known only for little old ladies never
would have appeared on my itinerary had I not married a man
who went to college there. John told me about Dubuque on our
first date…after I told him about my trips to India, Nepal, and the
Yucatán.

"Of course, you'll never want to go back there to visit," I said,
taking care to phrase a statement of fact.

"I'd go for the pizza," he said. "Best pizza I ever had was at
Marco's in Dubuque." I thought he was daft, but cute, and since we
lived in New York City, where four-star pizza is as commonplace
as heavy traffic, I figured we could live happily ever after with no
more talk of Dubuque.

I was wrong. Every time I asked John, "Where do you want to
go to dinner tonight?" he said, "Marco's in Dubuque."

I tried to tempt his palate with home-style pizza made by moms
and pops in the far corners of the city's outer boroughs, and with

13

gutsy Manhattan street corner pies. We sampled pizza with exotic vegetables and rare mushrooms fashioned by chefs of international renown, but John still said, "Dubuque," when we discussed plans for dinner.

I had no choice. When it was time to celebrate his fiftieth birthday, I put aside fantasies of a sojourn *a deux* in Tuscany or Madeira to plan a surprise trip to Dubuque. John couldn't bear the thought of putting yet another decade behind him. I would help him ease the trauma with the comfort food of his youth.

My travel agent was not impressed with the plan. "You must be joking," she said. "What about some little Caribbean hideaway? Or how about the California coast? I'll get you a place with spectacular views."

I assured her my sense of humor had nothing to do with the trip, though I thought she was joking when she quoted the airfares.

"We could fly to London for that," I said.

"I rest my case," she said. "But it's your choice."

I thought about Harrod's, the Victoria and Albert, and long walks in Hyde Park, but I said, "Book the flight to Dubuque."

I had her arrange the flights so we would be in Iowa for just 24 hours. "Even that's too long," I told her.

Since she couldn't recommend a hotel, I called Marco's. The young man who answered the phone was shocked to hear about my plans.

"I thought they had good pizza in New York," he said.

"I did, too," I said.

"Long way to go for pizza," he said and recommended the Holiday Inn.

My next call was to John's boss, to see if John could get time off for the trip.

"Why do you want to go to Topeka, anyhow?" his boss asked.

"Dubuque," I said, and explained.

"My wife took me to Hawaii for my fiftieth," he said.

"Your wife is a lucky woman," I said.

"No problem with the time off," he said. "Have a good time in Omaha."

I got off the phone with a sigh. If only John had gone to Berkeley, I could be heading to California to dine at Chez Panisse. If he'd taken a junior year abroad, I might be planning a four-star birthday using the Michelin guide. Instead I was going to territory unknown to Fodor, Frommer, and Condé Nast. The discriminating traveler, I was sure, would find no stars in Dubuque.

"At least it's just for a day," I told my sympathetic friends.

I thought I couldn't become less enthusiastic about the trip until the day before our departure, when I learned that a record-breaking snow storm was due to touch down in New York around the time our plane was scheduled to leave. The airline advised me to change my tickets and take a 6 A.M. flight. Now I was not only going to Dubuque, I would have to rise before dawn to get there.

I took consolation in fantasy: I imagined the look on John's face when I told him about his birthday dinner, the way he'd hug me, his whoops of delight. I decided to tell him about the trip immediately, instead of waiting until morning as I'd planned.

I called him at work. "Meet me in the lobby in fifteen minutes," I said. "I have something to tell you."

I dashed out of my office and nearly skipped across town to meet him, replaying the fantasies along the way.

"What's up?" he asked when he saw me.

"It's about our dinner plans for tomorrow night," I told him. I watched him closely.

"What dinner plans?" he asked. "I have to work tomorrow."

"We have reservations at Marco's," I said. I was delighted to see that he looked puzzled.

"What are you talking about?"

Now came my big moment. I showed him the airline tickets. While he studied them, I shifted from one foot to the other, waiting for the hugs and whoops.

Finally he said, "You could have just had it sent Federal Express."

"Huh?"

"Maybe Marco's could have sent the pizza. You know, overnight mail. I wouldn't have minded if it was cold. I just occasionally get a hankering for their pizza. I really don't want to spend any time in Dubuque. It's pretty dull."

He didn't want to go either! I was left with a reluctant travel companion and two non-refundable tickets. I explained to John why we would be picking up the pizza ourselves, and consoled him by saying, "It's only for twenty-four hours."

The next morning, while plump snowflakes busily swirled around us, we took off. It was snowing with fury in Chicago, where we had to change planes. The airline employee who bussed us out to our plane had to take several turns around the runway before she could find the right one, a subcompact suitable for use as a crop duster. As we boarded the craft by stairs that shook in the wind, John said, "I wasn't dying to go to Dubuque, if you know what I mean."

"I do," I said.

Our captain had good news for us. "It's not snowing in Dubuque," he announced soon after we were aloft. Then came the clinker: "Local temperature is five degrees. The wind chill makes it feel like ten below."

We were greeted by a display in the terminal that bid us to "Discover Dubuque!" I sniffed. Surely even Columbus would have turned back if he'd stumbled upon *this* burg.

But I was surprised when we arrived at the hotel. What it lacked in charm, it made up with its swimming pool, exercise room, and proximity to the banks of the Mississippi.

Up in the room, John thumbed through the phone book. I noted a few smiles escaping his lips, then some outright grins. "It's still here!" he kept shouting. The restaurants and shops he remembered from his college years were still in business. "C'mon," he said, "I'll show you Dubuque."

I stifled the urge to suggest we spend the afternoon in front of the heat vent, and let John lead me out into the stinging cold.

"They used to say that Dubuque was like Rome," he said. "A city with seven hills."

I rolled my eyes. But as we walked, I looked around. Graceful Victorian-era houses perched on the bluff above us. John showed me how he used to negotiate the hills, on the Fourth Street elevator, a one-car railway with almost vertical tracks, now open only for tourists in the summer.

"Well, I must admit, I've never seen anything like that," I said.

We had lunch at the Maidright Cafe, where the hamburgers were square and spiked with barbecue sauce and onions. I told the waitress they tasted like the sloppy joes I remembered from my Ohio childhood.

"We're better than sloppy joes," she said.

For dessert we went to Betty Jane's Homemade Candies, where we were greeted by white-aproned clerks and the smell of simmering chocolate. Then we strolled along Main Street, past dress and florist shops, a store that sold religious articles, and a billiard hall. Despite the new pedestrian mall, Dubuque looked like the all-American town, circa 1955.

We wound up the afternoon at the Redstone Inn, a sprawling, turn-of-the-century, red-brick house, now a bed and breakfast, where we sipped tea in an antique-filled drawing room and basked in the sunshine that streamed in through the delicate lace curtains.

That night at Marco's, John was greeted by a waitress who remembered him from 30 years ago—when he could down a large pie without concern for his midsection. He ordered his usual: a large pizza with sausage. The waitress presented it with a flourish, and the rich smells of Italian home cooking settled around our table. I snapped a photo as John took his first bite.

I waited to see his reaction, but he merely smiled and took another bite, so I tried the fabled pie myself. The sauce lacked punch, but the crust was cracker crisp, and the homemade sausage lively with pepper and fennel. The pizza was carpeted with high-quality mozzarella that dripped from my slice.

With my second bite, I fell in love. It may have been the pizza, or maybe it was the candles, the friendly waitress, and the neon signs over the bar—or whatever it was that made Marco's look just like the old-fashioned, hometown restaurant it was. It wasn't anything akin to New York's *trattorias* or bistros, its four-star culinary temples, or even its neighborhood coffee shops.

In some ways, eating at Marco's was as foreign to me as dining on street food in Bangkok, and Dubuque was as exotic as Nairobi, Prague, or Istanbul. I'd forgotten that travel is itself romantic, and that, to the traveler, even the most ordinary destination can feel faraway.

John reached across the table and took my hand. "Thanks for bringing me here," he said. He smiled in a way that gave me more than the whoops of delight I had craved.

"I've got an idea," he said. "Let's see if we can change our flight back."

Twenty-four hours weren't enough. I'd just discovered Dubuque.

Fredda Rosen is a New York City-based freelance writer and a previous Travelers' Tales contributor who frequently writes about travel and food. Her articles and reviews have appeared in Cosmopolitan, The Washington Post, *and many other U.S. newspapers and magazines.*

KELLY SIMON

Doing Rumours

*A lone traveler discovers one thing
is always on the menu.*

THE IZMIR PALAS IS HARDLY THAT. IT'S A BUSINESSMAN'S HOTEL that gives promise of hot water. Other than me, there's not a single woman in sight. Good women (it seems there are no other kind in Islam) disappear into their homes at nightfall and never appear in public unescorted, especially women over fifty, like me.

I ask for a seaview room. The clerk narrows his eyes at my Western clothes —rumpled pants the worse for wear after the five-hour bus trip from Istanbul. A sea-view room will set me back an additional 17,000 lira, he cautions, tearing his eyes away from my sandals, whose perforations reveal bare skin. I wave my hand in a last-of-the-big-time-spenders gesture to indicate that $1.83 is no object.

The room is spartan and straightforward—the pistachio-colored walls I have grown used to after a week in Turkey, the monastic single bed draped with a white cotton spread, the granite floors. Taped to the mirror, a placard urging guests to "avoid dirting and doing rumours in the room."

I open the window and breathe in the briny air. Below me, the Aegean laps against the seawall. Through the laces of a blue awning, I see the lights of a cafe whose damasked tables spill along the quai.

Music trickles upward through the balmy night. I shower off the grime of the bus trip in tepid water, change my clothes and hurry downstairs, praying that the restaurant won't close before I get there.

Only one other table is occupied at that hour. A moustachioed business man and three cronies sit around an overflowing ashtray and a half-empty bottle of *raki,* the local liquor. A pall of blue smoke hangs over their table. They stop talking and follow me with hungry eyes as I walk to the opposite side of the room. From among such mysteries as Steamed Fish with Butterfried, Samlet with a Bunch of Custards, Two Yellow Yolks on a Sword, and Crushed Spinach, I order fried eggplant with yoghurt and grilled lamb kidneys. "*Finis,*" says the waiter of the lamb kidneys. Disappointed, but accustomed by now to menu as hyperbole, I order, instead, Mussels à la Maitre d' Hotel, translated on the menu as Metro Hotel's Mussels, plus a self-congratulatory *raki* and water—I have survived the first leg of my trip alone! The moustachioed businessman tries to make eye contact with me and I look away—directly into the hot eyes of the cook who is sizing me up from behind the glass refrigerator case.

I sip my *raki* trying to look chaste, feigning absorption in a bus schedule. (Good women in Turkey don't drink spirits.) The potent anise-flavored liquid nips my tongue and warms my throat. When I have just about polished off the last of it, the cook comes rushing out of the kitchen elbowing past the avuncular waiter, whose face darkens. With a sweep of his arm and a flourish of a napkin, he sets a silver salver on the table before me and slowly, theatrically, raises the domed lid. On the platter are two perfectly grilled lamb kidneys, charred on the outside, oozing rosy juices. With his hands clasped to his bosom as if he has just presented me with the treasures of the Ottoman Empire, he stands at my elbow, waiting for me to take the first bite.

"*Çok iyi,*" I say, in my best Berlitz Turkish, making a thumbs up gesture. And, indeed, the kidneys are moist, and pink, flecked with rosemary and thyme, hinting of garlic, each crisped by a thin veil of suet. The cook beams and rushes back to his post behind the refrigerator case, watching me steadfastly as I eat.

When I finish the kidneys, the waiter brings the rest of my meal. The eggplant, drizzled with tangy yoghurt and bathed in pale green olive oil is buttery and soothing, the orange mussels are plump as eggs and fragrant with fresh herbs. The air is a warm bath and a sigh of a breeze stirs the awning overhead. Halyards tinkle against masts. The tide every now and then spills onto the mosaic esplanade with a flash of white spume.

"You like our *raki?*" the waiter asks solicitously. I nod, grateful for his platonic concern. Being a sex object after all these years is no bed of roses. It requires constant vigilance. I know it's not my glamor that draws these flies to my honey, it's my availability. Like Everest to Mallory, they want to climb me because I'm here. The waiter returns with a tumbler of *raki* filled to the brim. "*Gratis,*" he says, lowering his eyes. He removes a shiny red apple from his pocket and polishes it, in some slow, deliberate ritual, on his pants leg. Then he leans forward and places it in the exact center of my dessert plate as if setting a Topkapi jewel. "I finis' working ten o'clock," he whispers.

When I stand to leave, I spy the cook outside, leaning against a streetlamp, arms folded over his bloody apron, waiting for me. I duck out the back door into the night and walk the unlighted backstreets that feel less threatening than the alternative.

When I think the cook's ardor has waned, I go back to the hotel. The lobby is brightly lit and cozy. I sit in an overstuffed chair and watch the late news on television with a gold-toothed man who sucks his teeth loudly, the hotel manager's wife and children, and the hotel manager who tsk's at each news bite. I feel relaxed and comfortable. That is, until I look up and see the cook, now gussied up in a stiff white shirt and flowered necktie, watching me from under the overhang.

I bid the manager's family goodnight and go to reception to get my key. A sign over the desk reads, "Travellers who leave the hotel are bagged to advise Management till thirteen hrs." The moustachioed businessman from the restaurant stands beneath the sign watching me approach. His elbow, which rests on the reception desk, is crooked around a highball glass. He leans toward me unsteadily, presenting me with a nosegay of violet capillaries and peach-pit pores.

"Excuse me, Madame, you travel alone?"

"My husband is in Istanbul," I lie, pointing to my bogus wedding ring. "He'll be arriving tomorrow."

His damp lips part to reveal discolored teeth. "Please to have a drink my guest."

"Thank you, but I really must get some work done," I say, and go upstairs.

I sit on the balcony of my room, bare feet on the rail. Music drifts across the water through the still night. Below, a watchman's dinghy cuts through the bay, the oarsman's shirt luminous in the darkness. He makes his rounds, circling the boats, then, responding to a low whistle, heads toward the pier to pick up a passenger.

I take the apple from my pocket and bite into it. The sound, I think, must carry for miles. When I finish, I lean over the railing and loft the core as high and as far as I can over the awning of the restaurant below, tracking its end-over-end arc, waiting for the small column of spume to break the surface of the sea.

Kelly Simon's work has appeared in The Washington Post, The Quarterly, Ploughshares, The Norton Anthology, *NPR and elsewhere. She has traveled for many years and is currently at work on a series of stories about the darker side of travel. She is the author of* Thai Cooking *and has just completed a memoir entitled,* The Day We Put On Clothes.

HEATHER CORINNA

* * *

Eat, Drink, Man, Woman

Nourishment is a many-splendored thing.

I COULD MAKE A MEAL OF HIM, ONE SAYS. SHE IS GOOD ENOUGH
to eat, a feast for the eyes, I can almost taste him. More often than
not, I have mingled that taste with perhaps an acid shot of tequila,
a post-bliss peanut butter and jelly sandwich, an early morning cup
of coffee almost as warm as the body under the sheets beside me
was. More often than not, the city I am in vanishes, shifts when my
senses take the helm. More often than not, "food" is simply not an
apt description for what I take in with my mouth, and where my
mouth takes me.

He is new to me, this one, this time, and the taste of him. A day
has passed between lapping his skin with my tongue, and the new-
ness lingered freshly in my mouth. We sit across a white-spread
table, in a restaurant as new to me as he is, vacant for the night. He,
by trade, is as much experienced in the intimately different tastes
of one actual meal or another as I am in the infinitely different
tastes of one proverbial meal or another.

A wide-mouth glass is set on the table, with liquid within as
thick as molasses, but clear as water, a single bean suspended in it
mysteriously. Set to my lips, the scent of anise filled my nostrils,
attached itself to his eyes, watching a full mouth balance a drop of

23

syrupy liquor. There is, in Chicago, where I live, a sweets factory, deep in the industrial section of the city. As I drive through the area from time to time, I will think, in the frazzled way that I do, of a thousand things: bills that need paying, jobs that need doing, flat tires, and poems I can't finish. I will do this until I drive exactly one block past the sweets factory, and at that moment, none of these things exist. There exists only the sweet, overwhelming incense of anise and coffee and roasting chocolate, more evocative of sweaty sheets and midnight tangos than overdue bills and old factories.

This is no glass in my hands, this is skin. This is not liquor, but is longing I drink in.

The silver of tableware jingles, set down. A plate is delivered: rich swirls of tomato lingering round steaming mussels, shells coal grey and smoking. Cilantro tickles my nose, transports me to a sunset years back, in Mexico, on the coast, where my blue eyes and fair skin won me a free bottle of poison nightly, a smile appeared everywhere I turned, even in places my fair skin was sunburned. His fingers open the shells with deft grace, nimble soft fingers as strong as both my hands held together. The fork is cold on my mouth and the meat of the mussel on it slippery and smooth. His lips were like that, cool and hot all at once, smooth to slide on and easy to swallow.

This is no sea treasure on my lips, this is a kiss. This is no appetizer, but remembered and impending bliss.

The table is clean again, the vaguest spots of drizzled sauce hide amidst the slightest crinkles, folds. Silver bowls arrive, chairs are moved closer. Frost confuses itself with steam, making fog on the shimmer and sheen of the metal dish. Inside, a spoon teases a glacier of gold, capped with red berries cold on the icy peak of the sorbet. It is as frigid and as rocky as the cliffs were the night I spent in Lands End in England, aptly named, when I felt the wind rip at me and still stood, tangled in my hair, delirious with the possibility of being pulled over those desolate cliffs and into the icy, mermaid-infested waters below. The wind was a siren song saying, "Go." The long sloping fall of his nose and those hollow cheeks

rise cool above the frost of this second course, above the south end
rocks of Lands End. I remember that face, coiled back like a snake,
mouth closed tight, as tight as it clasps around the spoon, swallowing harder than at this moment, and not near as quiet.

This is no intermediary cleansing of the palate, this is delight.
This is no frozen berried ice, this is a ghost of last night.

Plates juggled again, a black sea bass arrives on a bed of peppers
green and dandelion yellow, slivers of reddest tomato, paper-thin
slices of almonds rolling a finger around and around the steaming
flesh. Once, as a child, in the hot valley in California, I was determined to see if, indeed, the sidewalk was hot enough to fry an egg
upon. It was hot enough to sear the tender bottoms of my feet so
that I had to sit on the grass to watch. I watched, slowly, as the soft
albumen sat and began to simmer, yolk staring at me like a lost eye.
And I watch you watch me slide forkfuls into my mouth, humming with delight, touching my tongue to try and add to one
sense and inflict them all upon me. I watch as you watch like you'd
watched the night previous, slipping my fingers in and licking
them off one by one, tasting the two of us mingled, after we'd
come undone.

This is no supper, this is seduction. This is no feast, but the
vaguest reflection.

Table cleared, the tray of sweets is held out for observation. The
richest of chocolate cakes makes a place for itself before me, a fork
sets itself to my lips, the scent of the chocolate infuses with the
scent of the hand offering it. My eyes close automatically: any sense
more than taste is too much when my mouth is filled with such a
sweetness, such overbearing richness I can feel melt unto my
tongue. I am not in Chicago, I have been transported. My grandmother, whose face, shining, is the only thing of her I truly remember besides her sweet alto voice, sits at her kitchen table, a tall
window overlooks the streets of Venice. Her fork is filled with the
same chocolate mine is, and the air is heady with chocolate and
her strong espresso. With the sweetness in her mouth, she is not in
Venice. She is not in a kitchen alone, plagued with an unhappy
marriage and a war-torn country. She is in a restaurant in Chicago,

where a man with the face of an angel sets his fork to her lips and feeds her spoonfuls of rich chocolate cake.

His eyes are as bright as stars, and the scent of him overrides the scent of chocolate, cilantro, anise, peppers, or bass. She looks to the empty plate with a soft smile, knowing the feasting here is done. Knowing there remains a feast to be had, in another place, in another time, that has not yet begun.

This is no finale, this is only a prelude. We describe so very little of what we feast upon when we merely call it food.

Heather Corinna is a writer, poet, musician, and artist who lives in Chicago, Illinois. She is a primitive sensualist at heart who loves to savor every passing scent, sight, and flavor, yet tries to stay pragmatic enough to avoid oncoming traffic.

MICHAEL PATERNITI

∗ ∗ ∗

The Last Meal

An imperial appetite knows no bounds.

THE NIGHT BEFORE THE LAST MEAL, I VISIT A STONE CHURCH where mass is being said. In the back row, a retarded boy sits with his mother, his head tilting heavenward, watching, in an unfocused way, the trapped birds that flutter and spin in the height of the church vault. About a hundred yards away, in the immense holy hangar, tulips bloom on the altar. It's the end of December—gray has fallen over Paris—and the tulips are lurid-red, gathered in four vases, two to a side. A priest stands among them and raises his arms as if to fly.

Last I remember, I was on a plane, in a cab, in a hotel room— fluish, jet-lagged, snoozing. Then, by some Ouija force, some coincidence of foot on cobblestone, I came to a huge wrought-iron door. What brought me to France in the first place was a story I'd heard about François Mitterrand, the former French president, who had gorged himself on one last orgiastic feast before he'd died. For his last meal, he'd eaten oysters and foie gras and capon—all in copious quantities—the succulent, tender, sweet tastes flooding his parched mouth. And then there was the meal's ultimate course: a small, yellow-throated songbird that was illegal to eat. Rare and seductive, the bird—ortolan—supposedly represented the French soul. And this old man, this ravenous president, had taken it whole—wings, feet, liver, heart. Swallowed it, bones and all. Consumed it beneath a white cloth so that God Himself couldn't witness the barbaric act.

I wondered then what a soul might taste like.

Now I find myself standing among clusters of sinners, all of them lined in pews, their repentant heads bent like serious hens. When the priest's quavery monotone comes from a staticky speaker, cutting the damp cold, it is full of tulips and birds.

Somewhere, a long time ago, religion let me down. And somehow, on this night before the last meal, before I don a white hood, I've ended up here, reliving the Last Meal, passing my hand unconsciously from my forehead to my heart to either shoulder—no— yes, astonishingly pantomiming the pantomime of blessing myself.

Why?

When it comes time for communion, why do I find myself floating up the aisle? Why, after more than a decade, do I offer my tongue with the joy of a boggled dog and accept His supposed body, the tasteless paper wafer, from the priest's notched, furry fingers? Why do I sip His supposed blood, the same blood that leaves a psychedelic stain on the white cloth that the priest uses to wipe my lip? Why am I suddenly this giddy Christ cannibal?

At the end of mass, the priest raises his arms again—and the retarded boy suddenly raises his, too, and we are released.

Then I find the hotel again. I lie awake until dawn. Fighting down my hunger.

That's what I do the night before the last meal.

On his good days, the president imagined there was a lemon in his gut; on bad days, an overripe grapefruit, spilling its juices. He had reduced his affliction—cancer—to a problem of citrus. Big citrus and little citrus. The metaphor was comforting, for at least his body was a place where things still grew.

And yet, each passing day subtracted more substance, brought up the points of his skeleton against the pale, bluish skin. He spent much of his waking hours remembering his life—the white river that ran through his home-town of Jarnac, the purple shadows of the womblike childhood attic where he had delivered speeches to a roomful of cornhusks. He sat, robed and blanketed now, studying how great men of ancient civilizations had left the earth, their final gestures in the space between life and death. Seneca and Hannibal went out as beautiful, swan-dive suicides; even the comical, licentious Nero fell gloriously on his own sword.

Yes, the gesture was everything. Important to go with dignity, to control your fate, not like the sad poet Aeschylus, who died when an eagle, looking to crack the shell of a tortoise in his beak, mistook his bald head for a rock. Or the Chinese poet Li Po, who drowned trying to embrace the full moon on the water's surface. Yes, the gesture was immortal. It would be insufferable to go out like a clown.

So what gesture would suit him? The president was a strange, contradictory man. Even at the height of his powers, he often seemed laconic and dreamy, more like a librarian than a world leader, with a strong, papal nose, glittering, beady eyes, and ears like the halved cap of a portobello mushroom. He valued loyalty, then wrathfully sacked his most devoted lieutenants. He railed against the corruptions of money, though his fourteen-year reign was shot through with financial scandals. A close friend, caught in the double-dealing, killed himself out of apparent disgust for the president's style of government. "Money and death," the friend angrily said shortly before the end. "That's all that interests him anymore."

And yet as others fell, the president survived—by tricks of agility and acumen, patrician charm and warthog ferocity. Now this last intruder hulked toward him. He shuffled with a cane, stooped and frosted silver like a gnarled tree in a wintry place. It took him an eternity to accomplish the most minor things: buttoning a shirt, bathing, walking the neighborhood, a simple crap.

And what would become of the universe he'd created? What would become of his citizens? And then his children and grandchildren, his wife and mistress? Was this the fate of all aged leaders when they were stripped of their magic: to sit like vegetables, shrivel-dicked, surrounded by photographs and tokens of appreciation, by knickknacks and artifacts?

When he slept, he dreamed of living. When he ate, he ate the foods he would miss. But even then, somewhere in his mind, he began to prepare his ceremony *des adieux.*

I'm going to tell you what happened next—the day of the last meal—for everything during this time in December shaped itself around the specter of eating the meal.

That morning, I pick up my girlfriend, Sara, at Orly Airport. I've prevailed on her to come, as any meal shared around a table— the life lived inside each course—is only as good as the intimacies among people there. Through customs, she's alive with the first adrenaline rush of landing in a new country. But then, as we begin driving southwest toward the coast and Bordeaux, she falls fast asleep. It's gray and raining, and ocean wind sweeps inland and lashes the car. The trees have been scoured lifeless. Little men in little caps drive by our windows, undoubtedly hoarding bags of cheese in their little cars. And then a huge nuclear power plant looms on the horizon, its cooling towers billowing thick, moiling clouds over a lone cow grazing in a fallow pasture.

There is something in the French countryside, with its flat, any-time light, that demands melancholy. And I wonder what it means to knowingly eat a last meal. It means knowing you're going to die, right? It means that you've been living under a long-held delusion that the world is infinite and you are immortal. So it means saying sayonara to everything, including the delusions that sustain you, at the same time that you've gained a deeper feeling about those delusions and how you might have lived with more passion and love and generosity.

And then the most difficult part: you must imagine yourself as a memory, laid out and naked and no longer yourself, no longer you, the remarkable Someone who chose a last meal. Rather, you're just a body full of that meal. So you have to imagine your-self gone—first as a pale figure in the basement of a funeral home, then as the lead in a eulogy about how remarkable you were, and then as a bunch of photographs and stories.

And that's when you must imagine one more time what you most need to eat, what last taste must rise to meet your hunger and thirst and linger awhile on your tongue even as, before dessert, you're lowered into the grave.

It was just before Christmas 1995, the shortest days of the year. The president's doctor slept on the cold floor of the house in Latche while the president slept nearby in his bed, snoring lightly, looked down upon by a photograph of his deceased parents. He was seventy-nine, and the doctor could still feel the fight in him, even as he slept—the vain, beautiful little man punching back. In conversation with the president's friends the doctor had given about a 30 percent chance of making it to December. And he had. "The only interesting thing is to live," said the president bluntly.

So there were lemon days and grapefruit days and this constant banter with the tumor: *How are you today? What can I get you today? Another dose of free radicals? Enough radiation to kill the rats of Paris? Please go away now.* There was also a holy trinity of drugs—like blessed Dilaudid, merciful Demerol, and beatific Elavil—that kept the pain at a blurry remove, convinced him in his soaring mind that perhaps this was happening to someone else and he was only bearing witness. Yes, could it be that his powers of empathy for all his countrymen—were so strong that he'd taken on the burden of someone else's disease and then, at the last moment, would be gloriously released back into his own life again?

With the reprieve, he would walk the countryside near Latche, naming the birds and trees again, read his beloved Voltaire, compose, as he had thousands of times before, love letters to his wife.

He planned his annual pilgrimage to Egypt—with his mistress and their daughter—to see the Pyramids, the monumental tombs of the pharaohs, and the eroded Sphinx. That's what his countrymen called him, the Sphinx, for no one really knew for sure who he was—aesthete or whore-monger, Catholic or atheist, fascist or socialist, anti-Semite or humanist, likable or despicable. And then there was his aloof imperial power. Later, his supporters simply called him Dieu—God.

He had come here for this final dialogue with the pharaohs— to mingle with their ghosts and look one last time upon their tombs. The cancer was moving to his head now, and each day that passed brought him closer to his own vanishing, a crystal point of pain that would subsume all the other pains. It would be so much easier…but then no. He made a phone call back to France. He asked that the rest of his family and friends be summoned to Latche and that a meal be prepared for New Year's Eve. He gave a precise account of what would be eaten at the table, a feast for thirty people, for he had decided that afterward, he would not eat again.

"I am fed up with myself," he told a friend.

And so we've come to a table set with a white cloth. An armada of floating wine goblets, the blinding weaponry of knives and forks and spoons. Two windows, shaded purple, stung by bullets of cold rain, lashed by the hurricane winds of an ocean storm.

The chef is a dark-haired man, fiftyish, with a bowling-ball belly. He stands in front of orange flames in his great stone chimney hung with stewpots, finely orchestrating each octave of taste, occasionally sipping his broths and various chorded concoctions with a miffed expression. In breaking the law to serve us ortolan, he gruffly claims that it is his duty, as a Frenchman, to serve the food of his region. He thinks the law against serving ortolan is stupid. And yet he had to call forty of his friends in search of the bird, for there were none to be found and almost everyone feared getting caught, risking fines and possible imprisonment.

But then another man, his forty-first friend, arrived an hour ago with three live ortolans in a small pouch—worth up to a hundred dollars each and each no bigger than a thumb. They're brown-backed, with pinkish bellies, part of the yellowhammer family, and when they fly, they tend to keep low to the ground and, when the wind is high, swoop crazily for lack of weight. In all the world, they're really caught only in the pine forests of the southwestern Landes region of France, by about twenty families who lie in wait for the birds each fall as they fly from Europe to Africa. Once caught—they're literally snatched out of the air in traps called *matoles*—they're locked away in a dark room and fattened on millet; to achieve the same effect, French kings and Roman emperors once blinded the bird with a knife so, lost in the darkness, it would eat twenty-four hours a day.

And so, a short time ago, these three ortolans—*our* three ortolans—were dunked and drowned in a glass of Armagnac and then plucked of their feathers. Now they lie delicately on their backs in three cassoulets, wings and legs tucked to their tiny, bloated bodies, skin the color of pale autumn corn, their eyes small, purple bruises and—here's the thing—wide open.

When we're invited back to the kitchen, that's what I notice, the open eyes on these already-peppered, palsied birds and the gold glow of their skin. The kitchen staff crowds around, craning to see, and when we ask one of the dishwashers if he's ever tried ortolan, he looks scandalized, then looks back at the birds. "I'm too young, and now it's against the law," he says longingly. "But someday, when I can afford one..." Meanwhile, Sara has gone silent, looks pale looking at the birds.

Back at the chimney, the chef reiterates the menu for Mitterrand's last meal, including the last course, as he puts it, "the birdies." Perhaps he reads our uncertainty, a simultaneous flicker of doubt that passes over our respective faces. "It takes a culture of very good to appreciate the very good," the chef says, nosing the clear juices of the capon rotating in the fire. "And ortolan is beyond even the very good."

The guests had been told to hide their shock. They'd been warned that the president looked bad, but then there were such fine gradations. He already looked bad—could he look worse?

It seemed he could. On his return from Egypt, he'd kept mostly to himself, out of sight of others; his doctor still attended to him, but they had begun to quarrel. The president's stubbornness, his fits, and his silences—all of them seemed more acute now. When he entered the room, dressed in baggy pants and a peasant coat, he was colorless and stiff-legged. He was supported by two bodyguards, and part of him seemed lost in dialogue with the thing sucking him from Earth—with his own history, which was fast becoming the sum of his life. He was only half physical now and half spirit.

When the dying are present among the living, it creates an imbalance, for they randomly go through any number of dress rehearsals for death—nodding off at any time, slackening into a meaningful drool. They ebb and flow with each labored breath. Meanwhile, we hide our own panic by acting as if we were simply sitting in the company of a mannequin. It's a rule: in the vicinity of the dying, the inanity of conversation heightens while what's underneath—the thrumming of red tulips on the table and the lap of purple light on the windowpane, the oysters on crushed ice and the birds on the table, the wisp of errant hair drawn behind an ear and the shape of a lip—takes on a fantastic, last-time quality, slowly pulling everything under, to silence.

The president was carried to a reclining chair and table apart from the huge table where the guests sat. He was covered with blankets, seemed gone already. And yet when they brought the oysters—Marennes oysters, his favorite, harvested from the waters of this region—he summoned his energies, rose up in his chair, and began sucking them, the full flesh of them, from their half shells. He'd habitually eaten a hundred a week throughout his life and had been betrayed by bad oysters before, but, oh no, not these! Hydrogen, nitrogen, phosphorous—a dozen, two dozen, and then, astonishingly, more. He couldn't help it, his ravenous attack. It was brain food, and he seemed to slurp them against the cancer, let the saltwater juices flow to the back of his throat, change champagne-sweet, and then disappear in a flood before he started on the oyster itself. And that was another sublimity. The delicate tearing of a thing so full of ocean. Better than a paper wafer—heaven. When he was done, he lay back in his chair, oblivious to everyone else in the room, and fell fast asleep.

Now I have come to France, to the region of François Mitterrand's birth and his final resting place, and on this night, perhaps looking a bit wan myself, I begin by eating the Marennes oysters—round, fat, luscious oysters split open and peeled back to show their delicate green lungs. Shimmering pendulums of translucent meat, they weigh more than the heavy, carbuncled shells in which they lie. When you lift the shell to your mouth and suck, it's like the first time your tongue ever touched another tongue. The oysters are cool inside, then warm. Everything becomes heightened and alive. Nibbling turns to hormone-humming mastication. Your mouth swims with sensation: sugary, then salty, then again with Atlantic Ocean sweetness. And you try, as best you can, to prolong it. When they're gone, you taste the ghost of them.

These are the oysters.

And then the foie gras, smooth and surprisingly buttery, a light brown pâté swirled with faint greens, pinks, and yellows and glittering slightly, tasting not so much of animal but of earth. Accompanied by fresh, rough-crusted, homemade bread and the sweet sauternes we drink (which itself is made from shriveled grapes of noble rot), the foie gras dissolves with the faint, rich sparkle of fresh-picked corn. It doesn't matter that it's fattened goose liver. It doesn't matter what it is. Time slows for it.

This is the foie gras.

The capon is superb—not too gamey or stringy—furiously basted to a high state of tenderness in which the meat falls cleanly from the bone with only the help of gravity. In its mildness, in its hint of olive oil and rosemary, it readies the tongue and its several thousand taste buds for the experience of what's coming next.

This is the capon.

And then the wines. Besides the sauternes (a 1995 Les Remparts de Bastor, a 1995 Doisy-Daëne), which we drink with the oysters and the foie gras, there are simple, full-bodied reds, for that's how Mitterrand liked them, simple and full-bodied: a 1990 Château Lestage Simon, a 1994 Château Poujeaux. They are long, old, and dark. Complicated potions of flower and fruit. Faint cherry on a tongue tip, the tingle of tannin along the gums. While one bottle is being imbibed, another is being decanted, and all the while there are certain chemical changes taking place between the wine and its new atmosphere and then finally between the changed wine and the atmosphere of your mouth.

This is the wine.

And so, on this evening in Bordeaux, in the region where

Mitterrand was born and buried, the eating and drinking of these courses takes us four hours, but then time has spread out and dissipated, woodsmoke up the chimney. Mitterrand, who was famous for out-waiting his opponents, for always playing the long, patient game, once said, "You have to give time time."

And so we have, and time's time is nearing midnight, and there are three as-yet unclaimed ortolans, back in the kitchen, that have just been placed in the oven. They will be cooked for seven minutes in their own fat—cooked, as it's gently put, until they sing.

With each course, the president had rallied from sleep, from his oyster dreams, from fever or arctic chill, not daring to miss the next to come: the foie gras slathered over homemade bread or the capon and then, of course, the wines. But what brought him to full attention was a commotion: some of the guests were confused when a man brought in a large platter of tiny, cooked ortolans laid out in rows. The president closely regarded his guests' dismayed expressions, for it gave him quiet satisfaction—between jabs of pain—to realize that he still had the power to surprise.

The ortolans were offered to the table, but not everyone accepted. Those who did draped large, white cloth napkins over their heads, took the ortolans in their fingertips, and disappeared. The room shortly filled with wet noises and chewing. The bones and intestines turned to paste, swallowed eventually in one gulp. Some reveled in it; others spat it out.

When they were through, one by one they reappeared from beneath their hoods, slightly dazed. The president himself took a long sip of wine, let it play in his mouth. After nearly three dozen oysters and several courses, he seemed insatiable, and there was one bird left. He took the ortolan in his fingers, then dove again beneath the hood, the bony impress of his skull against the white cloth—the guests in silence and the self-pleasing, pornographic slurps of the president filling the room like a dirge.

At the table now, three ortolans, singing in their own fat. We'll eat the birds because the ocean storm is at the purple windows;

because this man, our chef, has gone to great lengths to honor us at his table; because we're finishers; because it's too late and too far—the clock is literally striking midnight—to turn back.

We offer the third bird to the chef.

And so he's the first to go. An atheist, he doesn't take his beneath the napkin. He just pops the bird in his mouth, bites off the head with his incisors, and holds a thickly bundled napkin over his lips, occasionally slipping it from side to side to sop up the overflowing juices. Slowly, deliberately, he begins to chew. As he does, he locks eyes with Sara. For long, painful minutes during which we can hear the crunch and pop of bone and tendon, he stares deeply across the table at her, with the napkin to his mouth.

I believe the chef is trying to seduce my girlfriend, a scene mirrored by ortolan-eating lovers in Proust, Colette, and Fielding. But then I realize that he's not so much trying to take something from her as trying to find a still point from which he can focus on the chaos in his mouth. He's chewing, sucking, slobbering, savoring. And he's trying to manage all of the various, wild announcements of taste.

After he swallows and dabs his napkin daintily at the corners of his mouth, it's our turn. We raise our birds and place them in our mouths. I can't tell you what happens next in the outside world because, like Mitterrand, I go beneath the hood, which is meant to heighten the sensual experience by enveloping you in the aroma of ortolan. And the hood itself, with its intimation of Klan-like activity, might trouble me more if not for the sizzling bird on its back in my mouth, burning my tongue. The trick is to cool it by creating convections around it, by simply breathing. But, even then, my mouth has gone on full alert. Some taste buds are scorched and half-functioning, while others bloom for the first time and still others signal the sprinkler system of salivary glands.

And now, the hardest part: the first bite.

Like the chef, I sever the head and put it on the plate where it lies in its own oil slick, then tentatively I try the body with bicuspids. The bird is surprisingly soft, gives completely, and then explodes with juices—liver, kidneys, lungs. Chestnut, corn, salt—all mix in an extraordinary current, the same warm, comforting flood as finely evolved consommé.

And so I begin chewing.

Here's what I taste: yes, quidbits of meat and organs, the succulent, tiny strands of flesh between the ribs and tail. I put inside myself the last flowered bit of air and Armagnac in its lungs, the body of rainwater and berries. In there, too, is the ocean and Africa and the dip and plunge in a high wind. And the heart that bursts between my teeth.

It takes time. I'm forced to chew and chew again and again, for what seems like three days. And what happens after chewing for this long—as the mouth full of taste buds and glands does its work—is that I fall into a trance. I don't taste anything anymore, cease to exist as anything but taste itself.

And that's where I want to stay—but then can't because the sweetness of the bird is turning slightly bitter and the bones have announced themselves. When I think about forcing them down my throat, a wave of nausea passes through me. And that's when, with great difficulty, I swallow everything.

Afterward, I hold still for a moment, head bowed and hooded. I can feel my heart racing. Slowly, the sounds of the room filter back— the ting of wineglasses against plates, a shout back in the kitchen, laughter from another place. And then, underneath it, something soft and moving. Lungs filling and emptying. I can hear people breathing.

After the president's ortolan—he had appeared from beneath the hood wide-eyed, ecstatic, staring into a dark corner of the room— the guests approached him in groups of two and three and made brief small talk about the affairs of the country or Zola or the weather. They knew this was adieu, and yet they hid their sadness; they acted as if in a month's time he would still be among them.

And what about him? There was nothing left to subtract now. What of the white river that flowed through his childhood, the purple attic full of cornhusks? And then his beautiful books— Dostoyevsky, Voltaire, Camus? How would the world continue without him in it?

He tried to flail one last time against the proof of his death. But then he had no energy left. Just an unhappy body weighted with grapefruits, curving earthward. Everything moving toward the center and one final point of pain. Soon after, he refused food and medicine; death took eight days.

"I'm eaten up inside," he said before he was carried from the room.

We wake late and senseless, hungover from food and wine, alone with our thoughts, feeling guilty and elated, sated and empty.

The day after Mitterrand's last meal seems to have no end. Huddled together, we wander the streets of Bordeaux, everyone on the sidewalks turning silver in the half-light. And then we drive out toward Jarnac, the village where Mitterrand is buried—through winding miles of gnarled grape trees in the gray gloom. We visit Mitterrand's tomb, a simple family sarcophagus in a thickly populated graveyard, and stand on the banks of his childhood river.

If I could, I would stay right here and describe the exact details of that next day. I would describe how we watched children riding a carousel until twilight, all of their heads tilting upward, hands fluttering and reaching for a brass ring that the ride master manipulated on a wire, how the stone village looked barbaric in the rain, with its demented buildings blackened by soot from the cognac distilleries.

We just seemed to be sleepwalking. Or vanishing. Until later. Until we were lost and the streets had emptied. Until night came and the wind carried with it the taste of saltwater and the warm light in the boulangerie window shone on loaves of bread just drawn from the oven. And we were hungry again.

Michael Paterniti is a writer-at-large for Esquire. *His first book of nonfiction,* Driving Mr. Albert: A Trip Across America with Einstein's Brain, *will be published by Dial Press in the Spring of 2000. His work also regularly appears in various publications including* Harper's, *the* New York Times Magazine, Rolling Stone, *as well as on the radio program,* "This American Life."

✲ ✲ ✲

Jambo!

There's brotherhood in beer.

IT WAS MY FIRST TRIP TO AFRICA AND I HAD STEPPED INTO A neighborhood bar in Nairobi, Kenya, the kind of place ordinary guys stop in on their way home from work, or use as a respite from normal cares. You know: an African *Cheers* kind of joint. The place was crowded with regulars so I gingerly shouldered my way to the bar.

"*Jambo!*" the barman said, giving me the national salutation.

"*Jambo* back at ya, pal!" I said. "How 'bout a large Tusker lager?"

Tusker is a fine brew, and easy to spot among the others by its elephant head motif on the label. As I waited for my beer the guy sitting to my right said, "*Jambo!*"

"*Jambo* to you, too," said I.

"Would you like to buy me a beer?" he asked. I had quickly found this to be a common question in Kenya. No sooner would they *jambo* me than they'd ask for a drink. Even a woman accosted me so, out on the street in broad daylight. And she wasn't even pretty! She was an ugly, tobacco-toothed, over-the-hill, bone-in-her-nose *National Geographic* magazine cover girl in a Western-style dress, the kind that Richard Pryor has been known to call "a floppy titted zebra bitch." She cornered me between rush hour traffic and a gaping-open manhole. And I don't think she even stopped to *jambo* me, she just smiled her tar-and-nicotine smile and asked me to take her out for drinks. Drinks! Plural!

So by the time the guy in the bar asked me for a drink I was practiced in my polite refusal. "Thanks for the offer," I said, "but I'll pass this time." And I turned the other way. In front of me now sat a man named Patrick Chege.

"Uh...*Jambo*," I said.

"*Jambo*, friend!" he said with a broad smile. "Are you from America?"

"Yeah, from California. Does it show?"

"It's easy to tell. You Americans all stand at the bar like cowboys."

At that moment the barman set the Tusker lager in front of me, and Patrick nonchalantly laid down 40 Kenyan shillings to cover the cost. He said nothing, just smiled. "Well here's something new," I thought. I picked up the one-liter bottle, toasted him and took a long pull. Aarrgghh! I had forgotten to specify COLD Tusker. Kenyans generally drink their beer at room temperature, holding the belief it's unhealthy to drink too-cold drinks. I'm sure it's something they contracted from their former British rulers who taught them how to make and drink lager-style beer. As we all know, the Brits quaff their suds at room temperature. But a British room normally requires the wearing of woolens and huddling next to a coal fire. Your average Kenyan room sits a few degrees from the equator. And when it's packed with Kenyan good ol' boys and the odd American tourist, it can be sweltering. Beer is one of the most important things in daily life to me. It is one of the eternal verities and high virtues of civilization. I know and acknowledge that there are people in the world who use and enjoy it in ways different from mine. But I do not like their ways. I respect them, but I do not like them. It was only by an effort of will that I was able to swallow.

"We make a pretty good beer here in Kenya, don't you think?"

"Oh yeah. Good."

Patrick and I talked about our lives for a while, sharing our very different stories. I told him I was eating my way through the world and writing a book about it.

"I'm in the food game, too," he said. "I ship beef cattle to Saudi Arabia. We have very good cattle here."

So we chatted about the qualities of good beef and where to find the best. And I grimaced as I choked down more of the equatorially warm Tusker. Somewhere in the ebb and flow of our warm and beery chat a jolt of realization struck me. Though I had been in Africa, been in Nairobi, for three or four days, this was my first consciousness of it: every face I saw was black, except for mine.

Now, I live in Berkeley, California, the epicenter of political correctness (it's where the term was coined) and racial rhetoric. And only a few minutes' walk from Oakland, birthplace of the Black Panthers. I can hardly walk out the door of my home without being acutely aware of the "racial heritage" of everyone I see, including myself. Right wing radio talk Fuehrers and whining minority malcontents make it their mission in life to keep me so informed. And the blondest of blond guilty white liberal speechifiers and wavers of placards will take pains to remind me that I am "melanin deprived" and that others are not. And if I were to stumble into an "African American" bar in the wrong part of Oakland, well, I would likely stumble very quickly right back out. And as long as I'm telling the truth, any American who found himself the possessor of the only black face in a cowboy or biker bar would feel the same as I would in that bad-ass Oakland bar. For that matter, he might not feel at ease anywhere in North America except at home, behind locked doors, and maybe not even there.

We don't like to talk about this sort of thing. But there I was, at least three days in Nairobi, at the bottom of the tourist season, seemingly the only paleface in town, and in a bar full of "young black males." (Ooops! Was I supposed to capitalize "black"? We don't capitalize "white" do we? The nuances of the new racial order escape me.) And I had only just now noticed! It had taken at least 72 hours to notice that I was the lone European sort of guy in a sea of African sort of guys (and gals...grrrls...women...okay, Womyn! Don't hurt me!).

As I was being stunned by this revelation Patrick said, "You know, my younger brother is in your country."

"Oh?"

"In Texas. He studies there at the university. There are many Kenyans there. Oh yes. They all like to go to Texas, where the cowboys are."

"I guess cowboys are popular everywhere," I said, in something of a daze.

"Yes. But he says the Kenyans encounter a lot of racialism there."

"Uh..." Had warm Tusker lager destroyed my cowboy poker face? Was Patrick now reading my thoughts?

"Do you think there's a lot of racialism in Texas?" he asked.

Racialism. Damned British tutelage. Always got to stick in an extra syllable. "Well," I said tentatively, "I suppose it might depend on the region. I hope the cowboys aren't giving him too much trouble."

"Oh, it's not the cowboys. The cowboys are first-class fellows."

"Then it's the KKK?"

"The what?"

"Never mind."

"Actually, it's the black Americans that cause him the most trouble."

"Huh?"

The world was suddenly upside down. Here was I, perfectly at ease as the only white among a multitude of blacks; and there was Patrick's brother in Texas (In Texas, damn it!) getting grief from the "black Americans." (His words, not mine. I never heard an African African say "African American.") I took a slug of Tusker. Jesus, it's awful when it's warm! And I was beginning to wonder if it were a ticket through the looking glass.

"Um, I'm afraid I don't quite understand, Patrick."

"My brother writes to me that the black Americans discriminate against him because he is African."

Now this was just too much. And warm beer, too! I felt sure that if I took one more swallow of the hot suds it would cast loose all my moorings. Fortunately, Patrick called to the barman, "*Jambo!* Two more Tuskers."

"Make mine cold!" I shouted with an urgency that Patrick noticed.

"Oh, yes," he said, "My brother reminds me that the Americans insist on cold beer."

He laughed as he threw down some more notes, tipping the barman 10 percent. The two Tuskers appeared before us, and I could see from the beaded condensation on mine that it was as cold as a witch's tit, and as soon as I nursed on it all would be right with the world. I took a long pull and let the coldly warming liquid foam down my throat in an icy, reassuring froth. My balance restored, I said, "So, Patrick, would you kindly explain your last remark?"

"Well, my brother enjoys the company of the cowboys. They take him riding and teach him many things. This is good because he will come home to be in the cattle business like me."

"Uh huh." And another fortifying gulp of the cold one.

"But the black Americans shun him and the other Kenyans because they are ashamed of their African roots."

"No. No way. I see black Americans all the time wearing Africa medallions, and African clothes, and taking African names. And, and, oh, all kinds of stuff."

"Yes, yes. These things are all well and good. But when they meet an African they have another opinion."

"I don't get it." We each took a long bracing swig, the warm and the cold.

"When they meet an African they meet a Third World person. They meet someone from a country that has 50 percent literacy, 30 percent malnutrition and, I hate to say it but, a government that cannot or will not govern. A poor country that's going to stay poor a long time. They are ashamed to be associated with such a country. And I cannot entirely blame them. But when they meet a Kenyan or other African they make sure to tell them that they are Americans. And they make the Africans feel bad about it. Of course I'm not saying that all of the black Americans are this way. Maybe only a few. But enough to make the Africans feel bad, and to write some sadness into their letters home."

This gave me pause. And I recalled a brief item I saw in that morning's newspaper about a group of African Americans in a popular Nairobi restaurant. They felt they weren't being waited on quickly enough, so one of them stood up and proudly shouted, "We're Americans!" According to the report, they got quicker service.

"You know, Patrick, I finished reading a book recently. It's called *Schindler's List*."

"Oh yes. I saw the movie."

"Isn't it curious how some of the Jews helped the Nazis to pursue other Jews, because they were different kinds of Jews. Isn't that crazy?"

"Yes, of course. But then, I think we are a crazy species."

We took a thoughtful sip of the warm and the cold, rolling it over our tongues, enjoying it each in his own way, and lost for a moment in our private thoughts.

"Do you have racialism where you live, in California?"

"Uh…"

How could I tell him the truth without a social science treatise? How could I explain the racial balkanization of my home state without making it sound like race warfare? How could I tell him that the short walk to Oakland was a problematic, possibly dangerous affair, but the worst of the long walk to Africa was the occasional warm beer? Could I explain the oppressive idea of political correctness without sounding like a neo-Nazi, conservative, sexist, racist, homophobic, patriarchist, straight white male oppressor of women and people of color and the gay—lesbian—bisexual—multicultural alliance?

"Not officially," I said. "We have laws against it."

"Do the police enforce the laws?"

"Do the police enforce the laws here?"

Patrick laughed and said, "I'll ask you no more, my friend. *Jambo!* Barman! Two more Tuskers. And make them both cold. I'll try it your way this time."

According to Patrick Chege, Richard Sterling is a "first class fellow."

MARY ROACH

The Instructress

*An unflappable eater meets her match
in an Ecuadorian village.*

IN 1986, A PSYCHOLOGIST NAMED PAUL ROZIN TOOK A GROUP OF
toddlers and did a peculiar thing. One by one, he sat them down
at a table and presented them with a plate of what he said was dog-
doo and asked them if they'd like to eat it. (In fact, it was peanut
butter, scented with bleu cheese.) Then he did the same with a
sterilized grasshopper. Sixty-two percent of the children under two
happily dispatched the ersatz turd; thirty-one percent, the insect.
Older children invariably rejected both plates. His point: Disgust is
learned. Culture is our instructress. We are taught that horse meat
is disgusting but chicken embryos are not; that Slim Jims are tasty
and crickets are gross.

Espousing, as I have, a belief that nothing is inherently disgusting, that it's all a case of mind over culture, I have frequently, in my
travels, felt the need to put my money where my mouth is and my
mouth where it would rather not go. I have eaten walrus meat left
buried on an Arctic beach to "ferment" for a month, a raw fish eye
and its accompanying musculature, duck tongue, caribou marrow,
brain, flipper, ant. I am, yes, one of those annoying travelers who
boast about the disgusting food they've lived to tell about (and tell
about and tell about).

47

I am getting my comeuppance. I am getting it big time, in a small village in the Ecuadorian Amazon. I came here to do a story on an anthropologist named John Patton. Patton studies a tribe called the Achuar, notable for their skill in blowgun making and their long-ago rivalry with the head-shrinking Chuar. (If you've seen an authentic South American shrunken head, you've probably seen an Achuar tribesman.) Patton's base is Conambo, a scatter of houses along a fast, muddy river, reachable every now and again by a four-seater missionary plane. There is no hotel, no restaurant, no store. You eat what they hunt.

I am fast coming to understand that there is a huge difference, a vast yawning canyon of difference, between tasting something deeply unappealing and living on it. Anyone, if he tries, can suppress his disgust long enough to swallow a single fish eye or a mouthful of decaying walrus. Eating enough to live on is altogether a different matter. I am here for five days. I'm not doing very well.

My problem at the moment is a knee. It's a rodent knee, quietly genuflecting in a bowl of oily broth. Earlier today, the knee was attached to a happy, hairy, spaniel-sized rodent, gamboling and cavorting in the wee hours of the rainforest morning until our host happened along and plugged it full of buckshot. (Blow guns are only used on birds and pack animals like monkeys, wherein a gunshot scares off the rest of your chances for dinner.)

The knee is one of nature's marvels, a busy intersection of tendon, bone, cartilage. Be that as it may, marvel falls significantly short of an accurate description of my state of mind. Extreme psychic discomfort is close. The hunter and the chef are sitting directly across from me. Their generosity is heartbreaking. I have to clean my plate. I must force apart the gristly abomination with my teeth, work my tongue into its fissures and slimy orifices, extract anything vaguely chewable, and swallow it. I lean over to scout the contents of Patton's bowl.

He got the ankle. The thing about ankle bones, as schoolchildren everywhere know, is that they're attached to foot bones. And foot bones are attached to toe bones and toenails and those dirty little rubbery pads on the bottom of the foot. No matter how good a meat may taste, the experience is indelibly marred by the act of spitting ghastly unchewables out into your fingers.

Patton is undaunted. He has the entire thing in his mouth. He stops sucking and gumming long enough to say:"The foot pads are a good source of fat." He is enjoying his rodent soup, in the way that only a man who has been served steamed tapir fetus and live palm beetles can. A hail of tiny foot bones accumulates on the ground beside him.

The knee awaits. I've finished my broth. To stall any longer would betray my revulsion. I manage to locate a couple of pockets of reasonably normal-looking flesh. My inclination is to chew these slowly, forever if need be, until my hosts tire of sitting here and go off to tend the manioc garden. The problem with this tactic is that boiled rodent flesh isn't the sort of thing you want to have hanging around your tongue for any longer than is strictly necessary for purposes of not choking to death. It's not really that bad, it's just strong. As in overpowering, as in taste buds passing out and waving white flags. It doesn't, in short, taste anything like chicken. I find myself chewing with my mouth open, hoping my hosts will take this for an endearing cultural peculiarity, rather than an attempt to bypass the tasting portion of my meal.

I beg Patton to take my meat. (Our hosts speak no English.) Kind soul that he is, he relieves me of the knee. The man of the house makes a comment, which Patton translates:"She doesn't like to eat?" He has seen Westerners who don't have any children, who don't know how to shoot a rifle. Perhaps there are Westerners who don't like eating. "She had a big breakfast," fibs Patton.

It was in fact a big breakfast, but I didn't do very much having. Someone shot an alligator, and I had some leg. (It's a leg sort of day.) I have eaten alligator meat before, in Florida, but someone, bless him, had taken it upon himself to remove the scales before cooking it. I tried to pretend that the leg was something else, something bland and comforting. After several false starts— Melba toast? lettuce?—my brain, clearly shaken, presented me with "orange roughy."

Patton maintains that the bulk of an Achuar's daily calories do not come from meat. They come from *chicha,* a mildly alcoholic, vaguely nutritious, watered-down manioc mash. Achuar men drink up to four gallons a day. If you like *chicha,* you can live well in Conambo. In about an hour, I will get to try it. Patton's friend Isaac is hosting a *minga,* a work party for the villagers who helped Isaac's family dig a new manioc plot. It's similar in concept to the Amish barn-raising, with marathon *chicha*-drinking taking the place of square dancing.

I am of two minds about *chicha.* On the one hand, it's a beverage. In the land of scary food, the beverage is your friend. It's the Tecate that washes down the *menudo,* the swig of sake that makes the giant clam neck tolerable.

On the other hand, we are talking about a beverage fermented with human saliva. Achuar women chew boiled manioc into the desired mashed-potato texture, and then spit-spray the contents of their bulging cheeks out into the *chicha* urn. While I know that percentage-wise, we're talking a tiny fraction of the mixture, I'm having difficulty embracing the idea. I have a little agreement with myself: when spittle finds its way onto the ingredient list, I find a way to say no.

"You can't say no," says Patton, tossing ankle carcass to a cringing, harelipped dog. "It's just not done."

Patton and I are seated on a low log bench in the open-walled platform that serves as Isaac's living room. The man of the house whittles blowgun darts as he chats. A pair of black horn-rim glasses sits askew on his face. One lens is violently cracked, as though someone stepped on it, though no one here has the kind of shoes for that. The floor is dirty but uncluttered. Decor runs to parrot feathers and jaguar skulls, a government poster urging vaccinations for children. In the corner, a little girl has set up a *chicha* tea party with her dolls, the tenderness of the scene marred only by the knowledge that the tiny *chicha* bowls are made from howler monkey voice boxes.

Isaac's wife and mother are in constant motion, serving bowls of *chicha* to the ten or so guests. *Chicha* is the backbone of Achuar society. As with the ankle bone and the knee bone, you feel an unalterable pressure to accept. *Chicha* is the holy communion, the Maneschewitz, the kava-kava of Achuar life. It's present at every ceremony, every visit, every meal. A woman's desirability rests in no small part on her skill at *chicha* brewing and serving.

Isaac's mother dips a clay bowl into an urn of eggnog-hued liquid. Something slimy dangles off the bottom of the bowl, waving howdy-doo as she crosses the floor to our bench. Her hand is coated with a mucilaginous yellow fluid with flecks of manioc fiber. The sidewalk outside Ireland's 42 on a Sunday morning comes, unbidden and unwelcome, to mind.

"It's Miller time," says Patton as he takes the bowl. After ten minutes, he warns, she'll return to take the bowl away and give it to someone else, most likely me. It is considered irretrievably rude to refuse a bowl of *chicha*, or even to set it down. (In a maddening instance of form following etiquette, the ceramic bowls in which *chicha* is served are rounded on the bottom, so that the drinker cannot set one down without spilling the contents.)

A refusal is interpreted as a bluff and triggers a ritualized pas de deux: "No, really, I shouldn't." "Yes, yes, I insist." Woe unto the visitor: the host never backs down.

Which means I have ten minutes to talk myself out of the revulsion that's building in my gut, jostling for space among the pinworms and protozoa. My mouth is full of saliva anyway, I tell myself. What's a little more? Myself isn't buying it. Myself is noting the vast and unsettling difference between oral hygiene practices around the Amazon basin and around the basin in our bathroom at home. This isn't a matter of disgust, I tell Patton. It's a matter of gum disease.

Patton wipes manioc slime from his beard. Intelligent *chicha* drinkers, he holds, don't fret about the saliva it's made with. They fret about the giardia and amoebas in the unfiltered river water it's made with. It is at this moment that Isaac's mother gets up to retrieve the *chicha* bowl from Patton, fill it to near overflow, and present it to me.

The first thing that hits you is the smell. Fruity and fetid, a whiff of drinker's breath on a late-night bus. I put my lips to the rim of the bowl, bumpy-slimy with manioc pulp. I hold my breath and drink.

The taste is not awful. It's chalky, rummy, indifferent. But this was never about taste. It's about distaste. Did you ever drop something into a toilet and have to roll up your sleeve and retrieve it? That's how I'm feeling right now. Only I've got to keep going. I've got to lift the lid, step right in, and hunker down in the toilet bowl. As soon as the level of *chicha* lowers visibly, Isaac's mother will step up to refill the bowl.

I disappoint and surprise myself. I come from a tribe that eats Vienna sausages. I should be able to cope. But I can't. I cannot drink this bowl of *chicha*.

An idea alights. I ask Patton to hold my bowl and rummage in my backpack for the crinkle of airtight cellophane: a raspberry-chocolate Trader Joe's energy bar. The room falls abruptly quiet. Foreigner's backpacks are known to hold all manner of other-worldly wonders: sugar packets, earplugs, contact lenses. (The concept of bits of plastic aiding vision was not easily absorbed. A man pointed to a baby bottle nipple. "Could I as well put a piece of this in my eye?") The energy bar makes the rounds. A few of the men sniff at it. Only Isaac takes a bite. He chews vigorously at first, then stops, suddenly and with alarm, as though someone had snuck up behind him and put a gun to his head. His eyebrows bunch together like drawn drapes. His lips go all abstract and jumpy. He stands, grabs hold of a roof post, and spits forcefully. He coughs, arrghs, hawks, spits again. Every few seconds, he looks back at me, his face changing channels from disgust to bewilderment and back. After a good minute of this, he hands back the energy bar, grinning now that the taste is gone, shaking his head at the foreigner's unfathomable tastes.

The way I see it, permission has been granted to back out of the next bowl of *chicha*.

Mary Roach has traveled to all seven continents, yet to this day she cannot remember to order special meals. She has written about her travels for Salon, Islands, Condé Nast Traveler, Health, Vogue, *and* American Way. *She lives in San Francisco with her husband Ed and their three pieces of luggage.*

O. M. BODÈ

* * *

Etiquette, Schmetiquette

What would Miss Manners say?

I WEIGH ABOUT A HUNDRED EIGHTY POUNDS. TWENTY POUNDS too much for my height-weight ratio. Doesn't seem to bother me though. That is until I found myself on a boardwalk in a "Kampong Air": a Malay water village. All along the coasts of Borneo and the Philippine islands of the Sulu Sea, the water villages lie like myriad strings of pearls. They combine all the advantages of living on the water, such as cool breezes, few bugs, and the ability to go fishing and swimming whenever you want.

While researching material for a novel, I had been traveling through Borneo on river boats, mini-buses, and express boats that looked like 747s with the wings pulled off. I ended up in the port of Semporna at a tourist version of a water village in Sabah, Malaysia's northern-most province in Borneo.

The Semporna Ocean Tourist Center had look-alike cabins arranged in straight neat rows on military-like piers that were built over the blue-green waters of the Sulu Sea. It kind of lacked the anarchistic charm of a sea gypsy village with the chaotically added-on shacks of different sizes and shapes. To me those delicate Kampong Airs are works of art.

In the tourist center restaurant I mentioned to one of the pretty

Philippina waitresses that I was interested in seeing a real sea gypsy water village.

Carly said, "No problem. You come and visit my sister and husband. He's a Badjau (Sea Gypsy), Muslim, and she was Christian before. Now we all Muslim."

I was intrigued.

A tiny taxi took us to the edge of town past a shiny white mosque with golden minarets that seemed to point the way to paradise. We bounced up and down and sideways over one of the worst roads I'd been on in a long time. And at last we stopped at the edge of the Sulu Sea. There a long boardwalk zigzagged out to some rickety looking houses on stilts off in the distant haze.

There was a lot of spring to the boards as I walked on them. Maybe too much! I stopped and one board began to give way under my weight! Frightened I stepped onto the next board and it too began to bow. I thought I heard ominous cracking sounds. I sure didn't want to wreck the Sea Gypsy's village with my presence! From there on I sort of pranced light-footed like a lively baton major at the head of the parade. Laughing, Carly could hardly stay ahead of me.

At last we arrived at the end of the boardwalk and I was truly at the head of the parade leading a group of naked children with their eyes filled with wonder at the biggest white man they'd ever seen and who stepped so gingerly in their presence.

Two houses from the end of the Kampong Air, was the sister's house. She was amazed to see us. Carly had forgot to call her by cell phone. Yes, cellular phones are big-time in Southeast Asia. Everyone trics to have one.

The children, who were all smiles, begged, "Hey Joe, you got gum? Gimme gum?"

I had a few sticks on me and luckily as it so happened. So I passed out the few to the many little hands that were everywhere and a near riot ensued from those who received nothing, causing Biety, Carly's sister, to swat the hands away and shoo the kids off. Quiet returned except for the board I was standing on. It was giving off some bad sounds. I shifted my weight to another board,

but it too sagged and creaked. Later Biety's husband showed me
the secret of the boards: find a cross piece beam supporting the
boards and stand there.

I was ushered into a nicely decorated home with crocheted pillows hooked onto the thin walls and a thin Pink Panther with his
left arm missing sitting on a bamboo couch along with some other
toys. The arm seemed to have been torn off near the shoulder.
Maybe the veteran of some childrens' war. But his right arm remained and his tail was neatly coiled over the hand.

I was introduced to Mochtar, Biety's husband who ran a Shell
service station in Semporna with a big sign that said "JAM 24,"
open 24 hours a day. Mochtar was a thin, handsome man, five foot
ten, rather tall for a Badjau. He was burned dark mahogany like
everyone else who lived in the Kampong Air except Carly and
Biety who were surprisingly light-skinned. More like me who instantly got a nickname from the children: "Tuan Tahi-lalat," Mr.
Freckles.

Biety and Mochtar queried me about my home in America. I
told them that it was made out of stone and bricks and cement that
weighed many hundreds of tons. Mochtar told me that he was
going to build a garage out of concrete, for his new Toyota, on the
shore next to the beginning of the boardwalk.

He pointed to some cans in the corner that read: CAT SEMEN
and said, "I get ready, save necessary things for garage."

For a moment I thought he had a problem with too many rats
or mice and that Sulu Sea cats were too lazy to mate, but it turned
out that the can was really cement paint. Once I explained what
the words meant in English we all had a good laugh until a flash
of light was followed by a loud rumble of thunder that cut the air
like an ultimatum. I looked out the window and saw that a line
squall was rapidly advancing on the Kampong Air. The window
boards were partially lowered. Some faces of children peered up
through the spaces between the floor boards beneath us. They had
been fishing in a tiny canoe, and now they were under Biety's
house, sheltering from the first few drops of rain.

I noticed that the distance between the ocean and the bottom of Biety's house was much greater than at my cabin at the Semporna Ocean Tourism Center. When speed boats passed, their wakes caused big water spouts to shoot up through the floor boards of my cabin, like a geyser at a National Park. Unluckily, a couple of times I happened to be standing in the wrong spot when I heard the roar of a boat and the next thing I knew my crotch had been unnecessarily cleansed!

A few seconds later a tropical downpour splashed onto Biety's tin roof with a deafening roar. A small naked boy ran in and pulled a hose through the window, which he led to a big barrel in the corner of the room. Water shot out of the hose. I could see that it had been fitted onto the nozzle of an old plastic Fanta soda bottle that had been cut in half and grafted to one of the ends of the rain gutter. Well I guessed that solved the fresh water problem.

A fisherman with a thin rubber tarp covering him pushed aside the curtain at the doorway and dropped two big gunny sacks full of crabs on the floorboards. The surface of the bags rippled with movement.

"Do you like crab?" Mochtar asked.

"Do I like crab!?! Does the Sultan of Brunei like diamonds? I love crab!"

On a charcoal brazier Biety had a large pot of boiling water ready for some of the biggest crabs I'd ever seen outside of the snow crabs of Alaska. They had dark brown markings on them and fought like hell when they were brought to the pot. I felt sorry for them and hoped that they died fast. But I love the taste of crab meat!

Eventually, the table was loaded with a pile of boiled crabs two feet deep. It kind of reminded me of those restaurants on Chesapeake Bay that loaded your table high, from corner to corner, with cooked blue crabs. No plates needed.

They waited. Carly explained to me, that as the honored guest, I had to take the first bite before anyone else could eat. I nodded and started to grab the nearest crab. But my eye happened to catch the unblinking gaze of the Pink Panther. He sat there as if coconut butter wouldn't melt in his mouth. The little stump of his left arm hanging down, warning me that yes, I was in a Muslim household and I wasn't to touch any food with my left hand, my dirty hand. The hand that washed my butt. And if I did, it would be one of the unholiest of insults I could show. Hell, down in the Sulu Sea I might lose my left hand like the Pink Panther lost his arm! And I might even have the offending member suspended around my throat tied to a string. I thought of the axe coming down on my wrist with the hand nailed to a coconut stump. Or were they more civilized here and used a small specialized guillotine. Ouch!

A faraway crack of thunder resounded through the small shack as all the eyes on me waited patiently. The squall had passed.

"Umm, hunnh," I said as formally as I could and gingerly grabbed the smallest crab I could find with my right hand. My left hand was hanging out of sight as low as I could get it. It itched and I wanted to scratch it. "Why now, dear Allah?" I thought. "How was I going to break open this crab? I guess with main strength and awkwardness."

The silence was as heavy as the humidity. No sounds except for the last of the water gurgling out of the hose.

I smashed the crab down as hard as I could. Everyone jumped as the table and the mountain of crabs shook. Some of the crabs threatened to fall off.

Nothing, not even a hairline crack! I stuck my mouth under a dangling leg trying to maneuver it in. My teeth encircled the leg casing and I wrenched the crab away violently almost taking my molars with it. I ended up with a detached crab leg in my mouth. I tested the hard shell with my teeth. It was too hard to crack. There was a fury on my face that made the staring eyes around me grow even wider like the Pink Panther, who still sat watching me as if waiting for some faux pas to happen.

I jammed my elbow down on the crab's body. I was lucky the shell cracked. But, oh the pain, the electrical currents in my elbow buzzed furiously. Next, with my chin holding the crab down on the table I managed to pull up a piece of the top shell up with my fingers. Still using my right hand of course. But the piece of shell was like a metal spring, frustratingly winging back and forth from my pulls. I couldn't break it loose!

Mouths began to hang open like small children at their first circus performance. My left arm felt like a piece of lead. Totally worthless.

In unison, the faces of my hosts panned left to right as the crustacean slipped from beneath my chin and with the force of the pull on the piece of loose shell, it slipped from my greasy fingers and I neatly flipped the whole thing out the window, where it bounced once off the window board making a loud crack and then flew unceremoniously into the Sulu Sea. An accident waiting to happen of course. Even the eyes watching through the floorboards jerked seawards to see where the flying crab was going to land.

To draw attention away from my embarrassing action, I brought my fist down as hard as I could on the body of another crab. At the sound of the crash, from the window, the row of eyes still staring after flying crab, panned right to left, rapidly focusing on me again. I smiled. The crab shell had parted and I was able to fit two fingers under the carapace. Two shreds of crab meat hung on the cuticle of one of my finger nails. Remember I was still only using the right hand. I placed the tender morsels into my mouth like a king. I smacked my lips although the crab fragments were too tiny to taste. But I had done it! With only my right hand mind you.

Mochtar, the man of the house, grabbed the next crab and tore it apart in a matter of seconds. And one by one the rest of the family did the same, down to Biety's little five-year-old daughter, who needed some help from her mother, of course. The eating action was such a blur that for a few seconds I was unsure that what I was seeing was true. Everyone was using both hands!

I was shocked! But I managed to recover enough to get into the thick of things. And I'm sure that boards, as I stepped on them, on the way back to shore, sagged a few extra centimeters more than the first time.

O. M. Bodè has been around the world as a merchant seaman and holds a master's license in the American Merchant Marine. He has worked as a photographer, writer, and film editor, and currently lives in Hawai'i.

JOHN KRICH

* * *

The Revenge of the Snake People

Is that thing kosher?

QING PING MARKET IS NOT FOR ANYONE WHO HAS EVER FELT THE slightest urge to join an A.S.P.C.A. The bulk of this covered gallery, running crosswise through old Canton at its most crowded, is taken up with the world's greatest variety of exotica offered up as edible. The covered streets are claimed by sacks of medicinal herbs, a hundred types of dried fungi, aquarium fish, and tropical birds. It takes a bit of effort to spot anything offensive to foreign sensibilities, but of course, that's just what foreigners come here to do. On a good day, there are caged monkeys, raccoons, civets and, worst of all, fluffy kittens rubbing their noses against the wooden bars. They are not here to be sold to the zoo. Yes, Virginia, they really do eat anteaters by the truckload, wise old hoot owls, freshly stunned baby deer with open starlet eyes still seeking a gentler fate.

Everywhere, the leitmotif of Canton is the unidentified, decapitated carcass, all glazed and shiny; the hanging rodent flank, tail included; the steam-pressed pig head complete with steamrolled eyeballs. Though a number of overseas Chinese will insist that eating dog is entirely illegal, the bar-b-que shops of Canton are hung with stripped torsos too small to be pork and too big to be rabbit. "Woof! Woof!" is the explanation which I both expect and dread. Apparently, poodles and schnauzers are out. According to ancient texts, young "yellow dogs"—but not golden retrievers—are considered the tastiest brand of so-called "fragrant meat." One time in Korea, I'd been tricked into trying the stuff myself. As my hosts suppressed their giggles, I had nibbled on oddly stringy strips of flesh carefully disguised in a fiery sauce. The flavor had hardly been memorable, but that could be said about a lot of meals.

If "nature is one huge restaurant," as Woody Allen once put it, then no place in Canton makes the point so vividly as the Snake Restaurant. On our last night of furtive, vaguely creepy scavenging through China, Mei has to inquire three or four times to find the place. Of course, it's down a fittingly dark and serpentine street in the old city. But no identification is more obvious than this restaurant's ground floor entry. To get upstairs to a table in the cushy mezzanine, even one's own banquet room where the snake comes with electrified sing-along, you have to pass through a frequently blood-bathed and hosed-down area. This tiled butcher shop is lined with snake cages. But in the center are strikingly clinical dissection tables manned by more enthusiastic young snake handlers than could ever be found in an Indian bazaar. Each are certified trainers, we're assured, and deft slaughterers, choppers and strippers. Only in China would this show be meant to stimulate, rather than put off, one's appetite.

But Chinese appetites come from village life, as these snakes come from a farm near the Hong Kong border. As in ancient times, when Southerners were scorned for their love of frogs, a younger generation is enthusiastically carrying on the snake tradition.

"After you try it, you'll like it!" we are urged by an assistant manageress with a four-foot-high black beehive hairdo, a flashy, denture-regular set of choppers and cheeks as rosy and polished as a Washington State apple. So we follow her recommendations for a soup of snake, chicken, and cat, pieces of bar-b-cued snake, a stir-fried snake with greens, whole ginger in snake broth. A bonus comes in the form of snake spleen, excised with a knife from a caged garden snake brought to the table, then squeezed into a shot glass of mao tai. Talk about swallowing bile! But this bitter medicine is considered another boost for virility, one gamble which few men over thirty can refuse.

"The spleen contains vital element NA-3, C1," says the manager cheerily. But isn't that salt? Fortunately, she isn't pushing Stewed Three Different Snakes with Chicken Feet in medicinal herbs, the ever-popular Stewed Fur Seals, or the Stir-fried Ophicephalus Fish Ball and Stewed Frog.

"The entire snake is treasure," purrs the politburo Nefertiti on her return. "It increases blood circulation, cures cough, builds the blood and organ, tones the skin and hair. Make everyone feel energy, woman get beauty!" Apparently, we've come at the right time of year, too, since she hastens to rhapsodize, "When the autumn winds start, the snakes all grow meaty. That's the best time to eat!"

Now I know the origins of the term "snake oil." Not only is snake meat very *yang* or hot, in the Chinese system, but this woman claims it helped save the lives of some Cantonese injected with experimental serums by the occupying Japanese. And she herself seems unusually pumped up. For a state-run place especially, morale in the Snake Restaurant sure is high. The whole staff is its best advertisement—including several other *madchen* in uniform with severe expressions and scary bouffants.

"Is it a cult?" I suddenly whisper to Mei. All of the waiters and waitresses are acting like indoctrinated converts. Or perhaps, after so many years, they are merely addicted to the stuff they push. It seems that all of them are unnaturally preserved, with taut skin, a stunning profusion of hair and wildly bright eyes. I feel like we're dining in *The Village of the Damned,* that sci-fi flick where all the children have eyes that glow with an inner, alien light. I keep an eye on Mei to make sure she doesn't ingest too much cobra, lest she take on the same eerie glow. Now I fear that I'll catch her hissing each time we make love. Call this the Revenge of the Snake People.

"Can you guess how long I've been here?" the head snake goddess asks ominously. "Twenty year!" This grandmother doesn't look a single shred of skin over thirty-five. And she nods fervently when I ask if she regularly tastes of the serpent.

"One day, I'd like to open my own snake restaurant," she confirms. "With reforms, we have good pay and are able to travel abroad." But there's no place like home when it comes to snake.

"I'll bet you don't envy people abroad after a meal like this," observes our irradiated hostess. Willing to hear only one reply, the number one snake lady asks, "Don't you think Chinese people really know how to eat?"

I grunt my approval while munching on a morsel of cat. But in the morning, I wake with relief at having survived this final ingestion, relief at having survived China one more time. And it's only once we've arrived at the station for the train to Hong Kong that I really feel Canton's connection to the rest of the motherland's needy mass. Inadvertently, the town's greatest tourist sight has become an unstoppable deluge of blue-clad peasants with bed rolls, this stampede of poverty-arriving undocumented and unblessed to the new economic zones which stretch the borders of China's economy to bursting. But we've soon boarded our nonstop express from underdevelopment. Crossing this most abrupt of the world's borders, it felt like everything had gone from dim bulb to bright, as though the wattage of the world had experienced a sudden power surge. No doubt the transition grows less shocking every day. But perhaps it was best to come out of China gradually—walking the surreptitious routes, floating down the Pearl River, throwing one's self into the sea and the fate that awaited in the outside world.

A half-hour out of Canton, I already miss the dumplings and the fish-flavored shredded pork. I already feel farther from China than I ever wanted to feel. But with Mei by my side, I will always have a handy way back. Perhaps we should have started our search elsewhere, for it is going to be hard to top the mainland's flavor and punch—if not service. It was an amazing comment in itself—about Chinese history, about the relative prosperity and ingenuity of Chinese at home and overseas—that I should feel daring and heretical to suggest that the best Chinese food in the world might actually be found in China.

"You want Chinese restaurants?" asked the balding, shoulder-shrugging leader of an Israeli tour group in the seats ahead of us. "Come to Tel Aviv and try Moishe Peking. It's kosher!"

This is the strangest argument I've ever heard for convincing me to exercise my right of return. As for his impressions of my adopted homeland, the balding man bellows, "*Suzhou! Shmoo-joe! Enough already! We saw the whole schmear!*"

And we ate the whole schmear.

Award-winning writer John Krich is the author of two widely praised non-fiction books, Music in Every Room *and* El Beisbol, *as well as a novel about the private life of Fidel Castro,* A Totally Free Man. *This story was excerpted from his book,* Won Ton Lust: Adventures in Search of the World's Best Chinese Restaurant. *His travel and sports writing, reportage and fiction, have appeared in* Mother Jones, Vogue, Sports Illustrated, *the* Village Voice, Image, Commentary, California, The New York Times, *and many other publications.*

JAN MORRIS

When I Became a Gastronome

It was such a simple little thing.

I CAN RECALL THE EXACT MOMENT, IN THE AUSTRALIAN SUMMER of 1962, when I became a gastronome. It was a moment less of metamorphosis than of revelation—as though a veil had been lifted from my eyes, a muffle from my tongue, releasing my responses for pleasures I knew not of. I was in my thirties then, and had never taken eating and drinking very seriously. For the most part I simply wanted to get them over with. There may have been something in my family background (we have a Quaker strain to us) which forbade me to enjoy them too much, and anyway I always had more interesting things to do. It had never much worried me when food was bad, and I was never greatly excited when it seemed better than usual.

Everything changed, however, on that Australian summer day. I was being entertained to lunch by an Australian of Hungarian origin, on his garden terrace overlooking Sydney Harbor, looking inland to the bridge. The day was fresh, warm and bright as only an Australian day can be. The harbor glittered. Ships sailed by, the green of the garden was almost unnaturally green and in my memory the flying wings of the opera house seem to have been soaring with an especially buoyant air of elation.

Into this setting, seductive and half-hallucinatory (for the green was probably no greener than any other, and the opera house had not yet been built), the Australian brought our lunch. It was nothing elaborate—fresh rolls, pâté of some sort, cheese, I think, apples and a bottle of local white wine. In substance it was not so different from the family meal I once shared with American evangelists in Afghanistan, which consisted of peanuts and water. Its spirit, though, was not the same. It seemed to me that my friend laid out the plates in the garden purringly, unguently, and when he came to eat the food he did so with a seductive crackling of bread, a voluptuous spreading of pâté, the coolest possible draughting of white wine in the sun. It reminded me of Andrew Marvell—

> What wondrous life is this I lead!
> Ripe Apples drop about my head;
> The Luscious Clusters of the Vine
> Upon my mouth do crush their Wine...

As it happens nobody could be much less pretentious about food and wine than my epicurean host that day, and he would have been astonished to know, as he ate his usual simple lunch before going back to the office, that beside him I was enjoying a moment of new vision; yet so it was, and since than I have approached my victuals with a far less Quakerly dispassion.

The Friends need a meetinghouse to bring out the best in their silence, and for myself I need a restaurant for the full experience of gourmandism. Eating domestically can be fun, can be satisfying, can be technically or artistically excellent, but for me it can never match the rounded ample pleasure of a good meal out. Whether my company has been a lover, a friend, a family party, a group of colleagues or a book—alone or with others, especially since 1962 the stir of the restaurant, the preparatory bustle of the waiters (I am generally the first guest, preferring to go to bed early), the anticipation of the menu and the fulfillment of the dish when the cover is, preferably with a flourish, removed, have all been perennial joys of my life.

I suppose my ideal restaurant is one of the old French bour-
geois kind, Madame in black bombazine and serious long-aproned
garçons pressing on one another's heels out of the kitchen, pursued by herbal fragrances and the clatter of dishes. They are hard
to find nowadays, but French restaurants of other categories continue to give me pleasure in the old tradition. My partner and I
once spent a week in the French Alps, staying in a comfortable
family hotel, eating each day gargantuan breakfasts and satisfying
suppers, walking the mountains in between. At the end of our stay,
driving down to the airport at Geneva, we found ourselves passing Le Père Bise, in those days one of France's supreme restaurants,
and scruffy as we were in jeans, boots and anoraks, we decided to
stop for lunch.

I shall always remember the welcome they gave us—a table at
the lake's edge, a plate of small lake fish with salad, little wild rasp-
berries and a carafe of white wine, served with all possible subtlety
of attention. Kindness has always been a specialty of the best
French restaurants, and nobody could have been kinder to us than
the staff of Le Père Bise (since then alas fallen into harder critical
times). We were not in the least affronted, did not in the least re-
gret our little luncheon break, when we found that the cost of it
was rather greater than that of our entire week's holiday in the
mountains, room, dinners, giant breakfasts and all.

Not kind exactly, but certainly genial is the ambience of
another excruciatingly expensive restaurant I have long been un-
wisely fond of, the Four Seasons in Manhattan. "Hey," cried the
busboy to my guest when I took an eminent journalist to lunch
there one day, "hey, great to see ya, you're looking great, how's the
game?"—for it turned out, in the American way, that they were
members of the same squash club. The Four Seasons occupies one
of the very grandest rooms in all New York, in one of the most
elegant of all skyscrapers, but it is urbanely relaxed of style. "Be
easy," Lord Melbourne once told an aspirant politician who
sought his advice about tactics, "I like an easy man." I agree, and I
like an easy restaurant, too.

By now there can be few international celebrities, in any walk of life, who have not had a meal in the Four Seasons' magnificent pool room, so that while unaccustomed guests spend half their time wondering at famous faces, the management oversees its clientele with a worldly lack of excitement, conveying messages here and there, wryly amused by pretension and reasonably tolerant of eccentricity, if sufficiently worldly itself. I was there one day when two amazing women entered with slow purposeful tread, like gangsters in an old movie. They were fiercely made up, but dressed all in black, black hats, black dresses, black shoes—stiffened black it seemed to me, as if for some macabre medieval ritual—and heavily and with a sinister dignity they lowered themselves upon a banquette, to survey the room side by side in majesty. The staff observed this stately progress as awestruck as everyone else, but nobody batted an eyelid when an elderly diner at a nearby table, hardly less majestic himself, asked of nobody in particular: "What d'you suppose they're wearing underneath?"

Oh, there are many restaurants the very opening of whose doors warm me with the promise of happy hours to come. For forty years and more—yes, since long before my Sydney revelation—I have been catching the experienced eye of the barman at Harry's Bar in Venice, looking up sidelong from opening a bottle or pouring a glass as I push through the famous swing doors. I caught that eye of sophistication somewhat nervously as a young soldier long ago, I caught it all too often when I lived in Venice, I even caught it unawares once when, making a film about the city with a German television crew, I swung into the restaurant preceded by the crouching cameraman, pursued by technicians trailing wires and microphones, and supervised anxiously, as the door closed behind me, by a director in a long black coat with a velvet collar like Diaghilev. The barman was for once in his life transfixed, the diners stared with scampi on their forks, when we appeared in such wild gallimaufry! In Harry's Bar one night a group of friends and I, being young and heedless, enjoyed our meal so much that we ordered the same thing all over again;

twenty years later a woman I met in America said fastidiously that she remembered the occasion well, having watched our performance from the next table.

Drinking is something else. Drinking for me means only wine, and I did not need my Australian to persuade me of its pleasures. I like to brag that I have drunk a glass of wine every day since the second world war, and though this is not true in the fact, since I have spent much time in places where there is no wine, it is true in the principle—the chance of war introduced me to wine, and I never turned away. I believe in wine as I believe in Nature. I cherish its sacramental and legendary meanings, not to mention its power to intoxicate, and just as Nature can be both kind and hostile, so I believe that if bad wine is bad for you, good wine in moderation does nothing but good. If I am ever challenged, I refer people to that seminal work, *Wine Is the Best Medicine*, in which the great Dr. E. A. Maury, pictured on its jacket looking terrifically healthy with a glass of champagne in his hand, prescribes a suitable wine for almost every ailment—Entre-Deux-Mers for rickets, young Beaujolais for diarrhea, two glasses of Sancerre daily to lower the blood pressure...

When I was very young I drank, like most of us, with a lack of discrimination and an unvarying enjoyment that I now envy. Thinking of myself then, I am reminded of the great Sherpa mountaineer Tenzing Norgay, who I witnessed drinking, I rather think, his very first glass of wine of any kind. It was at an official banquet in London. I sat next to the very old-school and gentlemanly functionary who had arranged the occasion, and early in the evening he remarked to me that he hoped I would enjoy the claret, not just the last of its vintage in the official cellars, but perhaps the last in London. I was much impressed, and looked across at Tenzing, who was most certainly enjoying it very much indeed, having as a standard of comparison only the species of alcoholic porridge the Sherpas call *tsang*. His was a princely figure, and as the lackeys filled and refilled his glass his face shone with pride and pleasure. It was a delight to see him. After a while the old boy on my left turned to me again. "Oh, how good it is to see," he said with the true warmth of approval, "that Mr. Tenzing *knows a decent claret when he has one!*"

My own first wines were all Italian, and nearly all red. The fact that un-Italian wines existed at all was first brought home to me in Port Said, when, on disembarking from a troop ship from Trieste in 1946, I went to a restaurant for dinner with the young commanding officer of my regiment. "Rhine wine!" exclaimed the colonel in delight—"after all these years, Rhine wine!"—and though it has since occurred to me that he must have been hardly more than a schoolboy when he had last tasted it, still his savoir faire made it clear to me that there was more to wine than plonk Chianti.

Since then I have drunk wine of more varieties than my colonel could have conceived. I have drunk Egyptian wines made by Greeks, and Chinese wines made by Frenchmen, and Zimbabwean wines, and Canadian wines, and Peloponnesian draught retsina served in tin bowls, and Scottish wines made from the sap of silver birches, and two wines at least that I swear I will never taste again—the Indian-made wine called Golconda and the kosher cabernet that is bottled in downtown Manhattan. Believing as I do too in the mythic meaning of wine, its role as a messenger from the *genii locorum*, I have also followed it to some lovely places. In the days when we could still afford to be addicted to the burgundy called Echeseaux, I once set out to trail the wine from bottle to source, from my wine rack in Wales to the exact patch of vineyard it came from. I hoped that I would find there some more explicit declaration from the earth gods—and so I did, for when I drove up the stony track to the half acre of hill-slope from which every single bottle of Echeseaux has been derived, the solitary Frenchman working there looked up, saw the Welsh plate on my car and started talking about rugby football.

But I must admit that the best of all my vinous moments have been with the old Italian red after all. We drank lots of it when we were living in Venice, and sometimes after dinner, if friends were with us, we would take a bottle or two and sail the boat out into the darkness of the lagoon. This was magic. It was not that we were drunk, only that the wine's benevolence had made us better, happier people for the evening, had opened our hearts more receptively to beauty and emotion: so that out there in the purple night, watching the lights of the ships, passing the looming tripods of the sandbank stakes, and seeing unfolded before us the grand luminosity of Venice itself, its towers and palaces radiant above the viscous water—absorbing all this in wonder and merriment, we really were touched by the gods of the place.

Perhaps they sound gross, these pleasures of food and drink— frequenting extravagant restaurants, eating dinners twice over, navigating in semi-inebriated dream among the waters of Venice: but believe me, even as I indulge myself I relish in memory the loaf of bread, the simple pâté, the cheese, the apple and the white wine that changed my life so generously beside the sea in Sydney.

Welsh essayist Jan Morris is the author of more than 30 books, including Hong Kong: Epilogue to an Empire, The World of Venice, Long Ago in France, *and* Fifty Years of Europe.

You Are Where You Eat

*Food can be a landmark as surely
as any monument.*

SHOULD TASTES GET LANDMARK STATUS? SOME PEOPLE REMEMBER the first time they saw the Tour Eiffel. I remember the first time I had tournedos Rossini at Maxim's. A filet mignon on a slab of pâté on a tuffet of brioche soaked in sauce *marchand de vin*. How could cold steel compare with that?

When you're traveling, the challenge isn't just finding a good place to eat. It's finding the place that tastes like the place you're in, what you eat when you're there that tells you you're there. I'm talking stone crabs at Joe's in Miami or baby backs at Flynn's Dixie Ribs, a shack near Key West on U.S. 1. I'm talking steamers at Louie's in Port Washington; fry bread in Kayenta, Arizona; New England clam chowder with its spreading knob of brilliant butter at the Black Dog on Martha's Vineyard; the late, great abalone sandwich at Nathan's on Coney Island; sugar-dusted Kaiser *schmarrn* in the Tyrol, and *soupe á l'oignon* at the old Palmier in Les Halles in Paris at 3 A.M.

Once you get the ur-dish thing, you have a sense of purpose no matter where you are. During a business trip I took in Los Angeles, New York got snowed in and the group I was traveling with had to make a decision. Where should we fly that night so we could get to New York in the morning when the weather lifted? The entire Midwest was open to us. We could have gone anywhere.

"How about Wisconsin," I asked. "Isn't Taliesin there?"

Nobody knew.

"How about Columbus? We could see James Thurber's house."

Nobody cared.

Then I remembered Calvin Trillin's *New Yorker* piece about Arthur Bryant's.

"What about Kansas City? We could have ribs."

Jerry, the businessman who could do anything, made a few calls. What had been a delay turned into a quest. We flew to Missouri. A limo whisked us to Arthur Bryant's with our suitcases. It was ten minutes before closing. Mr. Bryant stopped sweeping and flicked the lights back on. The ribs were big, black, and crusty, the taste of Kansas City, and each of us got an Arthur Bryant's mechanical pencil with a floating steer on top.

Arthur Bryant's is subtitled "The House of Good Eats." Restaurants with subtitles are usually ur. Take Mother's, "World's Best Ham." Their Famous Ferdi Special is to a sandwich what a sub is to a canapé. A long roll gets layered with ham, roast beef, gravy, shredded cabbage, pickles, mayo, yellow mustard, creole mustard and a ladle of "debris" (fat-logged shreds of rump meat that fall to the bottom of the pan). The Ferdi is sweet and sour, hot and cold, soft and hard. It's crunchy, smooth, and full of contradiction. Forget chicory. Forget beignets. Forget crawfish étouffée. This is the real New Orleans.

The taste of Los Angeles used to be the McCarthy salad (Charlie? Joseph? Eugene?) at the Polo Lounge in the Beverly Hills Hotel. It was California's answer to chef's salad and seemed quintessential L.A. because the pieces were chopped so fine it was already chewed for you. I thought I'd lost my favorite salad when the hotel was sold. I kind of went into mourning. Then somebody told me about the Gotham at Cafe on 5 at Bergdorf's. It is the identical salad chopped the identical way with the identical Russian dressing a mere 38 blocks from home.

London is Welsh rarebit at the counter of the Fountain Restaurant at Fortnum & Mason. Listed on the menu under Toasted and Savory, this is molten cheese at it's cheesiest—hot, dripping, and Day-Glo orange. If you're not sure what piquant is, Fortnum & Mason's Welsh rarebit is the defining dish. Do not order an ice cream soda to go with it. An ice cream soda in England means something entirely different from what it means here. You get something stranger than what you get when you order an ice cream soda in Boston, where what you want is called a frappé.

Ireland is oatmeal, rich as a nut. You can't get a bad bowl of oatmeal in Ireland. I know. I've stayed in B & B's like jails with shower curtains for doors, but the oatmeal is never less than chewy and full blown, as satisfying as a steak. A bowl of oatmeal in Ireland with a little milk and unrefined sugar, and you're fueled, you're ready for a revolution.

Sometimes the ur-dish is what a town is famous for. Other times it's the association the food has with the place, so that even a frankfurter at The Roadside Rest can resonate. When I was little, the taste of the thrilling ride to Long Beach on Long Island was a Rangeburger at the Texas Ranger. This sloppy, flappy burger was piled high with mayonnaisey slaw and a thick slice of tomato. It told us we were almost at the bridge that led us to the beach. The taste of the beach itself was my mother's famous "chopped egg." The eggy mayonnaise seeped into the sun-warmed Wonder Bread. No matter how carefully the sandwiches were wrapped in wax paper, there was always a little sand.

Some people will swear the taste of Atlantic City is James's or Frailinger's saltwater taffy. My husband says it's hot peanuts from Mr. Peanut on the boardwalk. For me, Atlantic City will always be the Miracle of the Club Sandwich. When I was eight, my grandparents drove my sister and me there. We checked into the Shelburne, a gray whale of a hotel with taps in the bathroom for your choice of sea water or artesian well, then went to the Traymore for lunch.

"What's that?" I asked my grandparents.

"A club sandwich," they said.

Two kinds of water in the bathroom! Two kinds of sandwiches in the sandwich! It came toasted on white in four sections with a frilly toothpick in each quarter and the good kind of pickle spear.

A triple whammy is when the food, the place, and what's going on in the world all tie in together. This happened on Aug. 4, 1962, aboard the SS *United States.*

"You can have anything you want at any meal," Dad explained.

"Anything?"

"Anything. Even if it's not on the menu."

To test the waters, I ordered something I'd seen only in comics: pheasant under glass. I got pheasant under glass. Once I knew I really could have anything, I only wanted one thing: caviar—tubs of it with piles of decrusted perfectly toasted white bread. I was on the sea eating what tasted of the sea and reading *Hawaii,* an island born from a coconut bobbing in the sea.

Finally I understood the meaning of sublime. Then the news came over the wire. Marilyn Monroe was dead. I can never eat caviar without thinking of her. Or think of her without wanting caviar.

Thanks to fusion cuisine, it's hard to get the pure taste of anyplace anymore. Where will it end? Thai-Inuit? Franco-shtetl? Pirogi con salsa?

Not that I mind that the taste of Florida has become Crackling Togarashi Spiced Chicken Salad with Asian Greens at The Heights in Coral Gables instead of a scary place called Pickin' Chicken where Granny Ethel took me in the '50s and the waitresses dressed like Mammy in *Gone With the Wind.* Or that Boston, which was once the taste of lobster rolls at Faneuil Hall, is now Lydia Shire's Duck Grilled Over Cherry Chips, Pan Juices Spiked with Pomegranate.

Besides, it doesn't do you any good to get attached to a taste. In fact, it's dangerous. Ask anyone who ever loved Schrafft's fudge. Dense, velvety, dark, and winy—was the secret ingredient...Cointreau? Coffee? Cinnamon? Is it true that Julia Child is constantly trying to duplicate it? Schrafft's fudge was the taste of

New York, my favorite taste in the world. Every place I go, if there's a candy store, I stop and buy a piece of fudge, hoping. Nothing comes close. People who fall in love with a taste are asking for culinary heartbreak no matter where they are. I can't find Flynn's Dixie Ribs anymore either. Must have blown over in Hurricane Andrew.

Patricia Volk is a novelist, essayist, and teacher who lives in New York.

* * *

Go Fish

Be fluid, like water.

AT MY APARTMENT ON CHOPINA STREET, THE SPARTAN DECOR exudes the same communist style as the plain bricked exterior of the building. My Chagall calendar is nailed next to the doorway in the hall, in order to give the place some color. The ethereal painting of the month appears eerie; or maybe it is the juxtaposition of deep blue paint strokes against vintage wallpaper that is unsettling. There are three weeks left without black Sharpie Xs through them—only three weekends left to see the rest of Poland. The pile of scrap paper with names and nine-digit phone numbers, neatly penned in Polish-style cursive, stares at me.

My next-door neighbor, Michael, is home. I have been teaching his mother, Halina, first grade level English for two months already. Michael has been like the younger brother I never had, and Halina my Polish mother. In the icy winter, Halina knits an intricately patterned cardigan for me. Later in the spring, twenty-year-old Michael shepherds me on and off the trains, insisting upon hauling my suitcases for me. The two of them are my family in Gliwice, a college town in lower Silesia.

The Poles pronounce Michael's familiar name with the foreign sound of "Meehau." His English is smooth and effortless, as is his

Polish, German, and Russian. Once again, I ask him for another favor. He dials the unfamiliar phone number and asks for Agnieszka, "*Dzien Dobry. Tak. Tak. Pani* Restivo..."

As the conversation ensues, I slightly decipher it with the aid of his gentle nod and eyes that reassure mine with comfort. "Renée, what will you be wearing on the day you meet them?" he asks.

"A forest green sweatshirt with a big paisley R on it," I decide as I realize no one in Poland will ever know that the R stands for Rutgers University. People back home never know what it means either.

Michael relays the information to Agnieszka in Polish, and then hangs up the red, five-and-dime quality telephone. With no answering machine, reliable operators, or flair for rather archaic language I rely upon him with trust. I thank him, offer him an Italian-American style dinner of baked ziti and garlic bread, and say goodnight all in one breath. "*Dobra noc*," he whispers back. I close the door between us and inhale the sweet smells of garlic, tomatoes, and the basil that I hand-imported from the farmers' market in Vienna the weekend before. Dinner is going to be just like home tonight.

Before I go to sleep, I daydream of the South Baltic Sea, shipyards, the Solidarity movement, lumber, metalworking, and Malbourk Castle. What does a place look like when it is exactly 1,000 years old? Taken by Teutonic Knights, captured by Russia, ceded to Prussia, Nazi-controlled, then returned to Poland again; such fascinating history must have produced an exuberant mix of architectural styles and culture. The seven-foot high, smooth, tiled furnace interrupts my thoughts as it hisses at me, until I fall asleep in a maddening sweat produced by the smothering heat.

During the five-hour train ride from Katowice to Warsaw to Gdansk, I devour hearts made of chocolate-covered gingerbread, with strawberry jam in the middle. The tattered fabric booths of my second-class seat call my attention to them. Somehow, the train ride enables my mind to smell and feel an aura that belongs more to the 1920s or '30s. There is a distinct atmosphere here; I've only encountered it before in films or books. The distant hum of the horn blows as the wheels spin on the tracks below me, transforming the present into the past for an instant. Hours of struggling to converse with fellow passengers in first grade Polish and English pass by. The train comes to a full stop.

When the train arrives at the Gdansk station, Agnieszka kisses me firmly on the lips and embraces me as if I'm an old friend and she hasn't seen me in years. It seems like we've met before. Her plump hands insist upon taking my backpack, as her sisterly smile meets mine. There is a bond between us. Her devoted mother, Maryska, had cared for my grandfather until the day of his passing. Still, it is hard to believe that we are just two strangers from distant countries, meeting one another because our families insist upon it.

Three tram rides, ten zloty, and one hour later we arrive in the suburb of Gdansk, where she has lived her entire life. Agnieszka takes me by the hand and guides me up, down, and around coarse cobblestone streets that seem familiar and distant at the same time. As we walk, our pace is relaxed yet efficient. Agnieszka is neat in appearance; her secondhand sweatshirt, jeans, and sneakers hint at her meager income, yet she continues to splurge on anything edible at the kiosks and street vendors along the way. She grasps my backpack in one arm, juggling it along with plastic bags of miniature cucumbers in fresh pickling brine, loaves of rye bread wrapped in brown paper, herbed farmers' cheese, and packets of mixed chocolates. Soon, my one free arm is filled too—with fresh cheese, potato pierogies, *jagoda* berry jam—the other arm still clings to hers. Our cornucopia of goodies makes it impossible to thumb through our Polish-English dictionaries, so we barely speak. Her guiding eyes and hands pull me in the right direction; my smile indicates my contentment, as we communicate without words.

Although Agnieszka's scanty apartment is the size of a small garage, her proud expression upon our entrance reveals how content she is there. She fluffs up the old pillows that are scattered upon the couch and gestures towards it for me to sit down. She pushes a bowl of spring strawberries and stemmed cherries towards me to pick from. We struggle to speak word by word, letter by letter, sound by sound, as we encounter frustration and accomplishment at the same time.

Hours later, Agnieszka's husband, Tadeusz, oversees her preparing dinner in the shared kitchen outside in the hallway. Soon they appear in the doorway, bestowing plate after plate—heaped up higher than any I have ever seen in America—upon me. The string beans topped with butter-drizzled bread crumbs entice me, as do the fluffy mashed potatoes. My eyes engage a thoughtfully arranged pile of sliced cucumbers in dill cream sauce.

Unable to bear the suspense of the entree any longer, I fidget around in my seat and regard the bounty of food before me. Meehau had mentioned my strict vegetarian diet, during their brief conversation just days ago. I do not expect Agnieszka and Tadeusz to come out next with a plate stacked high with grilled quinoa tempeh, or tofu sautéed with fresh ginger, minced garlic, and organic shoyu sauce. The native Poles rarely use fresh garlic in their home cooking; as for ginger, only fanatics like me look hard enough to find it on the shelves of the health food stores here.

Meehau had mentioned that Agnieszka and Tadeusz were at first concerned with what they should prepare for me, but he told me, "Not to worry. They figured it out."

Tadeusz soon emerges from the aroma of butter and onions, his arms heavy from the plate of herb crusted fish that he presents before me with a bow of respect. A smile immediately emerges on my face, as nausea invades my gut. A vegetarian for eight years, I have not touched "anything with a face" to my lips since I became an animal rights activist in high school.

Tadeusz serves me diligently, as he positions a piece of the fleshy main course, sprinkled with just-chopped parsley, on my plate. Agnieszka surrounds the dead breaded entree with the more lively green beans, potatoes, cucumbers, pickles, and exotic Polish salads. The beans and bread crumbs bring my taste buds to a climax, as I contemplate whether or not to eat the fish.

If I indulge in its taste, I become a hypocrite. If I refuse to eat it, I become an ungrateful and difficult dinner guest from America. Agnieszka and Tadeusz probably spent half a month's salary to feed me...a spoiled American. I can't help but wonder if the carrots and potatoes are organic. Am I so privileged as to refuse the main course, which they prepared and revealed with such care? Maybe my digestive system is no longer capable of breaking down the flesh of an aquatic vertebrate.

Wondering where the fins and scales are, I can't bring myself to consume the filet.

"So, what kind of fish is this?" I ask Tadeusz, adding "Everything looks delicious!" and thanking Agnieszka with a *Dziekuje Bardzo!*

"I don't know how to say it," Tadeusz declares.

"Is it flounder, bass, carp, or trout?" I ask.

"No, I don't think there is a name for it in English," he replies. Agnieszka looks bewildered. She doesn't understand much of our conversation, because it is flowing too fast for her dictionary.

On to the sweet creamed, shredded carrot and raisin salad; the tastefully sour beets; the fresh baked rye bread; a homemade Polish meal that reminds me of a Thanksgiving at home.

Tadeusz with his mouth full, his plate almost cleared says, "Renée, fish is good, yes?" Without thinking, my fork breaks the flesh of the fish and I shovel it into my rather herbivorous, virgin mouth.

"*Bardzo Dobry!*" I say, telling him how delectable everything tastes. The fish doesn't taste like fish to me though, it tastes the way I remember a savory chicken breast did. The flesh tastes fresh and fulfilling, unlike the dead taste I thought about minutes before.

My belly comfortably full, I finally understand the Polish phrase that Agnieszka utters over dinner, "A guest is like God in the house."

Finishing the last seasoned morsels of fish from my plate, I wonder if I will die later that night. Maybe my stomach will become violently agitated, as I go to sleep that evening on Agnieszka's snug couch. I struggle with the uncertainty that crops up before me, as I fork the remaining crumbs of fish from my plate and let them greet my mouth.

Renée Restivo traveled solo through eastern Europe in 1997 while teaching English as a second language. She was the only American woman living in Gliwice, Poland at the time. She holds a B.A. in English from Rutgers University, and is currently pursuing an M.F.A. in creative writing at New School University. She has studied vegetarian cooking at the Natural Gourmet Institute for Food & Health in New York, and has made many memorable journeys throughout western Europe, the Caribbean, the U.S., and South Pacific.

DARRYL BABE WILSON

Daddy and the Porcupine

It always tastes better in the woods.

WE TOOK THE .22 RIFLE AND WENT UP NEAR THE SPRING. HE knew *ha'ya'wa* (porcupines) lived there. There were several in the nearby trees. He fired, and after a few moments one dropped to earth, thud. He picked it up by the long claws of its left hand, and we hurried back to the fire. As I followed, I kept a wary eye on that animal that grew way over a million needles and could throw them a mile! At least that's what Old Uncle said that he heard, one time up near Alturas.

Being a butcher, Daddy magically sliced the porcupine here, then there, then pulled the entrails out. He chopped some onions, potatoes, and carrots that we had carried over the pass in a paper bag. He threw some salt and pepper inside the cavity of the porcupine, then worked in the whole mixture he had chopped up. Finally, he took a piece of baling wire and sewed the porcupine closed. I watched carefully, but still don't know how he kept from being poked to death by a million porcupine quills.

Next he scooped the coals from the fire pit, put the porcupine in the pit, belly up, laid some dampened oak leaves on the belly where he had sewn the animal together, then covered it lightly with dirt and threw the glowing coals back on top of it all. We then went to the barn, harnessed the horses, and took them, harnesses jingling softly, on the old road down to the field to pull the rusty plow.

The team all hooked up, we began laboring. Daddy made it look easy. Cap and Fox (the horses) pulled and he aimed the plow, turning the black, mushroom-sweet loam. Meanwhile, I was walking along, picking up worms for fishing, and searching everywhere for responsibility.

For some reason, about noon, I remembered the porcupine and panicked. I thought it must have been all burned up. I threw a clod of dirt in front of Daddy; between him and the horses. He hollered "Whoa," leaning back and pulling on the reins. With a sigh and snorting through their huge lips, the horses stopped.

"*Ha'y;'wa! Ha'ya'wa!* Daddy! The porkey-pine! The porkey-pine!"

He laughed, unhooked the horses from the plow, tying them to a nearby scrub oak where they could both water and eat. We then hurried up the hill to the fire pit and our porcupine, which I was certain had burned to an absolute pile of nothingness. We approached the fire. I could see that it was out, not even smoking. Daddy scooped off the dirt and dusted the powder from the expired coals. Where the leaves had been piled on the porcupine's belly, the hair was barely singed. Where the coals had come directly into contact with the quills and the skin, they had crusted like bubbly pork rinds, with the texture of charred leather.

We broke the porcupine open, discarding the plasticlike, burned skin, and began eating the dark, sweetly scorched meat. Lightly salted, it was sooo good! After eating that meal cooked in "the old way," Daddy reburied the porcupine in the pit, then we went back to work with the horses and the plow, turning the earth for a few more hours.

Eventually, I had a can half full of worms for which I felt responsible. Quitting work, we took the horses back to the barn, unharnessed them, led them to the water trough, watched them drink deeply. After retiring them, we went back to the fire where Daddy dug up the porcupine again. It was still hot! Like starved coyotes, we ate again.

Born in 1939 at the confluence of the Fall River and the Pit River in northeastern California, Darryl Babe Wilson is a member of the Achumawe and Atsugewi tribes. He earned a Ph.D. in 1997 from the University of Arizona at Tucson. The father of seven sons, Wilson currently lives in San Jose, California, and teaches American Indian history and literature at DeAnza College. This story was excerpted from his book, The Morning the Sun Went Down.

JIM HARRISON

The Raw and the Cooked

Life is a banquet, so don't starve to death!

IN GEOLOGIC TIME EVERYONE NOW PRESENT ON EARTH WILL BE dead in a few milliseconds. What a toll! Only through the diligent use of sex, and, you guessed it, food, can we further ourselves, hurling our puny I *ams* into the face of twenty billion years of mute, cosmic history. With every fanny glance or savory bite, you are telling a stone to take a hike, a mountain that you are alive, a star that you exist.

A few of you of a critical bent and a firm memory of third grade are asking, "What about shelter and clothing?" Not at all an interesting question, and to which I pose another: Would you rather camp in a pup tent at Lutéce with Elle Macpherson or spend your pathetically short time on earth with real estate agents and haberdashers?

Now that we have returned to earth from the nether reaches of the cosmos, we can address certain dilemmas of dislocation and free-floating anguish, to wit, is there an American cuisine? Of course not. Have you forgotten the melting pot, a notion that also tends to be sprung on us in the third grade? Melting pots don't produce specific cuisines, or do so only inasmuch as directed by region and ethnicity. In terms of eating, you are far luckier if your

grandmother is French, Italian, or Cajun rather than Scotch-
English, Irish, German, or Swedish. The frontier tended to be
pork-ridden and verminish after the game was gone. Farther
west, no buffalo cuisine evolved except among the plains natives
because we slaughtered twenty million buffalo within a scant
thirty years for their tongues and hides and to make the area safe,
as Phil Sheridan said, for "spotted cattle and the festive cowboy."
Cuisines don't evolve in thirty years, or out of movement for that
matter, but out of bioregions maintained in good health by their
inhabitants.

Societies like our own and Germany's, burdened as we are by a
soul history dominated by the fetishists of pragmatism, tend to eat
for function—a meal is mere fuel for the realities. It is interesting to
note that now that our drive toward dominance has become somewhat enfeebled in the direction of a service economy, the food is
getting better. You are liable to find an acceptable, if not good,
restaurant in any American town of more than ten thousand. Travel
is not nearly the culinary mud bath it was even ten years ago. In
fact, our past wretchedness is no doubt the cause of our current relative inventiveness. The truth—that most of our best efforts still fall
short of a French truck stop—must not discourage us. For those of
us who have just passed fifty, our daily prayer should be that our
guts hold out for the coming new age of American food. I just
came to a painful, jolting stop, remembering a college trauma. A
kindly professor drew me aside while I was in the process of flunking out of graduate school and told me that while I might someday be a poet or storyteller, it was certain that I would never be "a
thinker," that I was far too interested in "the textural concretia" of
life itself. In a trice I hitchhiked the thousand miles to Greenwich
Village and had an Italian-sausage sandwich with fried onions and
green peppers. By the next day at lunch, Kant and Wittgenstein had
dissolved in the marinara on the 50-cent spaghetti plate at Romeo's.
I returned to Rimbaud, Apollinaire, and Char for wisdom, abandoning forever the academic pursuit of trying to answer questions
that no one ever asks. Just recently I made a difficult three-day trip
to Paris. As you have no doubt noted, scarcely anyone calls it Gay

Paree anymore, evidence that the myths of our youth have been further dissembled. How I craved to go there as a Midwestern high schooler (Haslett Rural Agricultural High School, now a suburb) flunking chemistry while trying to read Sartre's *Being and Nothingness*. The book was inscrutable, but that meant nothing, as I intended to carry it into a Left Bank café and meet a dark-eyed girl wearing a turtleneck. Back in her garret I would drink wine while she bathed in the sink without tearing it off the wall. Errant details always ruin fantasy. The sink *does* tear off the wall, and she dies from knocking her head against a table leg. I'm convicted of murder and spend the rest of my life on Devil's Island. The bell rings and chemistry class is over.

Frankly, Paris has always somewhat frightened me. I hadn't been there in fourteen years, and on three brief earlier trips I had been broke, traveling on the generosity of friends. Once at Faugeron's I estimated the bill to equal three months of my income. When alone I feared ordering a meal because they might spring some sort of 500 percent tax on me. People were so beautifully dressed and appeared to be on important missions, even while sitting at cafés. Despite two years of college French, I could not bring myself to say anything, though I was expert at the menus. Paris is far and away the most gorgeous city on earth, but it chills the blood when you're broke. Only up in Normandy with the familiar smells of hay, earth, and cow shit did I feel comfortable.

On this brief trip I discovered both of us had changed. This time I flew first-class (expense account) and was somewhat nervous that someone I knew would discover me doing so. As the wag Garrison Keillor has pointed out, Midwesterners hate to be discovered at pretension. Naturally, I was caught by an intellectual acquaintance who glared at me, said hello, and headed for steerage. I could barely swallow my first drink but got over it when it occurred to me that I no longer believe that a plane is more, or less, likely to crash into the ocean because I am a passenger, a specific relief from ego.

At my not-very-humble quarters at the Plaza-Athénée, I napped from the overnight flight, waiting for lunch and my first meeting with a prominent actor. In three days our meetings took place at lunch, dinner, while taking walks, and at nightclubs, actually accomplishing a full hour of work. Such are the ways of the movie business, where 99 percent of anything accomplished is derived from mutual wordless assumptions. In this case the sole irritations were the paparazzi, who grew in number until by the third evening I was close to pointless violence. Rather than being perceived as a sensitive writer, I was mistaken several times for the actor's "security," probably due to my moderately burly physique and crummy Midwestern clothes. This has happened before, and I merely pat my breast as if carrying heat, perhaps the 9-mm Walther I stole from Hunter Thompson ten years ago in Key West after he ruined a beach picnic by shooting dead jellyfish.

But anyone can have meetings. It takes real attention to eat well. The first lunch at the Lipp was late and a bit rushed. Since it was a hot day, I ate an enormous plate of their famed *choucroute garnie.* In that the French are not exactly pro-German, this is considered to be strictly an Alsatian dish. We lightened up that evening by going to the Stresa, where *choucroute*-bloat allowed me only pasta *al'oglio* and a wonderful salad of chicory and watercress.

Very early (jet lag) the next morning I managed a three-hour walk, got lost, and finally took a three-block cab ride to the hotel, after being misdirected several times by friendly folk. Since it was hot again we went to Gourmet Ternes, owned and operated by the former head of the butchers' union in Paris and reputed to have the best beef. In consideration of the heat, I skipped the rillettes I desperately wanted, had a lentil salad and an enormous chunk of filet. So much for American beef pride—this was as good, if not better, than the Palm or Bruno's Pen and Pencil. We delayed dinner until late, waiting for the heat to subside, which it didn't. At the Voltaire I went ahead with foie gras and *tête de veau,* a preparation from the tongue, cheek, and brains of a calf with a wonderful sauce *gribiche.*

During the next day's dawn walk my whole system seemed to be backing up, as it were. A wise man would have fasted and communed with pigeons, but at lunch at Faucet's I started simply with an eggplant fan and *oculus,* letting down my guard with a confit of goose thigh accompanied by potatoes fried in goose fat. The saving grace is that these restaurants are not of the "all you want to eat" variety. Dinner at Belecour moved gracefully into the top-ten-of-a-lifetime category, which is no mean thing. I had not heard of the chef, Gerard Goutagny, who is a genius of the simple—which, of course, is tremendously complex. I had a salad of poached ray on a bed of *passe-pierre*, a kind of wild seaside string bean, followed by the roast pigeon I should have communed with, followed by a grand fresh fig tart.

For some reason, at dawn I felt crisp and lean with nary a stomach burble. On the way to Orly it occurred to me, as it had on my three previous trips, that the singular French gift is to allow each ingredient to taste like its essence while marrying it with another. Their poet of the Resistance, René Char, said that "lucidity is the wound closest to the sun." This is certainly true of their good restaurants, where clarity of intent informs every move.

Naturally it was hot when I got home, so I barbecued an Amish chicken using Sweet Baby Ray's ("the boss sauce") as a base. I have heard that Paul Bocuse heads for barbecue shacks in America. A full day out of Paris I headed for my cabin for detoxification. Since it was hot in the Upper Peninsula, I made a mouth-blasting Thai curry out of a low-cal turkey thigh. That evening at the tavern there was much talk of a huge marauding black bear that had entered the village, destroying the beehives of Stan, Mike, and Willard. Rich had brought his hounds to town and was running the bear. We could hear them baying in the distance through the screen door of the bar. The trouble was that the bear was too big to "tree" and was safe in the night. Suddenly I was a very long way from Paris.

Jim Harrison lives with his family on a farm in northern Michigan. He has written two collections of novellas, Legends of the Fall *and* The Woman Lit by Fireflies; *six novels,* Wolf, A Good Day to Die, Farmer, Warlock, Sundog, *and* Dalva; *and seven books of poetry. His work has been translated and published in nine languages. He also wrote* Just Before Dark: Collected Nonfiction.

PART TWO

Some Things to Do

ROBERT L. STRAUSS

The Ceremony of One Chip

What they are is what they are.

THE OLD STONE DINING ROOM AT THE TASSAJARA ZEN MOUNTAIN
Center, twelve miles inland from Big Sur, was filled to capacity and
busy with conversation. The moment Edward Espe Brown entered, draped in the robes of a Zen priest, the quiet chitchat
stopped. Author of vegetarian classics such as *The Tassajara Bread
Book, Tassajara Cooking,* and co-author of *The Greens Cookbook*
(with Deborah Madison), Ed was about to give an evening lecture,
one of three I would hear while participating in his workshop
"Cooking as a Spiritual Practice."

I had gone to Tassajara hoping to overcome my performance
anxiety in the kitchen which for years has made every dinner
party, every entertaining occasion, something to fear and dread
rather than enjoy. In his workshop, Ed concentrated on the very
basics. We tasted salt. We tasted pepper. We sharpened knives. We
meditated. At Tassajara, snuggled deep into the rugged Santa Lucia
mountains, there were no carbonated beverages, no meat, no junk
food. We ate beautifully prepared vegetarian meals. We thought
about food at its most elemental in our attempt to appreciate more
deeply the joy and pleasure it can give.

Although Ed is highly regarded as a chef it seemed at Tassajara

93

he was more respected for his knowledge of dharma than of food. The room remained quiet as he settled into his chair, adjusted his robes, and pulled the microphone close. I didn't expect instantaneous enlightenment from Ed's lecture but was hoping for something thought-provoking and profound. After what seemed like a very long time, he finally said, "I really don't have much to say this evening" and chuckled to himself.

The room grew quiet and solemnity had reestablished itself when Ed reached down and began fidgeting with something in his bag. Although I couldn't see what it was, the crinkly sound was unmistakable. Ed had a bag of potato chips.

"Tonight we're going to perform the ceremony of eating just one chip," he announced. Something, however, was already amiss. Someone had gotten into Ed's nine-ounce bag of Lay's and he wasn't sure if there would be enough chips for the hundred or so people crowded in the room. That problem appeared to be solved when several closely shorn Zen students raised their hands and asked the master what to do if they didn't want to eat even *one* chip. "Then you will celebrate the ceremony of *not* eating one chip," Ed answered. "In Zen," he noted, "the eating of one potato chip and the not eating of one potato chip are kind of the same thing."

When the bag finally came our way, the Zen student next to me rummaged around at the bottom and found the tiniest shard which he placed on the end of his finger as though it was a silicon chip and he was part of an Intel ad. My other neighbor dropped his chip. It broke in two. He looked at it mortified and then had to stifle a laugh. This was, after all, the ceremony of eating one, not two chips.

Ed instructed us how to approach our chips. Foremost was concentration. "Collect your mind," he said. "Attune your mind to the chip. Pay attention to the chip." We were to use all our senses, our fingers, our eyes as well as our taste buds. He reminded us to be aware of our ears because "there will be some crunching going on." And we were to be mindful, meaning that we needed to be fully aware of what we were about to do.

Usually it is only foods that we don't care to eat or are repelled by that we give such close attention to. I'm sure that I had never before been mindful of even one of the thousands of chips I have eaten. I took a good long look at my chip.

It was shaped like a girl's tongue caught in mid-giggle, a cute squiggle with a thin corona of gold running around its blond edge. I smelled it and my nose filled with the familiar scent of grease and starch. I ran my tongue over its rough surface and felt its salty effervescence. There seemed to be a lot of un-Zen like giggling going on as people inspected their own chips.

When we were finally told to eat our chips there was a crunch more than worthy of one of Jay Leno's old Dorito's television ads that used to shake the screen. After digestion had begun, Ed asked people how the experience had been for them.

Some commented on the salty aftertaste. Others noted how well the fingers and the mouth worked together. One person said holding the single chip had made him very nervous about the whole enterprise. Several others were still working on the residue caught between their teeth. The conscientious objectors said they were surprised by the loudness of the crunch. A lone dissenter didn't quite get the point, commenting, "But chips are meant to be eaten quickly and absentmindedly."

Ed told us that chips are perfect for what they are but because, like so many things in life, we take them for granted. We don't have a sense of them no matter how many we have eaten. The whole notion, he explained, was to take the time, to have a careful awareness of whatever we are doing or eating or cooking and not assume that one already knows all that there is to know. Not even about the simple guilty pleasure of a single potato chip.

After carefully observing a chip for the first time and fully experiencing its salty, greasy, pulpy "Buddha nature," Ed told us he was able to walk away from potato chips for several years. "But now," he said, "I'm thinking they're pretty good again." Me too.

Robert L. Strauss is the author of more than four dozen television documentaries and has worked as a management consultant in over fifty countries. His articles have appeared in the Chicago Tribune, Saveur, *the* San Francisco Examiner, *the* Los Angeles Times, Salon, *and other Travelers' Tales books.*

THERESA M. MAGGIO

Love on a Plate

Sicily's abundance from the sea and garden
is a communal feast, served up and
savored right on the street.

WHEN I GO TO SICILY I EAT STREET FOOD. IT'S CHEAP, IT'S GOOD, and it's a way to watch Sicilians. Street food feeds a need there much deeper than hunger—their need to be close. Sicilians telephone each other from the back of the bus to the front, and seek out the crowded beaches, the piazzas packed with people and markets where they're likely to get mauled. They must have company, or at least an audience, for whatever they do. In Sicily, where food is love and the street is a stage, street food is more than a cheap meal, it's communion.

Some of my fondest memories revolve around it. Twelve years ago I lived with a fisherman in Mondello, a beach town and fishing port just northwest of Palermo. In the center of the piazza there's a fountain with a bare-breasted mermaid facing the sea, her arms raised to the sky with a fish in one hand and a seashell in the other. Between her and the turquoise bay, there used to be a row of shacks selling *frutti di mare*: octopuses in tanks, pyramids of spiny *ricci*—the sea urchins that look like horse chestnuts—and raw oysters, steamed clams, and purple-blue mussels, all served on handpainted ceramic platters. At night in the huts on the water's edge, bare light bulbs hung low over steaming pots behind the cooks in their smeared white aprons. At their backs the black cliffs of Capo Gallo and Monte Pellegrino cuddled the moon when it rose shrimp-colored over the sea.

Evenings Piero and I used to sit outside Renato Bar beside the mermaid to watch the Palermitani come in from the city by the hundreds to graze at the seafood shacks. Men and women weighed down by gold and wearing their best shoes dragged their whiny kids by the hand that wasn't holding an ice cream cone. They'd stroll and stop to belly up to a counter, order a plate of *ricci,* seven of them for about $5. Leone, who dived for the *ricci* by day, cracked them open at night with a long, sharp knife. It was like cracking geodes—inside the brown shells were the orange star-shaped gonads of the urchin, shiny and wet, which his customers scooped out with a crust of bread. Most of the shacks are gone now because they blocked the view of the sea from the piazza, and when the World Cup soccer games were played in Palermo in 1990 the authorities ordered them removed. You can still find impromptu seafood booths in nearby Palermo, especially during religious feasts, but nowhere in such numbers and variety. Now tourists in Mondello have the sea view, but the locals lost something they loved.

I didn't eat seafood, so Piero, my fisherman, would walk over to the outdoor *friggeria* (the fry shop's still there, behind the mermaid) to buy me an *arancina,* a hot brown snowball of deep-fried rice filled with melted butter, béchamel and bits of ham. Or sometimes he brought back a white paper sack of *panelle,* crisp little squares of deep-fried chickpea flour to go with my glass of beer.

Back then, I was a kept woman. Piero supported us on what he earned fishing, and in the summer he worked as a lifeguard on Mondello Beach. All July and August I sat in his umbrella chair and watched Sicilians. We didn't have to leave the beach to eat. Every day a tanned towheaded boy from the city picked his way through the beach blankets with a cut-glass bowl full of iced co-conut slices balanced over his shoulder in his upturned palm.

"*Coco bello!*" he sang. Piero waved him down and chose two meaty white chunks, which the boy handed over with pincers.

Piero always overpaid and told him to keep the change. The boy was one of five brothers from a poor family in Palermo, Piero said, and their father was in jail but got released on weekends to work the beach with his family. An older brother sold hot corn on the cob, which Sicilians devoured without butter or salt but which tasted like overcooked cow corn to me. Another brother trudged the sand with a cooler of iced drinks. The strap dug deep into his bare shoulder and he sang. "*Acqua, aranciata, birra,* Coca-Cola, Sp-r-r-r-ite!"

In the winter I'd take the bus into Palermo to walk through the Vucciria, a souk-like market off the Piazza San Domenico in Via Roma where the specialty is fresh fish but you can buy almost anything edible. Its main street is a narrow down-sloping canyon bordered by four-story tenements. In late morning, spears of sunlight strike the cherry-red tarps stretched taut above the vendors and glossy black slabs of marble shine under their feet, forever wet with melting fish ice. (A Sicilian who says he'll pay you when the Vucciria dries up means when hell freezes over.) Shoppers shoulder through the fray past mounds of black olives the size of quail eggs and cooked baby artichokes bobbing in cauldrons. Down at the base of the street, I once watched a man in a suit coat and fedora choose a small octopus from a tank, have it boiled, squeeze a lemon over it, and eat it for breakfast. In a corner of the cramped piazza two men stood behind a belly-high barrel eating *milza* and washing it down with tumblers of white wine. *Milza* is thinly sliced calf spleen, deep-fried and drizzled with lard and cheese and served on a bun. They wiped their greasy chins with their shirt sleeves, laughing and joking in the warm winter sunshine.

There were bushel baskets overflowing with *babbaluci*, tiny white snails that climbed over each other trying vainly to escape. In July, during the five-day feast of Santa Rosalia, men deep-fry them with garlic in olive oil on street corners. Revelers suck them out of their shells and chase it with a bottle of beer.

In the market I watched one man stop at what looked like a plate full of glass splinters. He grabbed a fistful, threw his head back and swallowed them. They were *neonati*, the transparent newborn fish that Sicilian women steam and sprinkle on pasta but men just eat raw, for virility, the man told me. A fisherman, he liked to scoop *neonati* live from his net, salted by the sea, "and feel them wriggle down my throat."

I preferred *pizzette*, the palm-sized pizzas I bought for a dollar in bars or bakeries. They have kept me alive on the road; if I eat one for brunch I'm good until afternoon. In Mondello we lived 50 feet from the piazza in a street just one block long. Summer nights, when it was time to eat supper but too hot to cook, Piero would stop at the foot of the Via Terza Compagnia to buy boiled potatoes and green beans that Filippo, the greengrocer, had cooked over a gas burner on the pavement outside his shop. While he rolled up a paper cone and filled it with our supper (just add vinegar and toss), I would choose a roasted red pepper from the pan it was baked in. Then we'd walk four doors up in the 9 o'clock twilight and eat on our second-floor balcony.

On hot nights the lady next door sat her 3-year-old twins on the hood of her car and fed them pasta below us. She twirled the spaghetti onto a fork and the girls sucked in their supper strand by strand. The noodles whipped their cheeks with red sauce and made their mother laugh—love from a bowl, in the street, where there was a breeze and people watching.

Theresa M. Maggio is working on a book about the tonnara, *the tuna trap which takes place off Favignama in Italy.*

STEPHANIE SARVER

The Solitary Scone

Bake it in your existential oven.

MAKE THESE SCONES, WHICH HAVE A BISCUIT-LIKE TEXTURE, WHEN you are alone on a Sunday morning. On a day when the sky is clear, rise at dawn, or even before dawn, and if the weather allows, open your windows and listen first to the silence of the early day, and then as light approaches, to the birds whose songs will rise with the sun. I prefer to prepare these delicacies in a kitchen graced with a window that faces east.

Begin with one cup of raisins. Place them in a bowl and cover them with boiling water. Consider the water. Trace its path from your tap back through time to its source. If, like me, you live near San Francisco, you may enjoy the sweet water of the Sierra Nevada. Imagine yourself as a link in a long chain of aqueous events that begins with the evaporation of water from the sea, which ascends to the heavens, where it condenses into great clouds that are driven to land by lofty winds. Envision the clouds snagging on the high ridge of the Sierras, where they drop their precious cargo as winter snow, which becomes the spring melt that trickles and then roars into an infamous reservoir that floods a valley of granite. Consider that water as it is diverted into pipes that carry it west again, to be deposited in more reservoirs strung over the San Andreas Fault close to the Pacific. From there, it is piped still farther to your tap, where it pours into your teakettle.

Then imagine the San Joaquin Valley of California, where your raisins might have grown. Imagine a vineyard near the Kings River in the heat of an August afternoon when the sun bears down and the only shade is among the vines, where the grapes hang in voluptuous readiness for harvest, among dusty leaves netted with the sticky webs of black widow spiders. Imagine yourself walking among the rows of vines, kicking up the silky powder of top soil. Feel the sweat rising on your upper lip as you struggle to breathe air that seems too hot to inhale. Now examine a raisin. Imagine it as a round, green grape swelling under a blistering sun cut from the vine by leathery hands, spread on paper trays, shriveling to deep purple.

This exercise is especially rewarding in winter.

Now measure two cups of flour and place it in a glass or ceramic bowl. A stainless steel bowl, while functionally acceptable, is too cold for this task. Consider your affection for the bowl you use; consider how many other recipes have been assembled in its shell; consider its contribution to your meal, its allegiance to your effort. Add salt, baking powder and soda, and nutmeg. While purists might argue for sifting, I've always forgone this step and have merely stirred together these dry ingredients with a fork.

Your kitchen should now be flooded with yellow sunlight as the beams enter at a low angle. The oven should be emanating a warmth that will grow with the heat of the sun. Close your eyes and feel the light pouring in through the east-facing window. Consider that this same sun shone on the first people who crossed the Pacific, on Emily Dickinson in Amherst, on Einstein in Princeton, and on the person you most love at this moment. Feel it warm your being. Now listen for mourning doves, or house finches, or perhaps the raucous squawk of an early jay.

Take a quarter pound of butter, now plastic but not too soft, and drop it into the flour mixture. Using your bare hands, gently massage the flour into the butter, pinching the soft mass into ever-smaller lumps. Close your eyes. Your fingers stir through the bowl, grasping the pliant lumps, mingling it with the flour mixture that bears the consistency of the silky San Joaquin Valley topsoil. The two essences, cereal and dairy, are blended into a homogenous whole. Feel love surging through your being at the sensations elicited by this divine mix. Marvel that your hands are a conduit to your spirit, which delights in this moment of essential being, whose perfection is heightened only by the anticipation of what will follow. Bask in the tactile delight of squeezing the dough, caressing these sweet products into what will become gustatory rapture.

Now cleanse your hands, and turn your attention to the egg. Cradle it in your palm and feel your fingers close over its roundness. Its fluid weight shifts within the shell. It is an *egg*, potential avian life reduced in your sensuous craving for weekend bread to a leaven, a glue, a decoration. Consider your mastery over the egg. Now hold it between your fingers and snap gently against the edge of a bowl, fracturing the shell. Using both hands, pull the egg apart, rend the inner membrane, and with confidence, separate the white from the yolk, and drop the yolk into the cup of unsweetened plain yogurt. Blend the yolk into the viscid pudding with a deft, calm stroke, watching as it breaks and stretches into a spiral before it finally surrenders to disperse through the yogurt, transforming its watery whiteness to a lemony yellow.

Drain the raisins and mix them evenly into the flour mixture. If you favor a sweet scone, add a tablespoon or two of sugar. Then, without hesitation and with great deliberation, pour the yogurt mixture into the flour and quickly fold them together until the flour is moistened throughout. Don't dawdle. Gather the dough into a ball, adding enough flour to make it workable, and then divide it into two balls, patting each into a flat, round wheel of about six inches in diameter. Take a large knife and press it firmly into the fleshly dough, cutting each round into six wedges. Transfer these to a baking sheet.

Return to the egg white, viscous and pale, and with a fork, whip it into a slight froth, beating it just enough to transform it into a stringy froth. Brush the egg white over the surface of each round, using a pastry brush that has a rich and varied history, one that has been with you for many years. Slide the sheet of scones into the oven. Bake them for eighteen to twenty minutes.

Spread a clean, starched cloth over the table (preferably one with matching napkins that you have ironed yourself.) Arrange a handsome cup and saucer, a plate, and silverware in an attractive display. Grind coffee beans grown in Jamaica or Columbia or Kenya, and brew a strong coffee. Heat milk for the coffee and pour it into an old, heavy pitcher that once belonged to your great-grandmother. Consider how pleased she would be to know that you are using her dishes. Imagine her in your midst, her hair drawn back into a bun as in her photographs; she is smiling a gentle smile from 1910. Introduce yourself as her son's granddaughter and imagine she is speaking English as you direct her into a chair at the table. She asks how you came to own the pitcher. Imagine your explanation as you turn to the oven to withdraw the scones. They have turned a golden brown and their aroma has permeated every corner of your abode.

Breathe deeply and conjure a vision of the past or a fantasy of the future and hold it in your awareness only long enough to utter a gasp of pleasure. Imagine pressing your face into the hollow of a warm neck. Then unfold the newspaper and pour the coffee. Pull a round of scones apart. Notice the steam rises from their spongy seams. Break one open and observe the flecks of nutmeg and the deep purply black color of the raisins. Dwell on the remarkable texture, the slightly flaky crust, and the soft, somewhat resilient center. Roll the dough in your mouth. Taste the butter, the egg, the yogurt, the nutmeg, and the raisins. Vow that you will eat no more than two.

Now think about what you will do after you have eaten your scones. Talk to the cat. Reflect on your solitude. Alternate bites of scone with sips of coffee.

When you have eaten your fill, freeze the leftovers. They will keep for many days. When you desire, heat then until they are hot.

Their consistency will be slightly different, but they will still taste good. Serve them to unexpected guests.

Stephanie Sarver is the author of Uneven Land: Nature and Agriculture in American Writing. *When she's not writing essays or baking scones she works as an editor. She lives in the San Francisco Bay Area.*

SHANE DUBOW

The Impulsive Chef

Does he have what it takes?

I DIDN'T HAVE A PLAN. I'D JUST BEEN DUMPED. I WAS 24; IT WAS Valentine's Day (depressing), and I felt like breaking rules. Don't date a co-worker. Don't call a co-worker to seek a date on the same night you wish that date to go down. Don't find your newly single self in your kitchen, with this just-graduated, impossibly fit, wide-eyed, new co-worker cabbing it over because she's spontaneous like that and because you wanted to assure a certain proximity to your futon and so you told her you'd cook something despite the fact that your on-hand edibles consist of salt, one half jar of pickled ginger and one wedge of pepper cheese sent by your dairy obsessed mother in Wisconsin.

Sudden Thought Number One: Order in.

Sudden Thought Number Two: Breathe.

Sudden Thought Number Three: Get thee to the store and wing it, you wussy, because you've done it before (remember super ramen?), and because this is a night to confront some fears and tempt some adult knowledge, and because you've already survived a few of life's hardships (dying father, lost love, the '84 Cubs), meaning nothing you do with a stove and God's bounty will ever risk the same sorts of lows. And besides which, good smells seduce, and hot kitchens shed clothes—and she'll be here in about eleven minutes.

So I booked to the bodega down my street, I bought the only perishables they had—cilantro, limes, garlic, olive oil, a baguette—plus two bottles of a trusted (and cheap) Chilean wine.

Sudden Thoughts Numbers Four to Six: When you shop hungry, you buy things, on impulse, you've never tried. But then, if you buy good ingredients and don't do too much to muck them up, shouldn't they stay good when combined? And besides, if you rely only on cookbook exactitude, what then of your soul?

Home again, my skimpy harvest spread before me, I started in on that wine, which was one of my habits at the time and which instantly put me in mind of my Chilean friend Marcello, currently out of town—a unfortunate bit of happenstance, since he was also the friend who'd introduced me to a certain simple dish, a relish (or was it a salsa?), that might accommodate my sweep of the bodega's sparse shelves.

And so I wung it. First I roasted the garlic to mellow its zip, because I didn't want dragon breath to discourage any kissing. Then I plucked the cilantro and squeezed the limes and made use of my blender for the first time in a long time. But the taste was too thin, too ungrounded, so I splashed in some olive oil (and wished for pine nuts) and tried again. Now it needed salt (I should have known), and so I added some of that. Meanwhile, the bread was warming, the cheese was sweating out, and I'd recued this Wes Montgomery record called "Goin' Out of My Head" that I'd inherited from my dad.

My date arrived flush-faced and giggling. She smelled like vanilla. We ate on the floor in the living room and burned a candle and drank the wine and ripped off crusty hunks of bread—lightly toasted—to dip in the sauce, which was just the thing, I thought, because the salty-limy taste woke up our tongues (and reminded me of tequila) while the thicker, richer, garlicky cilantro base made the sauce feel significant in our mouths when we first kissed.

"So what do you call this?" she asked later, after we'd taken a rest from our groping and returned to the dip with our fingers because we'd run out of bread.

Sudden Thought Number Seven: That's a good question.

It's years later now, and I hardly ever miss that girl. Or that job. But I still make that cilantro stuff all the time.

CILANTRO PESTO
SALSA-RELISH-DIP THING
Serves two to four

1 heapin' helpin' (call it 3 to 4 firmly packed cups) fresh cilantro, stems removed
4 to 6 cloves garlic
$\frac{1}{2}$ cup pine nuts
$\frac{1}{2}$ cup olive oil
1 to 2 limes
Salt to taste

Roast or sauté garlic until browned. Squeeze lime juice into blender. Add garlic, cilantro, pine nuts and oil (and don't fret the amounts, because staying loose is what it's all about). Blend and serve as a dip, spread or relish with toasted bread, grilled fish or raw or roasted vegetables.

Shane DuBow's work has appeared in Harper's, GQ, *and other publications. He lives in Chicago.*

ZACHARY TAYLOR

Greece and Water Mix

Drink from the well of history.

"HAVE A DRINK!"

I certainly was thirsty, and it was hot even here in the shade, but I could think of a good reason not to stick my head in a stream. Goats' bells tinkled somewhere in the brambles nearby. "I don't think I should," I said.

My host Kostas would not be put off. "*Malaka.*" He let the word fall casually, bemused and disdainful in the same breath. My command of modern Greek is shaky, but this particular epithet I know quite well—largely because the word is so crude. Besides, I had already heard Kos use it many times to describe me: because I couldn't find the ripest fig on a tree, because I made a mess when I peeled one with my teeth and fingers, because I didn't believe bees had left honey behind in the sweetest figs, because I hadn't ever eaten fruit grown without the benefit of pesticides. An apple from an orchard in Arcadia looks awful; mottled and pitted, its skin is as forbidding as the Arcadian mountains, burnt a dusty brown by the August sun. But the flavor…the apple doesn't taste sweeter, really; it just tastes *more*. And Kos had made fun of me because I wouldn't know how to survive in these mountains. "Someday, *malaka,* all the cities will be destroyed," he had assured me, his eyes twinkling. "Then those apples will save your life."

Even so, I had looked askance at the apples, just as I now worried about the stream, which flowed quickly, bounding over some stones, sliding between others. Here and there bugs skimmed across the surface where the water had collected in pools; according to Kos, who had been coming to the stream ever since he was a boy, crabs were hiding in the mud. Oaks lined either bank, forming a canopy that arced overhead. An idyllic spot, I granted, and when Kos put his lips up to a miniature waterfall and took a long, deep draught, all at once my resistance gave way. The water was cold and tasted very fresh.

What water didn't pour down my gullet continued through the valley until it reached the Alpheios, the river of Olympia, which flows by the site of the ancient games on its way to the sea. In antiquity that water might have refreshed athletes or victorious teams of horses, thus passing into Pindaric song. In more recent history, during the Greek War of Independence, Theodoros Kolokotronis's guerrillas might have found refuge from the sun at the very spot where I now kneeled. Karitaina, the hilltop stronghold from which they raided the Turks, is only a few miles away.

The stream's source on the slopes of Mount Lycaeos is a wellspring of myth. The ancient Arcadians who lived beneath the mountain believed it was the birthplace of Zeus. It is told that soon after his birth the future king of the gods was hidden from his father and given to three nymphs to raise. One of these was called Theisoa, and she gave her name to what is now Kostas's village—and to the source of the stream. The nymphs bathed the young god in those headwaters, for which the Theisoans called the stream Lusios, the bathing river.

So I learned while reading Pausanias's *Periegesis* months later in a library a world away, and once more I was immersed in those waters. Pausanias traveled throughout Greece in the time of the Roman emperor Marcus Aurelius and related, in minute detail, what he saw and heard. Pausanias considered the Lusios—known

as the Gortynios by the Arcadians who lived farther downstream—
to be the coldest river in the world. He was familiar with the
Danube and the Rhine, but he had a peculiar set of criteria according to which the Gortynios won the laurels:

> I call the water cold of those rivers which flow through a land
> with a warm climate and in summer have water refreshing to
> drink and to bathe in, without being painful in winter. The
> Gortynios surpasses all rivers in coldness, especially in summer.

The important thing, I thought, my mind drifting back to my
own experience of Arcadia, is contrast. I thought of the lovely apples with their ugly skins. I thought of the rugged, dry mountains
providing the sweets of life—mountains capable of providing for
humans as Mount Lycaeos once did for the greatest of the gods. I
thought of the present-day Arcadians, autochthonous, sprung from
the very earth on which they live, who with every draught from a
stream drink up millennia of history and legend.

*Zachary Taylor lives in Cambridge, Massachusetts. His work has appeared
in* Persephone, Living Hands, The Boston Book Review, *and*
Atlantic Unbound.

JIM LEFF

Cuckoo for Kugel

Grate a few pounds of potatoes…

EVERYTHING'S BEEN COMING UP KUGEL LATELY. KUGEL ("POTATO pudding") is sort of an oven-baked potato pancake. Its ingredients are ultra-simple: grated (using a hand or meat grinder, *never* a food processor) potato—and perhaps some onion—along with eggs, oil, salt, pepper, and an optional teaspoon of baking powder.

Like all soul foods, this is a dish born of poverty. But creativity flourishes under impediment, so destitution frequently leads to de-liciousness—and there are few things in this world as delicious as a well-baked kugel. It's a delicacy anyone even remotely fond of potatoes must adore.

I'm nuts about it; though starchy, inelegant kugel is the trashy underside of Jewish cooking, it's long been one of my most craved things. Of course, this might not have been the case had I been born a century earlier Over There, where potatocentricism stemmed from necessity rather than caprice. There's an old song that goes, "Monday, potatoes; Tuesday, potatoes. Wednesday and Thursday, potatoes. Saturday…maybe a potato kugel, then Sunday, potatoes again." It's only recently that I've come to understand that this was a blues song sung from poverty, not a hopeful song for a future utopia.

The dark side of the current klezmer music craze is that a musician who's learned the style finds himself qualified to make plenty *kesh* playing Jewish weddings. I don't mean swanky affairs at suburban catering halls with chopped liver sculptures and toupeed high school band teachers warbling "Wind Beneath My Wings"; I mean the hard-core stuff, Orthodox and Hassids dancing sweaty ecstatic circles while the band blares a nonstop succession of identical-sounding oompah tunes in snakey D-minor. Same-sex dancing and long curly sideburns. Blow your brains out for six hours of cacophonous mayhem in exchange for enough *kesh* to pay half your rent. It ain't bebop, but it's hard to resist.

And thus I found myself—stylishly tricked out in yarmulke and polyester tux—playing trombone for a particularly *frum* (religious) crowd upstate in Muncie, the Hassidic Martha's Vineyard in the foothills of the Catskill Mountains. They were too pious to drink much, though a bottle of Old Williamsburgh (I kid you not) Kentucky Straight Bourbon Whiskey was passed among the elders. The women were virtually locked away in the room next door; too observant to even wear wigs, they donned dowdy kerchiefs.

At the head of the dance floor, in a position of supreme authority, was a table bearing three large rococo silver trays. I watched, fascinated, as all attention came to focus on this setup. With a flourish, the top of one vessel was opened to reveal a kugel. The second lid was removed, kugel again. Third...kugel kugel kugel. There followed a feeding frenzy, as yours truly jumped off the bandstand to try to salvage a morsel amidst the kugelly commotion.

These, in truth, were not great kugels, but that's not the point. Kugel is intrinsically a Craved Thing: potato, egg, salt, grease. That's four of the Major Food Groups; you simply can't go wrong.

The Three Sacred Offerings had nearly been forgotten when, as we started another set, I detected the wafting aroma of fresh kugel. There was even more being brought out. Amazing.

We later stood around the starchy relics, debating the merits of the second kugel (eggier) versus the much-loved fifth kugel (very dense), when a waiter, with the earnest sense of duty and pride of purpose of a rabbi carrying the Torah, presented yet another tray.

I was deeply moved by this elevation of a dish far too homely to be served in restaurants or at less earthy soirees. My head spun at each new serving until I was overcome, thrown into such an emotional tizzy that I found myself screaming—from my spot between a horrified trumpeter and a bemused tenor saxophonist—"By Golly, I'm *proud* to be Jewish!" I was having one of those life-changing moments, catalyzed by the dizzying procession of Bottomless Potato Puddings.

The bandleader, a way-*frum* but pretty hip guy named Yochi (pronounced YUKHee; with a name like that he'd make a helluva food writer), impressed by my kugel catharsis, invited me home for a pre-Sabbath taste of rare Hungarian skillet-cooked kugel.

Brooklyn's Satmar Hassids are the most stalwart preservers of the Hungarian Jewish tradition, and so I found myself the following Friday in South Williamsburg, the turf of Orthodox Judaism's most xenophobic sect. Yochi's mom sat me down at the dining table in front of a huge slice…which I chomped nervously under the wary gaze of the entire hyperextended family.

It was surprising, wonderful stuff; very little oil was used, but a hennery of eggs lent a puffy, almost quiche-like texture. The polished exterior was too dry and greaseless to be crisp; rather it's a parchment to be worked through in your journey toward an almost erotically creamy, coarse-grained interior.

Hungarians cook their kugel in much the same manner as Spaniards make *tortilla espanola* (but they grate the spuds, rather than slice or dice). Here's the deal: combine 9 russets (hand grated through the small holes) with 8 eggs, salt and white pepper; fry in just $\frac{1}{4}$ cup of corn oil heated to smoke point in a 10-inch pan (nonstick works best). Reduce to low and cook uncovered 45 minutes. Transfer to a plate, smoke another $\frac{1}{4}$ cup of oil, then flip kugel back to pan for 45 minutes of low heat on the other side.

Not long after lunch at Yochi's, I discovered the Hall Street Kosher Cafe, a trailer parked in an abandoned lot across from the Brooklyn Navy Yards. This down-home spot cooks the kugel of my dreams: plump pillowy squares of hand-ground potato. The chef, Mario, is a religious Jew from Argentina who, despite sounding more Freddie Prinze than Jackie Mason, turns out pure Eastern European Jewish soul food just like my grandma used to make, with nary a Latino touch.

An Argentinian's kugel evokes my Eastern European grandparents while a Hungarian's evokes Iberia. Galicia, Poland meets Galicia, Spain—all courtesy of kugel. Clearly, that upstate caterer was right to have glorified kosher cuisine's most unglamorous dish; when eating gets this primal, archetypes rise to the surface. Grate a few pounds of potatoes and suddenly all men are brothers...and otherwise unbelieving trombonists turn *frum* for a night.

Jim Leff, a New York City-based food writer and jazz trombonist, is the author of The Eclectic Gourmet Guide to Greater New York City: The Undiscovered World of Hyperdelicious Offbeat Eating in All Five Boroughs. *He's also the Alpha Dog at his Chowhound Web site (www.chowhound.com).*

FRANCES MAYES

✦ ✦ ✦

Market Day

Like a fingerprint, a Tuscan market
is unique and indelible.

MARKET DAY FALLS ON THURSDAYS IN CAMUCIA, THE LIVELY TOWN at the bottom of Cortona's hill, and I'm there early before the heat sets in. Tourists pass right through Camucia; it's just the modern spillover from the venerable and dominant hill town above it. But modern is relative. Among the *frutta e verdura* shops, the hardware and seed stores, you happen on a couple of Etruscan tombs. Near the butcher's shops are remnants of a villa, an immense curly iron gate and swag of garden wall. Camucia, bombed in World War II, has its share of chestnut trees, photographable doors, and shuttered houses.

On market day, a couple of streets are blocked to traffic. The vendors arrive early, unfolding what seems like the whole stores of supermarket aisles from specially made trucks and wagons. One wagon sells local pecorino, the sheep's milk cheese that can be soft and almost creamy, or aged and strong as a barnyard, along with several wheels of parmigiano. The aged cheese is crumbly and rich, wonderful to nibble as I walk around the market.

I'm hunting and gathering food for a dinner for new friends. My favorite wagons belong to the two *porchetta* maestros. The whole pig, parsley entwined with the tail, apple—or a big mushroom—in its mouth, stretches across the cutting board. Sometimes the decapitated head sits aside at an angle, eyeing the rest of its body, which has been stuffed with herbs and bits of its own ears, etc. (best not to inquire too closely), then roasted in a wood oven. You can buy a *panino* (a crusty roll) with nothing on it but slabs of *porchetta* to take home, lean or with crispy, fatty skin. One of the lords of the *porchetta* wagons looks very much like his subject: little eyes, glistening skin, and bulbous forearms. His fingers are short and porky, with bitten-down nails. He's smiling, extolling his pig's virtues, but when he turns to his wife, he snarls. Her lips are set in a permanent tight half smile. I've bought from him before and his *porchetta* is delicious. This time I buy from the milder man in the next stand. For my husband Ed, I ask for extra *sale*, salt, which is what the indefinable stuffing is called. I like it but find myself picking through to see if there's something peculiar in it. Though the pig is useful and tasty in all its parts and preparations, the slow-roasted *porchetta* must be its apogee. Before I move on to the vegetables, I spot a pair of bright yellow espadrilles with ribbons to wind around the ankles; I balance my shopping bags while I try on one. Perfect, and less than ten dollars. I drop them in with the *porchetta* and parmigiano.

Scarves (bright Chanel and Hermès) and lined tablecloths float from awnings; toilet cleaners, tapes, and t-shirts are stacked in bins and on folding tables. Besides buying food, you can dress, plant a garden, and stock a household from this market. There are a few local crafts for sale but you have to look for them. The Tuscan markets aren't like those in Mexico, with wonderful toys, weaving, and pottery. It's a wonder these markets continue at all, given the sophistication of Italian life and the standard of living in this area. I find the iron-working traditions still somewhat in evidence. Occasionally, I see good andirons and handy fireplace grills. My favorite is a holder for whole prosciutto, an iron grip with handle mounted on a board for ease in slicing; maybe someday I'll find I need that much prosciutto and buy one. One week I bought hand-woven baskets made from dark supple willow twigs, the large ones perfect for kitchen supplies and the small round ones for the ripe-right-now peaches and cherries. One woman sells old table and bed linens with thick monograms, all of which must have been gathered from farms and villas. She has three mounds of yellowed lace. Perhaps some of it was made on the nearby island, Isola Maggiore in Lake Trasimeno. Women still sit in the doorways there, hooking lace in the afternoon light. I find two enormous square linen pillowcases with miles of inset lace and ribbons—ten thousand lire, same as the sandals, seems to be the magic number today. Of course, I will have to have the pillows especially made. When I buy some striped linen dishtowels, I notice several goat skins hanging from a hook. I have in mind that they would look terrific on the *cotto* floors at my house. The four the man has are too small but he says to come back next week. He tries to convince me that his sheepskins would be better anyway, but they don't appeal to me.

I'm wending my way toward the produce, but walk up to the bar for a coffee. Actually, I stop with an excuse to stare. People from surrounding areas come not only to shop but to greet friends, to make business arrangements. The din around the Camucia market is a lovely swarm of voices, many speaking in the local Val di Chiana dialect. I don't understand most of what they're saying but I do hear one recurring habit. They do not use the *ch* sound for *c* but slide it into an s sound. "Shento," they say for *cento* (one hundred), instead of the usual pronunciation "chento." I heard someone say "cappushino," for cappuccino, though the usual affectionate shortening of that is "cappuch." Their town is pronounced not "Camuchia," but "Camushea" Odd that the *c* is often the affected letter. Around Siena, people substitute an *h* sound for *c*—"hasa" and "Hoca-Hola." Whatever the local habit with *c* they're all talking. Outside the bar, groups of farmers, maybe a hundred men, mill about. Some play cards. Their wives are off in the crowd, loading their bags with tiny strawberries, basil plants with dangling roots, dried mushrooms, perhaps a fish from the one stand that sells seafood from the Adriatic. Unlike the Italians who take their thimbleful of espresso in one quick swallow, I sip the black, black coffee.

A friend says Italy is getting to be just like everywhere else—

homogenized and Americanized, she says disparagingly. I want to drag her here and stand her in this doorway. The men have the look of their lives—perhaps we all do. Hard work, their faces and bodies affirm. All are lean, not a pound of extra fat anywhere. They look cured by the sun, so deeply tan they probably never go pale in winter. Their country clothes are serviceable, rough—they don't "dress," they just get dressed. They wear, as well, a natural dignity. Surely some are canny, crusty, cruel, but they look totally present, unhidden, and alive. Some are missing teeth but they smile widely without embarrassment. I look in one man's eyes. The left one is white with milky blue veins like those in an exploded marble. The other is black as the center of a sunflower. A retarded boy wanders among them, neither catered to nor ignored. He's just there, living his life like the rest of us.

At home I plan a menu ahead, though I frequently improvise as I shop. Here, I only begin to think when I see what's ripe this week. My impulse is to overload; I forget there are not ten hungry people at home. At first I was miffed when tomatoes or peas had spoiled when I got around to cooking them a few days later. Finally I caught on that what you buy today is ready—picked or dug this morning at its peak. This also explained another puzzle; I never understood why Italian refrigerators are so minute until I realized that they don't store food the way we do. The Sub-Zero giant I have at home begins to seem almost institutional compared to the toy fridge I now have here.

Two weeks ago, small purple artichokes with long stems were in. We love those, quickly steamed, stuffed with tomatoes, garlic, yesterday's bread, and parsley, then doused with oil and vinegar. Today, not a one. The *fagiolini*, slender green beans, are irresistible. Should I have two salads, because the beans also would be good with a shallot vinaigrette? Why not? I buy white peaches for breakfast, but for tonight's dessert, the cherries are perfect. I take a kilo, then set off to find a pitter back in the other part of the market. Since I don't know the word, I'm reduced to sign language. I do know *ciliegia*, cherry, which helps. I've noticed in French and Italian country desserts that the cooks don't bother to pit the cherries, but I like to use the pitter when they're served in a dish. These I'll steep in Chianti with a little sugar and lemon. I decide on some tiny yellow potatoes still half covered with dirt. Just a scrubbing, a dribble of oil and some rosemary and they'll roast in the oven.

I could complete my shopping for this meal right here. I pass cages of guinea hens, ducks, and chickens, as well as rabbits. Since my daughter had a black angora rabbit as a pet once, I can't look with cold eyes on the two spotted bunnies nibbling carrots in the dusty Alitalia flight bag, can't imagine them trembling in the trunk of my car. I intend to stop at the butcher's for a veal roast. The butcher's is bad enough. I admit it's not logical. If you eat meat, you might as well recognize where it comes from. But the drooped heads and closed eyelids of the quail and pigeon make me stop and stare. Rooster heads, chicken feet (with yellow nails like Mrs. Ricker's, my grandmother's Rook partner), the clump of fur to show the skinned rabbit is not a cat, whole cows hanging by their feet with a square of paper towel on the floor to catch the last drops of blood—all these things make my stomach flip. Surely they're not going to eat those fluffy chicks. When I was a child, I sat on the back steps and watched our cook twist a chicken's neck then snap off the head with a jerk. The chicken ran a few circles, spurting blood, before it keeled over, twitching. I love roast chicken. Could I ever wring a neck?

I have as much as I can carry. The other stop I'll make is at the cooperative cantina for some local wine. Near the end of the sinuous line of market stalls, a woman sells flowers from her garden. She wraps an armful of pink zinnias in newspaper and I lay them under the straps of my bag. The sun is ferocious and people are beginning to close down for siesta. A woman who has not sold many of her striped lime and yellow towels looks weary. She dumps the dog sleeping in her folding chair and settles down for a rest before she begins to pack up.

On my way out, I see a man in a sweater, despite the heat. The trunk of his minuscule Fiat is piled with black grapes that have warmed all morning in the sun. I'm stopped by the winy, musty, violet scents. He offers me one. The host sweetness breaks open in my mouth. I have never tasted anything so essential in my life as this grape on this morning. They even smell purple. The flavor, older than the Etruscans and deeply fresh and pleasing, just leaves me stunned. Such richness, and big globes, the heap of dusty grapes cascading out of two baskets. I ask for *un grappelo*, a bunch, wanting the taste to stay with me all morning.

Frances Mayes is a bestselling author who has written for The New York Times, House Beautiful, *and* Food and Wine. *She is also a widely published poet and food and travel writer. She divides her time between Cortona, Italy and San Francisco, California where she teaches creative writing at San Francisco State University. This story was excerpted from her book,* Under the Tuscan Sun: At Home in Italy.

Fat Farm

Working the flesh was never so much fun.

WHEN I ARRIVED AT CANYON RANCH IN THE BERKSHIRE MOUN-
tains, I was coming down from an intense eating binge as *Vogue's*
monthly food correspondent. No sooner had I polished off a met-
ric ton of mail-order Christmas treats than I was on a plane to Paris,
where I had squeezed twenty-two restaurants into sixteen days.
Then it was off to Texas, roaming between Dallas and Fort Worth
in an extremely rewarding search for world-class barbecue joints.
My weight had climbed into a new zone, and I was getting nervous
about it. Five days later, Canyon Ranch had changed my life.

- From now on, I will always use conditioner after shampoo-
  ing. The shower room had pump bottles of conditioner,
  which left my hair so much softer and easier to manage.
  Where have I been all these years?

- I will become a serious weight lifter. See below.

- I will strive to become merely chubby again. That was twenty
  pounds ago.

- Until then, I will wear sweatpants as often as possible. They
  bind and chafe less than regular trousers and slip on so much
  more easily.

- I will become a spa junkie, if I can afford the habit.

Canyon Ranch's publicity material scientifically estimates that more than half of America's population has heard of the original Canyon Ranch in Tucson. I was vaguely aware that it was the first major coed fitness resort, not just another plush pamper palace exclusively for women. And that it was a magnet for socialites, movie stars, and CEOs, a lush oasis where you eat one thousand exquisite gourmet calories a day yet never go hungry. I also knew they were building a Canyon Ranch clone in Lenox, Massachusetts, near Tanglewood and Jacob's Pillow and, for those like me who are old enough to care, Alice's Restaurant....

Even if you've been a guest before (three out of four have), the first thing you get is a guided tour with lots of numbers.... Newcomers may find themselves winded before the end of the guided tour.

Next you fill out some medical forms. The final page strikes you as particularly bellicose and hypocritical. "Do you find yourself obsessing about food?" it asks. "Not at all," you reply, "but I think about almost nothing else." So, you soon realize, does everybody at Canyon Ranch, including the three hundred on staff. Then you meet with a program adviser who guides you through a bewildering range of possibilities....

I was growing acutely anxious about exercising in public. I flashed back to those agonizing afternoons in summer camp on the dusty baseball diamond—where three of us were always dispatched to far right field and spent two hours in the blinding sun praying that the ball would never come our way. My wife could hardly wait. A dancer and star high-school sprinter in California when she was young, she doesn't get much practice in either of them around me. She immediately signed up for a facial, three types of massage (cranial, sports, and shiatsu), body composition analysis, aromatherapy, and an herbal wrap, and filled in the rest of her schedule with classes in rhythm aerobics, flexibility, and strength training. Then she sprinted across the hall to the Canyon Ranch Showcase shop, unavoidable as you enter the spa building, where they sell athletic clothing, shoes, books, and tapes. She had not gone shopping for thirty-six hours and was beginning to show the strain.

As I had signed up for nothing but a late-afternoon tennis lesson (with an excellent pro), I rented a movie, and returned to our comfortable room after lunch. Except during meals, there is no coercion at Canyon Ranch, nobody following you around to make sure you are doing what you should....

On our second day, my wife's schedule was so crammed with exercise and pampering that we saw each other only at meals. By dinnertime, her skin was pink and smooth as a baby's. The skin-care person urged her to wear plastic bags filled with lotion on her hands all night. The skin-care person is divorced.

I spent my time wandering around, watching but not engaging, until I dropped into Gym 4, where they keep the aerobic and strength-training machines, beautiful glittering things in chrome and brass.... The fitness staff were unaccountably squandering their afternoon break lifting weights and futilely trying to climb the StairMaster; when they were done, I asked for a demonstration. Before you knew it, I had completed the full circuit, at modest levels of resistance, of course, and had mounted the treadmill for a snappy walk as I gazed through a huge picture window at the New England countryside. The Appalachian Trail passes just beyond the property.

When I had worked up quite a lather,...tried the men's sauna, steam, and inhalation rooms, I took a cool shower (individual curtained stalls), and, against my better judgment, felt almost terrific.

The herbal room was dim and warm. Calming New Age music seeped in through hidden loudspeakers. I lay on a table tightly swaddled in heavy, hot, wet canvas blankets impregnated with five herbs. The herbal therapist could not remember which five herbs they were—I would have preferred a little more tarragon—but promised they would detox me, get all the poisons out of my bloodstream. Like what? Oh, nicotine, coffee, chocolate, like that. With my sanguinary poisons oozing out all over the canvas blankets, I was surprised that she was not wearing a protective suit and helmet. I have always considered people who believe that chocolate is a poison to be twisted beyond redemption.

Then she left me alone. My arms were pinned to my sides by

the herbal wrappers, and for five minutes I considered going into a serious panic. At last I settled into a pleasant reverie. I was in Paris again, tucking into a plate of Joël Robuchon's ravioli of langoustines and his roasted rabbit under a fricassee of wild mushrooms. Presently the scene shifted to La Cagouille, where tiny mussels are grilled without oil on a bare open skillet. When the herbal therapist returned to unwrap me, I was sipping a dark morning coffee at the Café de Flore, biting into a crusty baguette.

Any of these delights would fit into the Canyon Ranch low-fat, low-calorie regime, yet none of them does. I knew I was in trouble at our very first lunch, the emptiest 285 calories I've ever frittered away. It was a "pizza" with a thin brown leatherette crust covered by a cheese mistranslated as mozzarella and some vegetables that don't even belong in the same room with a pizza. Coffee was a pallid version of brewed decaf. At dinner I would learn how to order a packet of instant Maxwell House to dissolve in my decaf, and the next day I would meet a waiter willing to smuggle out a cup of real coffee from the staff's real coffeepot.

Why all this fuss about caffeine? On my last day at Canyon Ranch, I read a delightful story in the newspaper. Researchers at Stanford have discovered that *decaffeinated coffee increases your bad cholesterol (LDLs) by an average of seven percent!* Real coffee has no such effect. The decaf crowd has got so powerful of late that you can no longer find a cup of real coffee at the end of a dinner party. Although these people have deprived me of pleasure for all these years, I now feel a profound sense of compassion toward them and am thankful to Whoever has guided me upon the low-cholesterol, caffeinated path.

I was never hungry at Canyon Ranch but never satisfied. Executive Chef Barry Correia has a strong background in modern American cooking, but he faces four insurmountable problems: the Canyon Ranch Nutrition Philosophy, the official recipes he is required to follow, the ingredients he uses, and the organization of the kitchen. The directors of Canyon Ranch should either start over from scratch or erase the words "exquisite gourmet fare" from all brochures, pamphlets, and advertising.

The Canyon Ranch Nutrition Philosophy is strict, though not as draconian as Pritikin: 60 percent carbohydrates, mainly complex, 20 percent fat, 20 percent protein, 1,000 to 1,200 calories a day, high fiber, no caffeine, oils high in polyunsaturates, two grams of sodium, almost no refined flour. Some of these rules are arbitrary, some outmoded. There is no medical reason whatsoever for healthy eaters to limit themselves to two grams of sodium a day. The tasteless gazpacho came alive after I had a little dish of salt brought to the table and added two tiny pinches. Though delicious crusty, yeasty bread is the most wonderful complex carbohydrate in the world, all the breads at Canyon Ranch range from boring to gruesome. All are store-bought but one, and this is made with baking soda instead of yeast. Great breads are not made with whole wheat flour and baking soda. Getting my knife into the whole wheat dessert crepes demanded more fitness training than I had undergone. The Canyon Ranch rule against refined flour (oddly they are happy to buy dried pasta made with refined flour) may raise your fiber intake a gram or two, but popcorn does the job twice as fast.

After straightening out their Nutrition Philosophy, the owners should get rid of half the Canyon Ranch recipes and many of the ingredients they buy. The vanilla extract is half artificial. The melons are unripe, the apples waxed, the bananas green. For at least two years now, polyunsaturated oils like soybean and safflower have been considered dangerous compared with monounsaturated oils like olive and canola. I have been told that Canyon Ranch in Tucson switched to canola last July; I saw no canola oil in my tour of the kitchens.

The ubiquitous rubbery skinless chicken breasts should be replaced with juicy low-fat free-range veal from Summerfield Farm in Virginia; the olive oil I saw in the kitchen was not extra virgin or even slightly virgin; the pasta was precooked and cooled, waiting to be reheated in boiling water; the vegetables were presteamed and reheated in the microwave; the "Maine lobster tails" were tough and dry and came frozen from New Zealand.

Why not steamed mussels, and tuna *tartare*, and cold briny

oysters opened on demand, and sashimi sliced at the very last minute, and concentrated, degreased veal or chicken stock for richness and flavor, and naturally low-fat game, and wild mushrooms, and hearty bean stews (a profoundly complex carbohydrate), and vegetables grilled with a little olive oil? What's needed are the freshest ingredients, recipes that go beyond the health-food theology of the sixties, and lots of skilled labor at the last minute. The Canyon Ranch kitchen is run with seven workers in the morning and five at night to feed a hundred guests three times a day. One restaurant kitchen I visited in Paris had a staff of thirteen for forty guests.

I gained at least one piece of nutritional information at Canyon Ranch that was worth taking home, and it may well change my life: your metabolic rate is directly related to the amount of lean muscle mass in your body. Doesn't this mean, I asked young Dr. Robert Heffron, that if I follow a program of weight lifting, I will be able to eat more? Heffron is one of the ranch's great human assets—up-to-date in both traditional and alternative medicine, open-minded and undoctrinaire, skeptical toward the Food Police and their current edicts. He found my theory unusual but grudgingly agreed. Aerobics may be good for your heart, but weight lifters use up more calories all day long, even in their sleep.

I hurried over to Gym 4 for a consultation with a weight lifter named Richard, who burns 2,600 calories before he gets out of bed in the morning. My goal is not to look like Arnold Schwarzenegger, I explained, much to Richard's relief. He taught me a series of home exercises with dumbbells and barbells and a padded bench. Now all I have to do is go out and buy a set of sixteen weights ranging from two to thirty pounds each. I am confident they will change my life once I have figured out how to carry them home.

Pumping up, purifying, and pampering, strengthening and slimming (I lost four pounds), and just plain thinking about your body for sixteen hours a day are inebriating experiences, and Canyon Ranch is a terrific place to do them all. The Berkshires are a land of calm and beauty, and after five more days there, I might even have believed that Yogurt Carob Parfait, the most comical dessert at Canyon Ranch, was really a hot-fudge sundae.

Jeffrey Steingarten is an award-winning food writer and the internationally feared and acclaimed food critic of Vogue *magazine. This story was excerpted from his book* The Man Who Ate Everything.

Out of Lunch

Forbidden fish is very sweet.

IN THE ARID DRYNESS OF THE CENTRAL BURMA PLAIN, LIES PAGAN. Between the 11th and the 13th centuries, as the site of Burma's capital, it was the location of magnificent architecture. Today 2,217 pagodas remain, along with more than 2,000 ruined temples in the country now known as Myanmar.

We had been out since dawn that morning to watch the colors of the sunrise spread across the plain from atop one of the ancient temples. Later, we had traveled for miles among the ruins but had scarcely met another tourist. Stopping at one of the huge ancient temples, we had passed through massive teak doors into the coolness inside. As our eyes adjusted to the semi-darkness of rooms made of thick stone impenetrable by sunlight, we began to see before us the giant, gold Buddha, sitting silently in the dark, as it had for centuries.

By noon, we were tired, hot and dusty. It was the dry season and the temperature was easily 115 degrees Fahrenheit. There was not a cloud in the sky. It was time for a midday break, some lunch and a rest. We headed back to our hotel near the banks of the Irrawaddy River and upon our arrival went straight to the dining room. There was no one there so we inquired at the front desk.

The desk clerk's lethargic shrug indicated that he didn't know, or care, the whereabouts of the dining room staff. Would he summon someone? we asked. Soon a rather heavy-set, though light-footed, man appeared. Breathlessly, he inquired if he could help us. We told him that we were hungry and would like to order lunch. He studied us a moment, then asked if we had ordered our lunch. Confused, we answered "no" we had not, but "yes," that was our intention now.

"Ah then, I am so sorry," was his reply. Slowly, from his broken English, we understood that it was impossible to have lunch served without prior notice to the hotel. The procedure was to order lunch in the morning, thus allowing the staff time to shop for food. In a country where few had refrigeration, everything was purchased fresh daily at a local market.

His apologies were profuse. But it was clear that lunch was an impossibility. "No order, no food," he said with a big smile, shaking his head up and down in the affirmative.

We had, in fact, inquired at the front desk that morning, whether or not the dining room was open for lunch. Yes, we had been told, it was open. Obviously, we had neglected to ask the next question.

But we were too hot and tired to argue or care. We picked up two warm 7-Ups apiece from the lobby bar and carried them up to our room. We turned the room's air conditioner on high. It made a horrible noise. We peeled off our sweat-soaked clothes, drank our soft drinks and were both soon asleep on top of the bed.

Knock. Knock. Knock.

My husband made himself presentable and opened the door. There stood the short but ample man from the dining room. Breathlessly, he began to explain the reason for this "unkind intrusion."

"Please, please, fifteen minutes, come." He was holding out ten fingers. "You will eat. Please. Please. Fifteen minutes," he said still gesturing with ten fingers.

My husband understood. "Yes. Thank you. Fifteen minutes," he repeated. "But," and now my husband had begun gesturing back,

"I don't eat meat," he said loudly as if volume might make what he needed to communicate easier to understand. "*No Meat.*"

The animated little man stopped completely and made steady eye contact. His smile was gone.

"No meat?" he asked.

"No meat," my husband answered.

"No meat?" was the incredulous response.

My husband elaborated. "Vegetables O.K. Fish O.K. Meat, no."

"No meat. No meat." We couldn't decide if he didn't understand the words or simply could not comprehend someone who did not eat meat.

"But fish O.K.," my husband tried again.

"Fish O.K.?"

"Yes, fish O.K."

"O.K. fish. No meat." He repeated the words again. He turned to leave. "Come, come. Fifteen minutes." He rushed off. We could hear the rapid slap, slap, slap, slap of his sandals down the long hallway.

We might eat after all. My husband closed the door, removed his clothes and had just stretched out under the grinding air conditioner which was beginning to sound seriously like it might not last the fifteen minutes to lunch.

Knock. Knock. Knock.

My husband groaned, redressed and opened the door. There stood our Burmese friend.

"Fish O.K. Fifteen minutes you come," he announced with a broad smile and scurried off.

We rested a few more minutes to the sound of the dying air conditioner, then took showers as best we could given the slow, thin trickle of water from our shower. The hotel had provided us with Cussons Imperial Leather soap from Indonesia, which promised "a little luxury every day" and left us smelling spicy with a slightly medicinal afterscent. Reasonably clean and refreshed, we put on dry clothes and went downstairs to the large dining room.

There was no one there. But one table was set, complete with a white linen tablecloth and large, freshly-pressed napkins. The room was not air conditioned. All the windows were shut tight to the oppressive heat outside. The ceiling fan over the table was on, circling at an alarming speed. Even so, it was sweltering.

We sat down. No one came. Finally, our friend scurried in— slap, slap, slap, slap. "Hello, hello. Please sit to dine," he welcomed us, seeming not to notice that we were already seated. "Soon you will eat. Just a moment, please." He scurried off.

We waited. I picked up a menu at another table. Reading the "European Louncheon" page, one entree caught my eye— Roasted Beaf with Mushed Potatoes and Baked Bears. I was glad that we had ordered fish.

Within minutes our waiter was back, now laden with bowls of freshly prepared food. We were elated to see that we were being served true Burmese food, which is very uncommon there. Traditional food is eaten every day at home, so the Burmese consider it a treat to eat something else when they dine out. For that reason, there is a prevalence of Chinese restaurants across the country and we had been eating a monotonous diet of clear soup, rice and stirfry twice a day since our arrival.

Before us our new friend was placing a large dish of freshly cooked white rice, a plate of hot salad, lentil soup with vermicelli, and spicy cracker bread. Then, with a great flourish, he proudly placed a bowl of freshly prepared fish curry in front of us. "Fish," he beamed. "This fish!" he reiterated. "Very good this fish," he went on. He hovered over us. "You like Burma food?" he asked but he didn't wait for our answer. "This fish, very good. Very good." He disappeared in the direction we supposed the kitchen to be.

We barely had time to taste everything before he was back with a pot of hot tea and two cups. Beads of perspiration were dripping down his face from his continuous exertion. He looked at us intently.

"Fish O.K.?" he asked. But without waiting for our answers he said, "This fish very good. Very, very good," he said definitively. We continued to eat and nod our heads. He seemed not to need our answers. Besides he had scooted off again.

What he did or where he went on his frenzied trips was a

mystery to us. There was no one else in the dining room. And the kitchen was either outside or in another part of the hotel because there were no kitchen sounds. No sounds whatsoever as a matter of fact. Except for the fan overhead whirling at full speed.

We had not realized how hungry we were. Even in the extreme heat of the dining room, we were beginning to feel renewed.

Our little man was back. His backless sandals slapping his feet with each quick step as he made his way across the large room toward us. "You like fish?" he asked as he picked up the now empty serving dish. "This fish, not bad fish. Bad fish like this," he gestured, "this good fish. This gudgeon. From Irrawaddy. Gudgeon. Spelled G-U-D-G-E-O-N. Gudgeon!"

It was delicious.

By the next time he had come back across the room—slap, slap, slap, slap—we had eaten everything. This pleased him a great deal. He started clearing our table.

"You drink tea? Tea very good. This Chinese tea. Most Chinese very thin. Drink lots of tea. Me? I am very fat." He patted his hefty girth. "I drink a lot of tea but I am fat." He laughed heartily seeming to enjoy his own joke.

He poured us both a cup of tea. "Tea very good for your health. Good for digestion. Better than water. I make you a bottle of tea to take with you. Weather hot. Tea very good."

He made yet another trip across the dining room, carrying out our plates. Returning—slap, slap, slap, slap—across the large room, he brought two small plates toward us. On each plate rested an unpeeled, green banana. This was dessert, or "fruit in season" as it was ubiquitously referred to. It seemed like the whole country had only one "fruit in season." We would add these to the growing collection of seasonal fruit we were carrying in our day packs.

Now that we were done eating and because he had delivered our bill, our waiter/adviser/friend had apparently finished all that was officially required of him. He seemed to be positioning himself comfortably for a prolonged conversation.

But just then, another couple walked into the dining room.

Slap, slap, slap, slap—he officially walked across the large room to greet them. They were French but he spoke to them in the same broken English. "You order lunch?" he asked them. When they replied yes, he seemed confused. "No order lunch," he replied as if making a statement. "Yes, order lunch." They were firm, "this morning, order lunch." "One minute," he said and scurried across the dining room. Soon he was back. Slap, slap, slap, slap. "No order lunch," he said firmly.

The French couple seemed not to be making much progress. "Order fish," one of them said loudly.

I doubt that our friend saw us leave. He was—slap, slap, slap, slap—making his way hurriedly across the dining room speaking to himself loudly in Burmese. What he was saying, we could only guess.

Upstairs, our air conditioner was noisily holding its own. After the stifling heat of the dining room, even at 95 degrees our room felt wonderfully cool. We rested, read, played endless hands of solitaire, and waited for the hot, intense sun to pass into the afternoon sky.

It was after 3 P.M. when, refreshed, we went back out onto the Pagan plain to spend the rest of the day visiting some of the most beautiful, ancient temples in the world. Before we left the hotel, we stopped at the front desk. And there, waiting for us, as promised, was a bottle of Chinese tea. Not just any tea. This tea was very, very good tea, I assure you!

Linda Rice Lorenzetti is a writer who will give up almost anything at a moment's notice to travel. Last year, she and her husband, photographer, Daniel Lorenzetti, traveled to five continents to complete work on their book, The Birth of Coffee. *They divide their time between homes in Florida and Montana and can be reached at www.imageexpedition.com.*

JACK LAMB

⋆ ✳ ⋆

Biscuits & Gravy

A soul satisfying search.

PERPETUAL MOTION, WORSHIP OF THE ROAD, A FIRE FOR THE American landscape—and an unfathomable desire to find the best biscuits and gravy in the Southwest—such is the trinity of ineluctable passions which delivered me from Newhall, California, to Phoenix-El Paso-Houston-Memphis-Oklahoma City-Amarillo-Raton-Taos and back to Newhall. A hell of a stretch to cover for no good reason besides cholesterol-laden vittles, but we did it, Moira and I. And I'm here for witnessing, for testifying, for thumping the gourd and stamping my feet to the sod, singing let it rain, let it rain, because down at Bing's Diner it rained sausage gravy all over my biscuits!

In the midst of my life, breakfast has become the most important meal of the day—one I appeal to in almost religious regularity—and breakfast has dominated those first pious moments as I stare at a new plate of B&G, with a coffee cup warming my hands, in anticipation of a sign, some message from the gods—kind of like my own personal Medgigorrie or California City.

At Bing's, after studying the lay of the gravy, the altar-like demeanor of the modest, assured biscuits, and the unctuous congregation of sturdy sausage chunks covering the plate, I had a vision (even without a smidgen of a taste)...I had reached my own personal Eden among the ruddy, green artichoke fields of the Salinas Valley in Castroville, California. Now, all this religious talk may have some folks wondering, What's this fella trying to push? Well, truth is, nothing but breakfast. And that's even questionable, considering the subject of worship here.

It's just that my family was too American in a sense. When they parked themselves in South Dakota, they put the Old World behind and tried to remake themselves by re-spelling the family name, and when my dear old Granny and her flat-bed truck of kids made it to California in '31, they didn't claim a religion either—so I was raised unbaptized, not knowing what religion we were or where the hell we came from. Fact is, closest thing I knew to religion was Bev's Country Kitchen every Sunday in Mira Loma, California, and Bev telling the cook, So help you if the gravy is cold again, to which Dad replied, Aaamen—and breakfast was served. So imagine my surprise, my astonishment and rapture, when sitting before me was a heavenly looking plate of grub, the steam rising off the gravy like angels on their way to tummy heaven.

But I have to backtrack a bit, because those of you who know your geography are thinking, *Castroville is nowhere near that Southwest loop from Newhall to Taos.* And you would be correct. Castroville came a few weeks after the tour de B&G, as Moira and I were visiting a friend in the Salinas Valley. On our way home, with pouring rain, howling wind, and the crack of lightning breaking through the full-bellied, low-lying gray clouds, the road signs were blurred by rain even though the wipers were on high speed. But I couldn't miss the World's Largest (twenty-foot-high cement) Artichoke in front of a restaurant aptly named The Giant Artichoke—which told me we were in Castroville.

We passed the artichoke restaurant, feeling certain B&G was not on the menu, and hoped to find a place which put its culinary efforts into breakfast alone. At the hazy edge of town, where artichoke fields opened and disappeared into the foggy distance, a good cafe seemed out of reach. But like a glorious mirage amid the fields arose a turn-of-the-century brick and mortar main street USA, now inhabited by stores catering to migrant workers. Admiring the old buildings and the steel banner across the road which announced "Castroville, Artichoke Center of the World," Moira yelled, "Turn around, turn around, you've got to turn around."

"I can't see anything back there," I said, "you're hallucinating."

She wouldn't relent. "You've got to see this...it looks like a trolley car diner!"

The storm and traffic were creating an oozing, hellish experience with headlight eyes. The gutters were flooded in foot-deep water, and semi trucks pounded the small street without concern for rain, pitiable pedestrians or our little compact car. But once we got turned around, as if it were neon lit in the shadows of Hades, I spied a trolley car painted white and red with curtains in the windows...it was Bing's Diner. I dodged through that valley of devilish elements and into Bing's parking lot, and though it was only steps to that dry solace threshold of a diner, Moira put her jacket over her head and we splashed through that squall and slammed the door behind us. Inside, I inhaled that coffee aroma, put my arm around my dear wife and stood proudly as I surveyed the placid, curtained window interior while the rain knocked out a Carmina Burana rhythm against that trolley car tin.

Surrounding wooden tables and chairs was sheet metal and rivets on every side, about twelve feet wide by forty feet long. The room was eerily empty at 8 A.M., except for the cook, the waitress, and the wall decorations. What's going on here? I thought. Trying to conceal my pure relief (from the weather) and terror (only the worst cafes are empty at 8 A.M.), I said "I'm looking for the best biscuits and gravy in town." The middle-aged cook looked up quickly, as if a disembodied voice had just popped out and said *bacon grease blows*! He stared at me for a second, then seemed to realize I was there to spend money. His face brightened. "You've got the right place, son. Take a seat and we'll pour you some hot coffee."

I settled into my seat expecting either a heavenly refuge or another weak-coffee-with-B&G-mash-and-goo rendezvous. Right off, a bad omen was before me: plastic flowers on the table. Plastic flowers means the owner would rather skimp than put the real article on the table—and the cook often follows suit with third-rate cooking. The waitress brought coffee to the table with work-worn hands and a friendly smile, saying "I saw you sitting in the car. It's good thing you didn't wait too long because the carhop isn't running today." She dropped the menus on the table and smiled. "The cook's working on your biscuits and gravy. What else would you like?"

"Coffee's fine. I think we still need a few minutes."

"Just one and not much more, all these people are waiting on you to order," she said as she gestured to the empty tables, then walked off.

"She's a little creepy," I said.

"She's just having fun," Moira returned.

Yeah, I assured myself, just exercising a quirky sense of humor. That's a good omen. Then I reached for my coffee, took a sip and winced. It was weak and damn near lukewarm. Bad omen. Bad, bad omen. Not counting on the cook's promise of fine B&G, I put a strategy together: order enough food so that at least one thing has to be good. When the waitress returned, I placed an order that was a personal challenge to the cook: pancakes, eggs, home fries, and full order of B&G (no half order offered). "Let's see you ruin all of those, buster," I said as the waitress left the table.

Moira tried to divert my concern for breakfast by reading the framed history of the trolley car that hung on the wall. "It was car number 49, and actually ran the streets of San Francisco until it was retired." Slowly, the diner began to fill up with morning stragglers. Perhaps the flood waters had kept them away, I thought. The waitress greeted the newcomers with the same "carhop and ghost" line. Good omen.

When the parking lot was full and the room was a-chatter, I began to relax. My uneasy feeling that we had somehow walked into an *Outer Limits* episode began to fade, and at the least, I was consoled by the fact that if the pit of hell did open up and swallow this glorious, out of place diner, all these other good folks were going with us. That was grim consolation, but it had been a rough morning.

Coffee refills came, and the coffee was warmer. Breakfast was ready with an "order up!" and ring of a desk bell. When the biscuits and gravy was set before me, I was astounded. "Look at this Moira, it's beautiful." She looked at my B&G appreciatively, assured me it was, in fact, beautiful, then went back to her veggie omelet. Sausage cooked to a sturdy, almost crunchy brown graced the entire oval plate—I simply had never seen so much sausage in gravy before. I was ecstatic. The gravy itself was a solid mixture of milk, flour, and grease with a hint of sweetness lurking therein, or maybe it was the biscuits. Either way, they complimented that gravy to perfection. The strangest thing about this plate of B&G was its size. In most cafes, it would be considered a half order. The oval plate it was served on was small, the two (halved) biscuits were almost diminutive, but the well-wrought gravy and the singular generosity of finely seasoned sausage made this plate unbeatable. In fact, there were full bites when all I got was a mouthful of heavenly sausage and gravy, and I felt like I was in the sun's light, floating above the storm on my own solar-powered cloud. For the rest of that afternoon, I didn't come down either. The whole drive home, the rain, wind, and crazy truckers didn't bother me a bit. Nothing got in my way, and I had only one place to go with one thing to do (a mission, you might say)—I was going home to write about Bing's.

So here I finish with a modest review of an unusual find and a damn heavenly plate of biscuits and gravy. All around, Bing's was mostly excellent, including the veggie omelet. While the home fries were undercooked and the coffee never did get stronger (or warmer), that B&G was simply tops. For its B&G, Bing's earns a top-notch spot in the *Biscuits & Gravy Quarterly*'s search for the Best B&G in the Southwest, with a 4-plate ranking (a magnum opus: 4 plates, 2 coffees). Pretty fair. Pretty fair. In the search for biscuits and gravy, it's just a rule that bad comes up more often than good, and Bing's concluded my purgatorial trip through the

Southwest, an American hajj on wheels you might say, and landed me at the gates of a promised breakfast-land that I knew I'd find, some day.

Jack Lamb publishes Biscuits & Gravy Quarterly *in Newhall, California, and is featured on the American Folk web site at: www.AmericanFolk.com/ BGQ. The B&GQ also features cowboy poetry, interviews with the "last old-time cowboys" and people who make biscuits and gravy. When he's not on the road doing, um, research, Lamb teaches at Santa Monica College.*

DAVID YEADON

* * *

Seeking the Secret
of Bird's Nest Soup

Do you really know what's in your bowl?

ONLY FORTY OR SO MILES TO THE WEST, BEYOND THE HAZY PROFILE
of Yao Yai Island, lay Phuket Island, one of Thailand's most over-
crowded bits of recreational real estate, packed with package tour
tourists. But here, on the eastern side of the bay, there's no one—
no distractions, no girlie bars, nothing but these beautiful beaches,
the occasional junk sailing by from Penang or Singapore, a few
fishermen, and dozens of scattered offshore islets, jungle-shrouded
and mysterious.

Oh—and the Phi Phi Islands.

In recent years this fantasy-shaped archipelago, full of soaring
limestone cliffs, crystal-clear coral reefs, and turquoise bays edged
with silver sand has become a little too "discovered" for travelers
seeking solitude. But in spite of a few small resorts and beachfront
restaurants, those willing to rough it can take off over the jungled
hills with a sleeping mat and a few basics and soon discover their
private corners of paradise.

I was taken by a local Phi Phi fisherman toward the southern
tip of this arc of islands. His pitch had been simple: "You like bird
ness soup?"

"Not particularly."

"You want see caves where ma' get ness?"

"Not really."

"Good. We go."

So we went.

It was hot on the main island and a breezy five-mile boat ride in a "longtail" didn't sound like such a bad idea. I'm a pushover for pitchmen anyway.

And what a strange world we entered.

Incised near the base of towering limestone karsts were dark caves, full of eerie shadows and dripping with enormous tiered stalactites. Our voices echoed in their murky interiors. As my eyes became accustomed to the dank gloom I saw a spidery web of bamboo pillars and catwalks, lashed together with rope and vines, rising from the floor of the cave and disappearing high into the darkness.

"For ness," the fisherman explained in his singsong English. "Ma' climb for ness. Ve' high."

"They climb these things?" I gasped. They didn't look strong enough to support a monkey—even a parrot.

"Li' bird. Swiss. Have ness."

"Swiss?"

He grinned, revealing a toothless mouth. He was having problems with the word and tried again

"Swisses? Lil' birds." He flapped his arms like wings.

"Oh—swifts!"

"Ya, ya. Ma', climb."

I must have looked a bit skeptical. Next thing I knew the fisherman leaped onto one of the vertical bamboo scaffolds and began climbing—almost dancing—upward, pulling himself up by the dangling vines, his toes outstretched like fingers. The bamboo poles creaked and swayed. I expected the whole gossamer construction to fall apart and placed myself to catch my falling guide.

In seconds he was up more than fifty feet, on the edge of the deep shadows. He pointed into the far recesses of the cave. The scaffolding seemed to be everywhere. "Ve' far. Two kilomet."

"Okay. I believe you."

"Ma', climb." His voice sounded miles away.

"Yes, I understand. Come on down now."

He was looking around. "All go. No swiss."

Then he spotted an object on the side of the high cave wall. He reached out, touched the mossy rock, and something white floated down to the floor. I picked it up. It was a bit like sponge tissue—webbed strands of soft fiber.

He was down again. I hadn't even heard him coming.

"Ness," he said.

It was a tiny fragment of a swift's nest, left behind by one of the pickers. Apparently the birds build them out of strands of saliva, which later coalesce into tangled rubbery strips, rather like transparent vermicelli.

"Ve' goo." He grinned and rubbed his skinny belly, then flexed a sinewy bicep. "Mak' stron."

I tore off a tiny piece and tasted it. Nothing. A texture like sponge with no discernable flavor whatsoever. It reminded me of the soup fiasco in Hong Kong when, unwittingly, I'd eaten a bowl of the most innocuous broth laced with gelatinous strips and been charged an outrageous amount for the honor of ingesting the finest shark's fin soup on the island. Birds' nests obviously fell into the same category. A dish for the purist, offering promises of virility, energy, longevity, and all those other virtues so anxiously sought by Oriental epicures.

It seemed like an awful lot of trouble and danger to go to for something so—well—bland.

The fisherman was now firing an imaginary machine gun at me and laughing. "If you ta', me go…" (more machine gun sounds). "Bi' dollas. Man', man', dollas. Much money."

Apparently these nesting caves are very valuable and jealously guarded.

The fisherman stopped firing. "Is alri'—no more swiss."

The cave had been abandoned by the birds. These were old bamboo scaffolds and presumably even more dangerous than they looked. The fisherman was even crazier than I'd thought. One or two rotten bamboo poles or some broken vine knots and the whole fragile construction could have collapsed. But he didn't appear to mind. He was firing his machine gun at invisible birds' nest looters again.

David Yeadon is author/illustrator of over twenty travel books, including Lost Worlds: Exploring the Earth's Remote Places *and* The Back of Beyond: Travels to the Wild Places of the Earth, *from which this story was excerpted.* He is a travel feature writer for National Geographic, National Geographic Traveler, The Washington Post, *and numerous other magazines and his work has been featured in many travel anthologies. He lives with his wife and cats on an idyllic lake north of New York City.*

Chai in an Unglazed Cup

Drink it this way while you can.

AT PHARLANI JUNCTION, A SMALL STOP BETWEEN JAIPUR AND Jodhpur, I heard the cry "*Guram chai*, hot tea," and swung off the train to patronize the Rajasthani platform vendor. He was serving his tea in traditional unglazed clay cups. I had been looking for this old-fashioned village tea since I started my journey.

No beverage is more satisfying or restorative than Indian *chai*. English tea and toast is a feature of hotel breakfasts, both in Western-style establishments and Indian ones, and uniformed bearers will present it to you with a flourish at the airport dining rooms. But the quintessential cup of *chai* is to be found on an Indian railroad station platform. The old-style earthen cups are made of unglazed red clay, and they are either glass-shaped or vase-shaped. My beverage cost only two rupees. "*Guram chai*, hot tea, *guram chai*," intoned the salesman, the sound passing through both nose and throat, "*Guram chai!*" I did not worry about germs; they had been boiled to death.

Drinking from clay is completely ecological. We smashed our cups on the railroad tracks. The monsoon rains dissolve the shards back into red Indian earth, dust to dust. There is no litter.

This sweet milk tea is made with tea leaves, water, milk, spices, and sugar—either the coarse white Indian sugar or a chunk of the unrefined sugar called *gur*. The ingredients are boiled together, then left to simmer over the charcoal fire, getting stronger and better throughout the day. Cardamom is almost always used, but *chai* is most delicious spiced with a combination of cinnamon, clove, nutmeg, ginger, cardamom, and black pepper. And there is an elusive ingredient in *chai* drunk from a clay cup, a slight earthy flavor.

Night had fallen in the desert, the dark broken only by a fingernail moon and occasional lights from villages along the way. As the train pulled into another small station, I again heard the nasal call, "*Guram chai*." Once more I sipped the satisfying familiar sweetness, mud-flavored. When will I have it this way again? The traditional vendor with his clay cups is disappearing; the large Indian plastic industry threatens to make the village potter obsolete.

Chai is sold everywhere in the large cities of North India, but only in plastic cups. A traditional host will serve the sweet milk tea, *deshi chai*, to his guests in glass or brass tumblers. It is always scalding, even when the weather is over 100 degrees. But it is surprisingly refreshing, boiling hot tea on a boiling hot day. Try it, you will see, but it is best in a clay cup. Look for it on the station platforms of Rajasthan, and the smaller Indian cities and villages. Enjoy it now, this year or the next, before it is too late.

I am sipping *chai* as I write, but, sadly, from a drinking glass.

Marguerite Thoburn Watkins was born and brought up in the foothills of the Himalayas, but has spent most of her adult life in the foothills of the Blue Ridge in Virginia. This piece was inspired by her recent visit to North India and Rajasthan.

NIGEL ANDERSON

⋆ ⋆ ⋆

Crocodile Hunting

Watch out, you too can be food.

FRIDAY EVENING IN HAUNA BASE, EAST SEPIK REGION, PAPUA
New Guinea. As the bruise of the sunset fades to black, the boats
moored in the middle of the Sepik River sparkle with bright
lights. The weekend party is just starting for the men who have
been flown in from their forest camps, ready for a cold beer and
some English-speaking company. I have finished in the radio shack
for the day. All the production figures are in and the helicopters are
tucked up for the night.

The boatman flashes me a grin as we skim across the soupy,
brown river to the accommodation boat. He, like me, is excited by
the thought of the crocodile hunt later. The native hunters have
spent the afternoon filing the points of their spears to needle
sharpness. There is a multiple-spiked one for smaller crocs. One
with a single, viscously barbed detachable point for anything
alarmingly big and a couple in between for any intermediate-sized
saurian we might come across.

Don, the skipper of the *Petaj*, our accommodation boat, meets
me at the top of the gangway. An ex-prawn fisherman in the Gulf
of Carpentaria, he is tall and wiry with shoulder-length greying
hair and quick, dark eyes. His nose, crooked from some barroom

brawl, leans out over a wicked grin surrounded by a bush of wild beard. He has a battery and powerful lamp for spotting our quarry. Their eyes always show red in the flashlight and you can tell the size of the croc by the distance between them. The further they are apart, the bigger the crocodile. There is also a roll of insulating tape to hold snapping jaws closed, a case of the South Pacific brewery's finest and the life jackets.

The Sepik River is wide and slow. It meanders in great loops which form narrow necked islands as it snakes through the dense rainforest. Sometimes these islands are cut off and oxbow lakes are created. Still, menacing backwaters, ideal habitat for the two types of crocodile found here. The dark-backed freshwater crocodile, huge and slow moving, and his faster, more aggressive cousin, the estuarine or saltwater croc.

At night the trees at the riverside stand in stark silhouette against the starlit sky, their reflections broken black on the swiftly flowing, mud thick water. Oxbow lakes are marked by a gap in the trees and whispering reed beds, called *pitpit*. When the river is high enough you can pole a canoe through into the mysterious world beyond.

Moonlight etches the trees in silver with mysterious, impenetrable black shadows. There are massive branches festooned with creepers overhanging the water. Dead limbs reach out like imploring hands. Frogs chirp and croak. A huge snake, the lamp reflecting red from its eyes slithers along a branch. Shine the light into the water and you can see tilapia fish swimming among the tree roots, chasing smaller fish and tadpoles. The hot, fetid air is alive with flying insects clouding around the lamp. We have to tie cloths around our faces to stop ourselves from breathing them in. Bats flit and dive, feeding on the nourishing cloud and cicadas chirrup in high pitched nocturnal frenzy from the encroaching bush. The rainforest cacophony breaks over us in waves. Insects and frogs create a symphony of croaks, their rasps and chirrups silenced only by the crash of a falling branch deep in the woods. After a few seconds of shocked hush the noise starts again, building into a crescendo of sound.

The hunters leave any croc bigger than about nine feet well alone. No one wants to take on a monster like that with a spear. Sometimes a wily old crocodile will see the potential of easy food near a village. He will notice habitual behaviour such as collecting water from the same place on the river bank every day or some-one dangling their feet off the school canoe. There will be a sud-den frenzy of thrashing water, a bloody swirl and silence.

When a croc starts taking villagers they call in a professional. These men are local legends and treated with enormous respect. Alphonse is one of these, a giant of a man at least six feet tall, un-usual in New Guinea. He works as a load master on the helicopters by day, but at weekends he takes his spears and goes hunting for rogue crocs. If he is not chasing monsters he can be persuaded to take the clumsy white men on a hunt for smaller quarry. He lives in a village called Kupkain about three miles upriver from the oil exploration camp.

The village is typical of Papua New Guinea. The houses, high on the riverbank, are arranged around a communal area of packed earth with a fireplace and logs to sit on. Each dwelling consists of one room about thirty feet long with a door at each end to allow the smoke from the cooking fire to blow through. The house is built on stout wooden stilts about ten feet high. Access is by clam-bering up a log propped against the doorway with footholds cut into it. The floor is made of split bamboo slats, springy under foot. The walls are low under a heavily thatched roof, blackened by years of cooking fires and festooned with drying fish, bows and ar-rows, hunting trophies and, deep in the darkest recesses, other more sinister artefacts. Pigs root around underneath, snuffling out food scraps while scrawny hens scratch and peck, keeping a wary eye out for the mangy dogs that slink slyly in the shadows.

When we arrive the whole family are sitting around the room in fire flickering gloom, their eyes and sweat shiny faces gleaming in the dim lamp light. The men with wild pig's tusks through their noses and dried grasses poking upwards from either side of their nostrils, wear cast-off western shorts or traditional arse-grass (a cluster of leaves hanging from a string around the waist). They have tattoos on their upper bodies created by taking pinches of skin and making small cuts in stylised crocodile head patterns. A mixture of soot and forest herbs is rubbed into the wounds to create raised scars. This process is incredibly painful and is a part of their initiation into manhood. The tattoos identify the village a man is from as surely as any passport. The women lurk shyly in the gloom, laughing at our clumsy attempts to get comfortable. Everyone has red-stained teeth from chewing betel nut. The interior of the building smells of people, wood smoke and fish.

Food appears in the form of smoked tilapia fish and a disgusting grey lump of gelatinous sago served on a leaf and eaten with the fingers. The dimness of the light is a distinct advantage when confronted by such a repast. Soon my eyes are watering from the acrid coconut husk smoke, used to keep mosquitoes at bay. After presenting the village elder with a gift of cigarettes and beer, the hunt begins.

The equipment is transferred from the aluminum speedboat to a thirty-foot dugout canoe. Alphonse takes overall charge of the hunt. There's also Little John, about five feet tall and immensely strong with a barrel chest and arms like legs. He is the spearman and spotter in the bow. The boat driver is Big John, taller and more slightly built than his namesake. An expert with the forty-horsepower engine he dodges the floating trees and other hazards with uncanny accuracy. Us ungainly white men sit on our life jackets amid ships, hunched into the narrow hollowed log and peering into the darkness, trying to keep up with the sweep and flick of the flashlight as John guides the driver up the inky black river. He stands on the flat top of the crocodile head carved on the prow, his toes gripping the smooth wood, balanced like a surfer and sweeping the powerful beam of light from side to side. The fallen trees floating down the dark river look unearthly, their roots like the writhing tentacles of giant squid. A flick of the light tells the driver which direction to swerve to avoid outstretched branches.

The air is thick with humidity. The temperature is only marginally less than the usual daytime 30 degrees (86 degrees Fahrenheit).

Clouds of tiny flies swarm in the shadows under overhanging bushes close to the river bank. Unfortunately, to avoid the swift current in midstream this is where we have to be. They clog our eyes and ears. Leeches, sensing our body heat, drop from the underside of leaves and make their unerring way towards unprotected flesh. Lightning flashes silhouette the rainforest giants on the riverbank against a flickering silver backdrop. The thunder is just a mutter from the far off hills where the storms are a nightly occurrence, leaving us to marvel at the fantastic light show without the misery of a tropical rainstorm.

A flick of the light. The canoe veers towards the *pitpit*. I can see the marker, a slender pole stuck into the mud at the entrance to a narrow inlet. John cuts the engine and we glide in. The sudden quiet is shocking in the darkness. We all help pole the dugout through the whispering reed bed, our ears tuned to any unexpected noise. Adrenaline surges, heightening awareness and sharpening reactions. Suddenly the silence is shattered. My heart leaps. Something thrashes off into the reeds, something very big. As the noise recedes into the distance the only sound is sloshing water and nervous laughter. Little John tells us it was a wild pig. Reassuring, unless you know what they look like with their coarse black hair, huge tusks, and ferocious reputation.

The *pitpit* gives way to the more open water of the oxbow lake. John sweeps the light back and forth. The bright beam pushes aside the darkness, illuminating a tangle of fallen branches entwined with parasitic vines and patches of floating lilies, their flowers closed to the night. A possum, dazzled by the light, blinks at us from his tree, interrupted in his nocturnal hunt for food. The light moves on, concentrating now on the muddy bank.

A flash of red. John swings the beam back. There he is, a crocodile, eyes gleaming like motorway cats eyes. The dugout surges forward as Big John dips his paddle in powerful strokes. The spearman, balanced like a dancer, lifts his spear. He leaps, plunging downward with the shaft. There is a slip slapping struggle, the smell of wet mud and finally the triumphant hunter rises like some fantastic creature, his arms raised, a snapping, grunting crocodile clutched firmly just behind its front legs. It is about six feet long and, like its captor, covered in a thick layer of stinking mud. He passes it to John and I keep as far from the snapping jaws as possible, staring at this prehistoric predator as its mouth is carefully taped shut. Taped and trussed it is placed in the bottom of the boat and lies there glaring at me, its strange, expressionless eyes seemingly fixed on mine. We open some beers, light cigarettes and pole our way back out into the main river. The earlier fears are forgotten as we all compare notes and already exaggerate the drama of the hunt.

When we are in open water again John slips over the side to wash off the mud, then the croc is washed as well. Its skin is silky smooth with raised ridges in patterns on its back, similar to the ones on the hunters' bodies. There are black and olive green-brown stripes fading to a pale creamy colour on the belly. The webbed feet on muscular legs have sharp claws to help propel it through the slippery mud. This is a sleek and highly efficient predator with a formidable armoury of needle sharp teeth. We continue the hunt for another two or three hours, collecting several smaller specimens, none of which is bigger than about three feet, much more manageable in the canoe.

The cramped seating position finally becomes too uncomfortable. We decide to call it a night and turn for home, Little John in the bow sweeping the light along the banks, looking for any we may have missed. He sees the telltale flicker of red on the waterline and directs Big John towards it. The outboard motor roars. Don and I crane to see the quarry. Excitement mounts again as we speed towards the patch of light held steady on the shore. Suddenly John yells to the driver to back off. He slams the engine into reverse. The croc has turned its head to see where the noise is coming from. What originally looked like two eyes close together turns out to be one big eye, with another about eight inches away. This is a very big crocodile, fourteen feet at least and the engine cannot reverse quickly enough. We slide over the crocodile's back pinning it to the river bottom and running the bow of the canoe up the bank. The huge beast, now enraged, arches its back. The head and tail on either side of the boat lift out of the water and slap down again in a welter of mud and spray. The outboard screams in protest as the prop tries to bite into the water. I am holding the sides of the boat in white-knuckled terror, watery mud running into fear widened eyes. Slowly the canoe starts to slip off both the bank and the crocodile, gradually picking up speed and taking us a safe distance from the crashing saurian jaws.

This is enough excitement for one night. The rush of shared danger loosens our tongues and it is a talkative crew that returns to the *Petaj*. The next evening there are barbecued crocodile steaks all round. The meat is a delicious mixture of pork and chicken with a slightly fishy flavour thrown in. We have it with salad, fresh bread and ice cold beer, wonderful.

I sit out on the deck under a dense cloud of stars, wrapped in the velvety warmth of the tropical night. The sound of music and laughter wafts to me from the bar and I let my mind wander. What have my friends at home in England been doing on their Friday evening?

Nigel Anderson first became interested in travel when he was little and sat on a beach in Devon, England, watching ships disappear over the horizon and wondering where they were going. Many years later he joined the merchant navy and since then has built boats, fished commercially, looked for oil in Papua New Guinea, driven overland expeditions from London to Zimbabwe and back, ridden a motorcycle around the edge of Australia, kayaked among the islands off Belize, and chilled out in Goa. He currently drives trucks to support his writing habit.

Great Expectations

Comfort comes in all guises.

"DOES IT COST A LOT TO EAT IN HONG KONG?"

"No," my boss said, "it doesn't have to."

Though he was an experienced traveler, I didn't believe him. He had money and I didn't—only 900 bucks to my name after airfare, and I was spending every last cent on this trip. For my first time overseas, everything had to be perfect.

I wanted to taste the Chinese recipes that had been handed down to my great grandmother, her daughter, my father, and now me. I wanted to dine with the locals and order for my friends in Cantonese. I wanted to eat the best dim sum in the world...

"The noodle houses are cheap," he encouraged.

Ahhh the noodle houses. I envisioned every street corner marked by bamboo carts with steamy mystery broth—old men in black pajama pants and mandarin shirts cooking dried egg noodles, grandmothers sitting on nearby benches chopping vegetables, live chickens in wooden crates waiting their turn to provide a fresh meal.

"And there's always McDonald's," he added.

"James! I am not going half way across the world to eat at McDonald's!" I yelled with my virgin travel nose 45 degrees towards the ceiling. The golden arches were *completely* out of the question. And off I huffed to go pack.

The next thing I knew, a beautiful Singapore Airlines stewardess was offering me a hot face towel, new socks, toothbrush, earphones for my personal TV with movie options, and a menu for a full-course gourmet dinner. This was the life, what international traveling was all about. The plane wasn't turning around, so I was officially "worldly."

I arrived to a quiet Hong Kong morning. Twenty-story tenements towered over clean vacant streets. Clothes dried on laundry lines outside the apartment windows. A man on a rickety black bicycle rode by with a large woven basket tied to the back. The sky was overcast and shops were closed. I headed down Nathan Road in Tsimshatsui to meet my friend.

All of a sudden, I stopped in my tracks. There they were. The golden arches. I hadn't even been in Hong Kong twenty minutes! A big shiny red and yellow sign staring me right in the face, bright and breakfasty for all of sleeping Hong Kong to see. I bolstered my international attitude, and walked on.

Our first day, we roamed through a Wanchai wet market. Live fish and crab swam in tanks, frogs and eels squirmed and slithered in tubs, chickens, ducks, quails and pigeons squawked from stacks of wooden cages. The sidewalks were full. The streets were loud. Chinese women pushed to get by, storeowners yelled for you to come in, cars honked to get through the crowds. Wanchai was busy and we were getting hungry.

I stopped in a bakery to get us some *Cha Shu baos,* (barbecue pork buns). When I returned with the buns, I almost turned into a pig—gobbling down the feed before I could even smell it. Almost. I couldn't turn into a pig because I had already transformed into a cat. A finicky feline sniffing her food and turning her nose. These weren't like the *baos* I ate at home. These *baos* were small and cold and doughy. My nose was back in the air. One loud whiny meow and we had returned to the hunt for lunch.

It was 3:30 and we hadn't eaten all day. Half bent over and cranky as can be, I stopped looking for the perfect back street dim sum cafe and begrudgingly settled on a restaurant advertising menus in English. They had the basics, and we ordered them. Chow mein, baby bok choy, egg rolls, steamed rice, and hot tea. There were other tourists in the restaurant, identifiable by their fanny packs, and they wouldn't leave us alone. Smiling and telling us what to order, and where to go. Clearly, I wasn't half way around the world. This could have been any old Chinese restaurant back home in San Francisco. I wasn't feeling worldly anymore.

The next 24 hours were a haze of tired swollen feet rambling mile after mile from Kowloon to Central, over to Admiralty, Wanchai, back to Kowloon, then over to Causeway Bay, back to Central and then back to Tsimshatsui and through the streets to our guest house in Jordan, all in the rain. Our log of the day read as a list. The Star Ferry, Hong Kong Park aviary, the government buildings, the Mass Transit Railway, Nathan Road, Mass Transit Railway, The Mandarin Oriental, Chater Road, The Mass Transit Railway, Nathan Road. All of our time was spent getting from one place to the next. Traveling.

The cell phones kept ringing and Calgon was nowhere to be found. I knew that I was wet, couldn't deny that I was exhausted, had Grouch stamped right across my forehead, and was hungry enough to eat a...hey! The light bulb of all light bulbs, the grand daddy of electrical know how, a billboard of Thomas Edison shot up in pink blinking neon above my head! I hadn't eaten since yesterday. Food—the ultimate mood-saver extraordinare!

The epiphany lifted our heads from following the feet in front of us.

"Thank God, a McDonald's!" my friend Alison said with an unbeatable sigh of relief. I, of course, went into the deep dark world of utter embarrassment.

"But, it's McDonald's," I whispered.

"Lucky for us, eh?" she replied.

"But, we're in Hong Kong," I attempted to reason, "we can't eat McDonald's in Hong Kong. What about dim sum? What about noodle houses?"

"What about next time," she said beginning to get annoyed

with me. My stomach was shedding its skin, throwing out its monogrammed lining, and nailing a "for rent" sign to my jacket.

"O.K., just this once," my hungry half surrendered.

She opened the door. I must have been delirious from the heat and famine, because there was no doubt in my mind that I had just set foot in the happiest place on earth.

"Didn't Disney merge with McDonald's?" I asked. But no one was listening. I couldn't move. I was paralyzed in air-conditioned bliss. It wasn't even raining in here.

The aroma of french fries and Big Mac's was sweeter and more fulfilling than any home cooked Thanksgiving dinner I'd ever set the table for. Happy Meal advertisements hung from the ceiling like white dreamy clouds. Everyone was smiling, everyone was eating. Except me. I woke up and went to order.

"Two of everything please."

The young Chinese woman ignored me and pointed at a picture menu for me to place a real order.

"Yut," I muttered the Cantonese word for one, trying to please my conscience. I could still bring some cultural experience to this magical Hong Kong wonderland.

"Do you mean Value meal number one?" she asked in perfect English.

"Yes, and a diet coke please," I replied, a little taken aback.

We sat down to eat the most rewarding meal of our lives. The fries had never been so perfect, Coke never as refreshing, and the special sauce, never so special. I couldn't remember ever being so gastronomically satisfied. What was happening to me? I was so relaxed and happy you'd have thought I'd just spent the last half hour being pampered at a health spa. But I wasn't in a spa and my health was of no consideration here. "Tomorrow, I'll redeem myself," I promised my conscience.

Sixteen hours later my words to James came haunting back, "I'm not going half way across the world to eat at McDonald's!" But there we were, starving at 7 A.M., standing in the rain in front of another Tsimshatsui McDonald's. A quick breakfast didn't count as a meal so I postponed my promise and ignored the ghost of

James while I followed Alison in to have the most delicious orange juice of my life. The rain had not let up and I wasn't going to either. I ordered more potato cakes and another large orange juice. Alison followed suit.

We didn't want to leave, but what would Sean, our other traveling partner, think? He was waiting for us to begin another blister-bursting-day of combing through more and more and more of Hong Kong.

One day led to the next and before I knew it the trip was almost over. We had found sanctuary in the dry friendly air-conditioned McDonald's almost once a day since the first acquiescence. Each visit had become more and more soothing to my tired body, but less and less agreeable with my conscience. But hey, on nearly every street, they were impossible to avoid.

For Sean's last day we were going to Macau. Alison had already gone back to the States, so we decided to take one last shot at giving up McDonald's for the rest of the trip. I *had* to start eating Chinese food.

After six days of true travel adventure wandering—the kind that never got us where we wanted to be, on time, or with energy to experience the landmark—we followed a simple map from the tourist authority. The sun was out, momentarily, and we were in search of the Monte Fort, built nearly four hundred years ago. We meandered up and down hilly backstreets, past mechanic closets and teak carpenters, seafood stalls and china bowl shops. There were clothes for sale, juices to drink, shoes to buy and jewelry to bring home for bargain prices. We were falling in love with Macau, but getting tired from not finding the Fort. And then, deja vú.

"Where is it?" Sean asked. By now I could recognize the early signs of misery.

"I don't know, according to the map it's supposed to be right here," I answered, equally irritated.

"I think we'd be able to see a Fort," he continued. I couldn't argue.

"Well, why don't we try this street." I offered.

Fifteen minutes later, "Sean, look, up there, I think that's it!"

"That's got to be it!" Desperately needed energy returned.

"How do we get up there?"

"I don't know." Hope faltered, but remained alive.

An hour later we still hadn't reached Monte Fort. Exhausted and frustrated, we saw some Americans up the street and relented to asking for directions. But they were fast and we were crabby. When we finally caught up, I froze in shock. Right behind the Americans was a corner McDonald's. I wasn't going to break our pact. No way, no how, no matter how hungry, hot and tired I was. Maybe if I didn't look over there, he wouldn't notice.

"Do you know where the Fort is?" Sean asked half cheerily.

"We can't find it either," the woman replied, "it's supposed to be right around this McDonald's."

Not the M word! Sean and I could only laugh. I knew that look in his eye. We were worn out, and she stood there beckoning with comforting golden open arms. I shook my head, but we were no match for her familiar charms. I kept my stubborn front.

"Sean, we said we weren't going to eat here anymore."

"Come on, just a shake," he compromised, "a chocolate shake." I could practically feel the relieving frosty cream on my throat. We were fighting a battle with desire much stronger than both of us, a calling far greater than the Fort we'd soon find.

"O.K. But only if it's to-go. A shake to-go isn't really like *eating* at McDonald's."

We walked into the air-conditioned paradise and forgot all about the archaeological treasure only minutes away.

"Two chocolate shakes," Sean ordered.

"And a small fry too," I added.

Jennifer L. Leo grew up in San Diego and graduated from the University of Southern California. She bicycled across the U.S., attempted to hop freight trains, and considered herself an adventure enthusiast before there were such things as X-Games. Now she lives, eats, and writes in San Francisco.

✦ ✦ ✦

Smokin'

They were cooking more than meat.

SLOWLY, MY HEART SINKING, WE INCHED PAST BAD BRYAN'S BUTT Rub, Bubba's Got A Top Secret, The Duck Stops Here, Tim & Todd's We Smoke But Don't Inhale, and So Good You'll Think You Died And Went To Texas. My eyes skittered from the signs to the hardware. One cooker must've been five feet high, in the shape of a Jack Daniel's bottle. Another was as big as a Civil War cannon and painted in lamés. A third was wide enough to swallow a four-foot pig splayed out like Grandpa's overalls on a backyard clothes-line. Many were so large you'd mistake them for trailers if you passed them on the highway. We braked at a grassy rectangle next to a lady wearing a shirt that read: I DIDN'T CLAW MY WAY TO THE TOP OF THE FOOD CHAIN TO EAT VEGETABLES.

"Looks like as good a place as any," I said to my father, "for Custer's Last Stand."

Above was a pure blue Tennessee October sky…somewhere behind all that pure gray barbecue smoke. The meat inspectors walked among us like sheriffs, making sure no Quick Draws sneaked a head start on tomorrow's showdown. Each of the fifty teams invited to the Super Bowl of barbecue, the Jack Daniel's

World Championship Invitational, had won a state title or a certified competition during the year. Then there was me and Dad.

I popped open the back door of the rental van. First things first: Stake the territory. On an easel, I carefully centered my sign.

BON APPETIT

THE PERFECT MAN'S RIBS

"C'mon," I called to my father, rubbing my hands together. "Let's set up the smoker." It seemed so puny now, considering the fume-belching monsters around us. Hard to imagine that less than 24 hours earlier, the two of us had nearly popped the veins in our foreheads lifting it into the van. Which made me feel a little guilty, knowing that my father probably hadn't wanted to come along.

A Samaritan noticed our predicament and asked if he could help. He got beneath the cooker with my father, but as I lowered it, 305 pounds of high-carbon steel fell and damn near imprinted the poor guy in the ground. "Jeeeez Loueeeez!" he yelped. "How much does this thing weigh?"

A snort burst through my father's nostrils, and a smirk lifted the left corner of his mouth, as if to say, Now you know what it's like to have a son like mine.

My eyes scanned the miniature barbecue city that had sprung up in the park bordering the Jack Daniel's distillery. Competitors in overalls and cowboy hats were shaking hands as if they knew each other's families, discussing the $15,000 in prize money, and scratching their heads over how it was against the law to sip so much as a light beer, because the home of one of the world's most famous whiskeys was a dry county. There did seem to be some winking over that.

It was hard to believe that tomorrow, 20,000 people would be descending on Lynchburg, a town that was no more than the distillery, an old-timey square with a hardware store and some souvenir shops, Miss Mary Bobo's Boarding House, and a sign that laid claim to 361 inhabitants. Folks would park halfway to Nashville in order to tour the historic distillery that charcoal-mellows Old No. 7, watch the greased-pole climb, and taste the world's best barbecue. And Dad and I, New Yorkers through and through, would be in the thick of it.

The woman who didn't climb to the top of the food chain to eat vegetables came over to introduce herself. Sharon and her husband, Don, had pulled up stakes in Kansas and joined the 10,000-mile weekend competitive barbecue circuit that began in May and ended here six months later, often squeezing in some shut-eye in the back of their car.

"The Perfect Man's Ribs. Hmmm," Sharon said. "Which contest did you win?"

"To tell the truth," I apologized, "I've been at this less that a month." Her forehead wrinkled, and I was already ruing that blast of bravado on my sign. I explained that I'd been trying to perfect myself and writing about the experience, going to experts like Jack LaLanne to take off weight, learning how to walk and talk properly, to eat with table manners, and to manage my time. Seemed only natural that The Perfect Man would know how to barbecue ribs that'd make his guests' tongues smack their eyebrows. So I'd tracked down the author of *The Barbecue! Bible*, Steven Raichlen, and after twenty-four hours of instruction and a few weeks of practice, I'd fast-talked my way into the Jack Daniel's contest to be judged on how well I'd learned. Only now was I fully understanding what I'd gotten myself into. My ribs could easily come out tasting like one of your uncle's loafers, and all of the major leaguers would cackle. Worst of all, my father would be there to witness it.

Sharon pointed at him. "Does *he* know how to barbecue?"

"No," he said, "I'm the guy who got suckered into helping lift the smoker because he couldn't find anyone else."

I let that one go.

"Well, if you need any help," said Sharon, departing, "let us know."

The championship was divided into seven categories: pork ribs, pork shoulder, chicken, beef brisket, whole hog, Jack Daniel's sauce, and dessert. I was entering only two: dessert, which I'd smoke that afternoon, and ribs, which I'd start the next morning, praying to time them just right for the afternoon judging.

I went about shaping a pyramid of charwood in the smoker's firebox. These coals weren't the supermarket briquettes that need to be doused with lighter fluid; they looked like dark, hard pieces of tree bark. Shipped by an outfit called Peoples Woods/Nature's Own in Providence, Rhode Island, they provided an even heat. They even sounded different from the supermarket kind as they took to the fire, reminding me of faint, faraway bells.

"Sure is a lot quicker and easier to do it with gas," my father pointed out. There it was in a nutshell: he saw life as smoothing out the bumps in the road; I went looking for Himalayas.

"Here," I said, handing him a bag of apples. "Core 'em to within a half inch of the bottom, then scoop out the seeds."

FIRE-ROASTED APPLES

8 firm, sweet Gala apples
$\frac{1}{2}$ stick unsalted butter at room temperature
$\frac{1}{4}$ cup dark brown sugar, firmly packed
$\frac{1}{4}$ cup dried cranberries
$\frac{1}{4}$ cup ground almonds

$\frac{1}{2}$ teaspoon ground cinnamon
$\frac{1}{4}$ teaspoon nutmeg, freshly grated
1 teaspoon vanilla extract
4 marshmallows, cut in half

I ground the almonds, wondering what he really thought about this Perfect Man business. Anytime a man tries to make himself over, isn't that like slapping his father across the face? Here I was at forty-one learning to do things that he was supposed to have taught me. The only time Dad had ever said anything about my quest to become The Perfect Man was after I'd learned about time management from an expert who charges corporations $3,000 a day. "I could have told you all that," Dad said. Probably could have, with his twenty-seven years as a manager at IBM, but he never *had*.

I sliced down the center of the vanilla bean and scraped out the extract. Then I tossed it in a bowl with the rest of the ingredients except the marshmallows, whisked, and spooned the batter into the apples Dad had cored. It was the ribs that worried me, not the apples. The dessert recipe, according to Steven, was idiot-proof. All you had to do was fill the apples up with the cinnamon-nutmeggy magic and leave them over indirect heat for about one to two hours until they were soft and squeezable as a homecoming queen.

THE RUB

$\frac{1}{4}$ cup paprika	1 teaspoon black pepper, freshly ground
1 tablespoon dark brown sugar, firmly packed	1 to 3 teaspoons cayenne pepper, to taste
1 tablespoon granulated sugar	1 teaspoon dry mustard
2 teaspoons salt	1 teaspoon garlic powder
2 teaspoons Accent	1 teaspoon onion powder
1 teaspoon celery salt	

"The ribs are going to be flavored in layers," I explained to my father, just after we'd watched some firefighters from Mississippi open up a whole hog like a hatchback and operate on the innards like surgeons. "The chunks of applewood we throw on the coals will give 'em a light scent, nothing harsh like mesquite or hickory. The rub'll give 'em a dash of Memphis. The mop sauce will add a curin' touch. Then the barbecue sauce I invented will top it off." It felt strange telling Dad what to do, as if he were my son, but dutifully he began measuring the peppers, powders, and sugars for the rub exactly as I directed.

Truth is, I probably *wouldn't* have listened to him about managing time even if he *had* told me. Hadn't listened to anything else he'd advised for nearly a quarter of a century. He'd said get a steady job and settle; I wandered across deserts and rain forests without health insurance. He'd said, just like his father before him, keep custom and marry a Jewish woman; I went to the altar with a half-Indian, half-African woman I'd met on a beach in Brazil. From the time I was seventeen, whenever Dad and I were in the same room, you could light an M-80 with the sparks.

Butterflies began to flit in my stomach as I mixed the seasonings into a rub. I was straining to match Charlie Vergos's legendary seasoning at the Rendezvous restaurant in Memphis—which, no matter if it was Monday or Friday, 2 P.M. or 10 P.M., was bound to make his customers' socks flap up and down. But no matter how many times I'd practiced mixing my rub, it seemed to come out different. When I didn't get the cayenne pepper just right, the taste ended up miles from Memphis, south of El Diablo, or, worse, lost way up in the Canadian tundra.

I dipped my finger into the bowl, brought it to my lips, and felt a smile lift my cheeks.

"Hey, Perfect Man!"

My smile grew wider. It was my professor, who'd been invited by Jack Daniel's to be one of the judges. Couldn't say exactly why, but in twenty-four hours of cooking lessons, Steven had become like a brother to me. Maybe it was because, philosophically, he stood square in the middle of me and my father. He loved to hit the road, going 150,000 miles across five continents for the better part of four years to learn everything a man could about barbecue for his 556-page *Bible*. But he also owned a house with a swimming pool and a library that had seventeen of his own books on the shelves. Me, I was still renting, and the fact that I'd yet to put a word between hard covers probably bothered me as much as it did my father.

Steven tasted the rub, looked over the apples, and nodded. The apples were almost ready, and I crowned each of them with half a marshmallow. Tomorrow, we'd reheat them and brush them with butter to make the judges' eyes shine.

It made me feel secure to have Steven peering over my shoulder as I sprinkled the rub over the ribs, wrapped the two racks in cellophane so they'd absorb the seasoning, and put them in an ice-filled cooler. People were going to be cooking all night, and I'd have loved to stick around, but I knew my father would be none too pleased stretched out in a cargo van. So we packed up in darkness, asked Sharon and Don to look after the cooker, and headed to a hotel.

"You know," Steven told me, "I wish I could do this with *my* dad."

MOP SAUCE

1 quart cider vinegar	2 teaspoons hot red-pepper
1 medium onion, thinly	flakes
sliced	2 teaspoons black pepper,
3 jalapeño chiles, thinly sliced	freshly ground
4 teaspoons coarse sea salt	

It looked like the dawn of the Battle of Gettysburg the next morning, with everyone scurrying around as if they were preparing for combat under a sky choked with smoke. I handed my father an apron, threw a couple chunks of applewood into a bucket of water to soak, and did what man's been doing for more that a hundred thousand years: started a fire to cook meat.

My Oklahoma Joe's cooker looked like an antique locomotive. It had a firebox at the back end for the wood and charcoal. An air passage conveyed heat to a chamber in the center so it could pass over and around the ribs on its way to the chimney stack in the front. This wasn't like baking, where you set the temperature, slide a pan into the oven, hum a happy tune, and pull out your apple pie. This was sport—every bit as challenging as throwing a knee-high curve on the outside corner. The recipe called for the ribs to cook about five hours, the trick being to maneuver the dampers and keep the temperature steady at 215 degrees, all the while replenishing the coal and wood until the meat shrank back on the bone and you could find the prettiest pink-red ring inside when you tore it open with your fingers.

I tossed the applewood, soaked to extract more flavor, on the fire, and Dad and I stood over the fire blowing into our balled hands, trying to keep warm. By 9:45 A.M., I was pulling the cellophane from the two racks of ribs and laying 'em on the grating, fatty side up, hoping that they'd be perfect when the judges sank their teeth into them at exactly 3:00.

"The mop sauce'll keep the ribs from dehydrating," I told Dad as he chopped an onion and I diced a jalapeño. "We'll mop 'em about once an hour." I poured the vinegar in a bowl, he sprinkled in some pepper flakes, and we tasted, smacking our lips at the lash of flavor. They'd make buckets of the stuff in the Carolinas, I explained, dip a mop, and slather the sauce over a hundred pieces of pork laid out over the fire like piano keys. He looked up and said, "Jeez." If I wasn't mistaken, he was beginning to grow curious.

Over the years, I'd tried to patch things up with him. I'd taken him on a car trip through the Dakotas, and there were moments when I almost thought we were finally going to connect. I'd even gone back to high school at thirty-seven to pass a chemistry final that I'd cheated on at seventeen, that having been the first wedge between us. Maybe he'd tried to patch things up with me, too. He'd come to accept the woman I married—once even introduced her as his daughter and me as his son-in-law! And when he found out we were in debt over our eyebrows after our first child was born, he'd offered to loan me the money to straighten things out. I didn't think about it back then, but it must've hurt him when I told him to mind his own business. My kids were what started to bring Dad and me closer. You can talk to your father through your four-year-old, tell your boy to do things that *you* didn't do, like: "Go give your grandpa a hug."

THE PERFECT MAN'S APRICOT HORSERADISH BARBECUE SAUCE

1 cup apricot preserves
$\frac{1}{4}$ cup dark rum
$\frac{1}{4}$ cup tomato paste
$\frac{1}{4}$ cup fresh lime juice
3 tablespoons cider vinegar
2 tablespoons ketchup
1 tablespoon soy sauce
1 tablespoon molasses
2 teaspoons Worcestershire sauce
2 tablespoons fresh shallot, minced

1 tablespoon fresh ginger, minced
$\frac{1}{2}$ to 1 Scotch-bonnet pepper, seeded and minced
$\frac{1}{2}$ teaspoon hot red-pepper flakes
Salt and black pepper, freshly ground
$1\frac{1}{2}$ to 2 teaspoons horse-radish, to taste

A guy competing for the Head Country Sauce team was boasting for the eighty-eighth time how he'd been stopped at the barricades by police who weren't letting any more vehicles into the cooking grounds, how he'd bribed the officers with jars of his Ponca City, Oklahoma, sauce, and how his liquid gold got him waved in like royalty over a red carpet.

That was the thing about sauces, I thought, lining up my ingredients. There were a zillion of them, and everybody swore theirs was king. There were recipes for fifty-five sauces in Steven's *Bible*, from North Carolina Vinegar to Vietnamese Apple and Shrimp. But I wanted a flavor that would distinguish my ribs from all others in the world. I wanted to combine the sweetness of apricot with the heat of horseradish, and it took Steven nearly all afternoon to help me find the fifteen perfect accessories to make them blend. "There are no mistakes in the kitchen," he'd said at every roadblock. "Only new recipes being created."

I turned over the ribs and mopped. Everything was going according to schedule; now it was time to make the sauce. I cut open one of the hottest peppers on earth, a Scotch bonnet, making sure to remove the seeds without touching them. If you did and you so much as grazed the skin near your eye, your corneas would be blazing for the rest of the day. I minced half the Scotch bonnet finer than a knife blade, tossed it into a bowl, then added exactly one quarter cup of rum. "It's all in the chemistry," I told Dad, shaking my head at the irony. For more than twenty years, we'd not been able to say that word to each other. I remembered Dad coming home after the teacher had told him I had no chance of passing the chemistry final, tried to recall the blowup that led to the bet. Fifty bucks on whether I'd pass. Pure bravado. Not only had I cut class all year, but I didn't have the money to cover.

As I grated the ginger, I tried to dredge up the details. They'd said it was impossible to cheat. The other students at each table were taking biology and physics finals. But then, the guy who signaled all ninety answers to me from the other end of the gym with the slightest positioning of his pen later went on to a career in law enforcement. I could remember the celebration when I passed, could see my father's face after word got back to him, via a neighbor, that I'd cheated. He didn't want trouble with school officials; he just wanted his fifty dollars back. "No way!" I'd howled.

The fights started every night when he returned home from work and grew so loud and viscious that my mother, in tears, finally said she'd leave the house if either of us mentioned the word *chemistry* again. We never did. But it didn't matter, because we were too busy arguing about everything else.

I added the molasses, ginger, and Worcestershire sauce, whisked, and was just about to taste what I'd wrought when a contest official approached. "There's been a slight change in schedule," she announced. "Since you're not a regular contestant, we're going to ask you to have your entries in at two o'clock. Hundreds of pounds of food are coming in at specified times, and there's no other spot available. We're terribly sorry for any inconvenience."

I glanced at my watch. It was almost one, and the ribs needed nearly two more hours of cooking. I felt as if somebody had just punched a hole through my chest. I looked to my father for help as if I were six years old.

COOKING RULES
Each contestant must submit enough food in a Styrofoam
container to feed six judges. Garnish is limited to green lettuce, leafy parsley, and cilantro. Any other garnish or decoration will disqualify the entry.

My father looked back. *You're* in charge, his expression said; what's the plan? Beads of moisture appeared above my lip, and I felt my toe kick up a clump of grass.

I recalled Steven telling me that some barbecuers in Texas were cooking like lightning at ferocious heat. But if I hiked the temperature, my ribs would surely come out like a worn black saddle. I turned to Don and Sharon. There was no choice but to risk it, they said: Stoke the fire, wrap the ribs in aluminum foil to help contain the moisture, and…pray. My dad flung wood into the firebox, I foiled the ribs, opened the dampers, and let the coals draw in a chestful of air. In no time, the thermometer needle was soaring to 400 degrees, and I was sure the flesh on the grill was mine.

We warmed the sauce on Don and Sharon's hot plate and the apples on top of the smoker. Onlookers snapped photos as we buttered the skins to a shine. At 1:50 P.M., there was no choice but to take out the ribs. I set them on the table, peeled open the foil, and exhaled in relief when I saw the meat shrunken back on the bone and I was able to pull off a piece with my fingers. We cut the six best pieces for the other judges, making sure they were equal in size and sliced along the bone, while more cameras clicked and I mopped my forehead so sweat wouldn't drip all over the meat. It was 1:55.

As I sprinkled rub over the ribs, Dad screamed, and I stopped short. "No!" he was whipping his head back and forth. "You're going to ruin them! You're putting on too much. They'll be too spicy!"

I looked into my father's eyes. Here we go again. Me wanting spice, Dad wanting safety. "Trust me," I said, sprinkling on enough to satisfy my taste without offending his. "Okay," he said the instant I stopped. "Perfect!"

It was 1:57. I stirred the remaining ingredient, the horseradish, into the sauce and layered it on the ribs. My father laid them out on a bed of lettuce, and together we closed the Styrofoam container, boxed the apples, and at 1:59 hurtled through the swarm to the judges' tent, without the faintest idea how those ribs tasted under the rub and sauce.

JUDGE'S RIB-TASTING RULES
Rate appearance, taste, tenderness, and texture on a scale of 1 to 9 (9 being perfect, 1 being dog's dinner).

Approaching us was a white-bearded, bespectacled man wearing a bowler hat, bow tie, and suspenders over a white shirt that, instead of buttons, had tiny barbecue bones down the center. There he was: Remus Powers, Ph.B., Kansas City man. Word was he knew barbecue like Einstein knew physics.

Remus *stared* at the meat for what seemed like hours. "Feels tender," he finally said, carefully peeling away a piece and inspecting. "Got the smoke ring." He began to chew, but it was impossible to read him, because his face was born to play poker. He took another bite, then another considerate chew, and finally, almost grudgingly, said, "I like the texture of the sauce. Very subtle heat." Another taste and a deeper nod, like he was really getting into it, but then he pulled his cards close to the vest so as not to influence Dale DeGroff, the bartender from Windows on the World, and Lally Brennan, owner of Commander's Palace restaurant in New Orleans, as they began to nibble.

Lally's eyes flashed. "That would get a 9 on my scorecard," she said.

"Absolutely—that's a 9!" added Dale. "That's a really unique flavor."

Lynne Tolley, the owner of Miss Mary Bobo's Boarding House, which attracts people from around the world with its down home cooking, amazed us by tasting and then reciting nearly every ingredient. "Only thing missing," she said, "is a little Jack Daniel's in the sauce."

When Clive Cussler, the best-selling novelist, lifted a slice of apple to his mouth, he crowed, "That's better than sex!"

Dad looked at me in disbelief. But I was still holding my breath. Steven, my professor, was last.

He studied my rib every bit as carefully as Remus Powers, Ph.B. had, then tasted. Chewed. "You done good," he smiled. "I'm a proud father." Another bite and he cocked his head, as if straining to hear a distant cry. "You know," he said, "I would have liked a little more rub on it."

Dad's eyes opened as if seeing the world for the first time. "*Really?*"

We laughed, he put his arm on my shoulder, and we walked light-headed in the sun to our booth, where a line of people were waiting for a taste of The Perfect Man's Ribs.

We drove home the next day recounting every sweat-soaked moment, happy that Don and Sharon's team had won first prize for pork shoulder and proud that the folks at Jack Daniel's had invited us to come back next year and judge. In the afternoon, amid the monotony of the interstate, my father's head sagged, and he dozed off in the passenger seat. I stared at him, looked at him closer than I ever had before, fixing upon the white hairs overtaking the black in his eyebrows. I saw the face of a man going on seventy and the face of my four-year-old son sleeping after a good time in the park. I tried to remember the fights, the simple comments that enraged me only because they'd come from my father's lips. But it was all gone now, like vapor. Nothing of importance had been said between us all weekend, really. But somehow, this was different from my other attempts at connecting with him. We had done something together. Maybe that's the only way with fathers and sons—never in talking, only in doing.

I glanced at my watch. At 1:38 P.M. on Sunday, October 25, 1998, I was at peace with my father. And it's a damn good thing, because two weeks later, while playing tennis he fell and damaged his left knee. And I could never sucker him into helping me lift a three-hundred-pound smoker again.

Cal Fussman is a writer for Esquire *and* ESPN.

THERESA M. MAGGIO

A Rite of Spring

*Ancient rhythms of life underlie
the reality of food.*

IT WAS MID-MAY WHEN I RETURNED TO FAVIGNANA, A SMALL
island off the northwest coast of Sicily. The wild capers were blos-
soming white in the cracks of the pink tufa cliffs, red-orange pop-
pies blanketed the island fields, and the fishermen were once again
preparing for the *tonnara*.

I had first come to the island many years ago, when I fell in love
with a Sicilian fisherman near Palermo. That May he left his own
nets and took me to Favignana to see the *tonnara*, the annual trap-
ping of the bluefin tuna. The fisherman, the *tonnaroti*, were his
heros, the best of his breed, he said, and he wanted me to see them.
He brought me to this slaughter as an act of love; that's what
helped me see it as a thing of beauty.

In spring the huge bluefins form schools in the Atlantic, then
pass through the Strait of Gibraltar to swim around the
Mediterranean coast and mate and spawn where they were born.
The *tonnaroti* use no purse seine, no sonar. Instead, as they have for
centuries, the *tonnaroti* wait for the fish to come to them. Every
year they set up two barrier nets, each about two miles long and
stretching down a hundred feet from the surface to the seafloor, to
funnel the bluefins into a chamber of death.

The bluefins have been a part of life here for thousands of years. On a cave wall on tiny Levanzo, Favignana's sister island, Neolithic paintings depict men, women, grazing animals—and the unmistakable diamond shape of a giant bluefin with its powerful, crescent-moon tail.

The earliest recorded tuna traps were Phoenician. Today the trap, whose basic design dates back almost 2,000 years, is a steel-and-rope cage larger than four football fields, with seven chambers connected by net gates. At the turn of the century, at least 50 such traps lined the coast of Sicily. Now Favignana's tuna station is Sicily's last.

On the north side of the island, along a small horseshoe bay, a famous 19th-century entrepreneur named Ignazio Florio built a boathouse and a cannery. A stone plaque in the now defunct cannery proclaims that in 1865, a record 14,020 bluefins were caught here. But the *tonnara* as a way of life is slowly slipping away. Today, due to overfishing and pollution, a thousand tuna is considered a good year.

Except during the height of World War II, the trap has always been set, despite the bluefins' dwindling numbers. As recently as 1996, however, the *tonnara* almost didn't take place. A local businessman who pays the fisherman (and owns all the fish caught) announced he could not afford to set the trap. Hearing this, some 20 *tonnaroti* chained themselves to the statue of Florio in the town square, and every shop on the island closed for a day of protest.

In the end the businessman relented, and the work began in late April, a month behind schedule. Relieved but worried about missing the migration, the 63 fisherman assembled to hear their orders from Salvatore Spataro, the *rais*. *Rais* means "captain," a title handed down from the Arabs who brought this method of fishing to Sicilian waters nearly 1,200 years ago. Every fisherman knew Spataro—he grew up on the island with them—but during the spring tuna season they would address him only as "*Rais*," and he would command them with nearly feudal authority.

As one work detail prepared the miles of rope and steel cable that form the trap's skeleton, others scurried up the mountains of stored nets, pulled them down piece by piece, repaired holes, and sewed seams. In a courtyard behind Florio's original boathouse, the nets were attached with ropes to more than 3,000 tufa blocks—the stone anchors that help hold the trap firm against the currents.

Finally, bouquets of flowers were tied to the bows of the work-boats, and the parish priest arrived to sprinkle holy water on the boats, the nets, the ropes, the stones, the anchors, and the sea itself.

Built at sea over three weeks, the trap was set about two miles off-shore. A beautiful old crucifix known as "I Santi" was raised above the entrance. The ten-foot-high wooden cross bore the image of the saints who protect the *tonnara*, with Christ above a small bronze statue of Saint Peter. It faced east, the direction from which the fish would come.

"Now, yes, we have a *tonnara*," the *rais* said as the cross went up. And with those words the waiting began.

Twice a day the *rais* and his men visited the trap. In the morning they rowed quietly up to the site and sent a diver into the trap to cut lose tuna that had died overnight in the net. They also killed any trapped swordfish, because they can panic the tuna.

In the afternoon the boats simply floated above the *camera grande*, the great room, for hours, the men counting the tuna through glass windows in the bottoms of their boats as the great fish circled far below them. At times the bluefins would flash silver as they turned on their sides to mate, oblivious to their fate.

The *rais* wanted 400 tuna in the trap before he called for the *mattanza*, the killing. He orders only four or five *mattanze* a season now; in earlier times, when the bluefins were plentiful, there was a killing nearly every day. The bluefins then sometimes weighed well over a thousand pounds; now they average less than 200.

And these days the islanders don't eat the tuna. Until the early 1980s the fish were packed in olive oil in Florio's cannery, but now the Japanese buy almost the entire catch.

On May 21 the *rais* returned from his afternoon check of the nets and announced the *mattanza* would be held the next day.

At seven the next morning the fishermen were gathered,

balancing long, steel-tipped gaffs on their shoulders, some somber, concentrating, others mugging for the cameras.

"The moment has finally arrived," said Gioaccino Cataldo, a tall bear of a man, his black beard streaked with grey, his massive hands scarred by tuna fins. At sea the *tonnaroti* herded the tuna from the sixth room, through a flower-bedecked gate into the *camera della morte*, the chamber of death. When the gate was closed behind the fish, the men assembled their boats above the chamber—the only one with a net floor—and began to pull the net up, hand over hand, singing the *cialoma*, a work song that is both incantation and dirge. One man chanted the ancient Sicilian verses:

Holy Savior
Who created the moon and the sun,
created men
created the fish in the sea
The tuna and the tonnara.
A promise is a debt!
This God must help us.

The fisherman responded, with a phrase perhaps derived from Arabic, "*Ai-a-mola, ai-a-mola*," the meaning of which is now clouded. The deep bass chorus sent chills up my spine.

As the net was drawn taut at the surface, hundreds of tremendous black forms loomed up from the blue water. Unnatural swells formed, like water about to boil. Suddenly, a dorsal fin sliced the surface. Allesandro, a ten-year-old island boy who had cut school to see his first *mattanza*, stood next to me on a boat, screaming with excitement, invoking the Mother of God, "Ma-ri-a! Ma-ri-a! *I tonni!*"

The fish rose in a mass, silver-blue, gape-mouthed, scuttling over one another, circling, lashing, trying to dive to safety. They beat their tails and sent up splashes ten feet high. The noise was deafening. Pandemonium. Shouts. The *rais* blowing commands on his whistle. Everyone getting soaked.

The *rais* gave the order to kill. Eight men to a fish, the *tonnaroti* leaned over the side of a boat to gaff the tuna. With eight gaffs in it, the first tuna was hauled upright against the boat, its great head held just out of the water. Shimmering veils of color, opalescent greens and pinks, washed over it as it was dying.

Then, on count the men heaved, their faces contorted into grimaces. They balanced the fish on the gunwale and rested, steadying it by its fins, waiting for one last tail thrash to propel it aboard. When it came, they leaped aside to avoid a blow from the tail that could break a man's back. The bluefin slid into the hold and, like thunder, thumped out its life.

When the chamber of death was at last empty, and 405 bluefins were on board, the current carried away the blood and the sperm and milky eggs expelled by the tuna in a last effort to procreate. The *tonnaroti* lifted their caps in unison and shouted "Jesus!"

The next day, the boats again resumed their morning pilgrimage to the trap. In the six *mattanze* this season, the fishermen would take a total of 1,635—the best catch in years.

Each day, Cristina Torre, a daughter of a *tonnaroto*, watched the slow procession of boats from her kitchen window. One time, she told me, when she was in the hospital and about to undergo anesthesia afraid that she would not wake up again, this was the scene that appeared to her. It remains the most beautiful memory a Favignanese can have.

Theresa M. Maggio also contributed "Love on a Plate" earlier in Part Two.

PART THREE

GOING YOUR OWN WAY

TARAS GRESCOE

Absinthe

It makes the heart grow, and then...

IT DROVE BAUDELAIRE TO BELGIUM, THEN TO AN EARLY GRAVE; IT
left Paul Verlaine a hollow-eyed wreck, wandering from bar to bar
in Paris's Latin Quarter accompanied by a misshapen shoeshine
boy named Bibi-la-Purée. The deaths of Vincent van Gogh, Oscar
Wilde, and poet Alfred de Musset were hastened by their inordi-
nate love for this poison, long-since banned by the thinking men
of all civilized nations.

Except, of course, in death-defying, devil-may-care Spain,
where 136-proof absinthe is about as common as orange Fanta.

I'd come to Europe determined to uncork the liquid muse of
the avant garde, the licorice-flavored, high-octane herbal alcohol
popularized by a French doctor in 1792. I'd discovered that in the
nation of his birth, absinthe's sale had been strictly prohibited since
World War I, but that in Spain, absinthe is considered just another
aperitif, as familiar as vermouth and Campari. I'd found what the
Spanish call Absenta in liquor stores in Madrid and in just about
every bar in Catalonia; hell, I'd even found liter bottles of the stuff
in the window of Can Canesa, the great grilled sandwich shop in
Barcelona's Plaça Sant Jaume.

And now I was in Barcelona's Barrio Chino—the infamous

warren of narrow streets where Jean Genet set *A Thief's Journal* and the Divine Dalí went slumming—finally face-to-face with my own glass of La Fée Verte, the 19th-century hallucinogen that, in its time, had ruined more lives than cocaine.

To tell the truth, I had been a little worried about my date with the Green Fairy. Before my trip, the only two people I'd met who'd actually tried absinthe—both mild-mannered Canadians—had gotten into fistfights after only a couple of glasses of the stuff. With this in mind, I'd chosen my drinking companions carefully: Mary, a Scottish painter who'd fallen in love with Barcelona in the '80s and stayed on through the booming '90s, and Henri, a gaunt Belgian pastrymaker with the sideburns of a rockabilly singer from Memphis. He'd left Ghent only two days before, using a Renault truck to transport 55-pound blocks of chocolate across France at a top speed of about 45 miles per hour, to fulfill his long-time dream of becoming the first trufflemaker for the sugar-loving citizens of Barcelona. As drinking partners, Mary and Henri may not have been Sarah Bernhardt and Arthur Rimbaud, but they had forged their friendship over countless glasses of absinthe, and knew its rituals. What's more, under their tutelage, I was pretty sure that I wouldn't finish the night in jail.

We had started the evening at midnight (this being Spain, after all) in the Bar Marsella, which, though recently purchased by two hefty Anglo-Saxons, has been preserved intact as a kind of monument to the fast-fading bohemia of the Barrio Chino. In the Marsella, yellowing posters for long-forgotten aperitifs curl on the walls, the paint peels suggestively and half-a-dozen different tile patterns jockey for space on the undulating floor.

A young waiter had brought us small brandy glasses full of clear, oily-looking absinthe, along with all the attendant para-phernalia: a bottle of water, paper-wrapped lumps of sugar and a three-tined trowel. In the classic version, one sets the trowel on the rim of the glass and slowly strains the water through the sugar cube into the absinthe until it dissolves. (Water wasn't the only mixer for absinthe, however: singer Aristide Bruant drank it with red wine, and Edgar Allen Poe took his with brandy. And died, incidentally, at the age of 40 of a heart attack after a prolonged drinking binge.)

Mary introduces me to a local variation: I allow a sugar cube, squeezed between forefinger and thumb, to soak up the absinthe, which is 68 percent alcohol. Then, placing the cube on the trowel, I light it on fire until the alcohol burns off. After stirring the dissolving cube into the absinthe, I fill the glass three-quarters full with water, provoking a remarkable transformation. The liquid turns milky green—a color Oscar Wilde described as opaline, though to my eyes it looks more like a happy marriage of crème de menthe and whipped cream. In the murky half-light of the Bar Marsella, my glass of absinthe appears to be glowing from within.

I pause before imbibing. Everything about absinthe, after all, is sinister. It proved the undoing of so many artists and writers that the best book on the subject—Barnaby Conrad III's excellent 1995 work, *Absinthe: History in a Bottle*—eventually starts to read like an obituary page. It's distilled from the grayish-green leaves of a shrub called wormwood (in Russia, the plant is ominously called Chernobyl) and in large doses, its active ingredient, thujone, is a convulsive poison. Even absinthe's Greek name, apsinthion, means "undrinkable." However, it was also one of the most popular aperitifs in *fin-de-siècle* France, the subject of a painting by Manet, a sculpture by Picasso and innumerable anecdotes by Hemingway. A favorite among the women at Parisian bars such as the Nouvelle-Athènes and the Café du Rat Mort, absinthe even made it to the New World, where Mark Twain and Walt Whitman drank it in New Orleans's Old Absinthe House. But the dead-eyed regard of actress Ellen Andrée, the barfly in Degas' 1876 painting "L'Absinthe," had always haunted me, and the more I look, the more the small groups huddled conspiratorially around the other tables at the Marsella resemble the doomed characters out of Emile Zola's *L'Assommoir*. I imagine myself embarking on a long slide into debauchery, followed by months of hydrotherapy—a *belle époque* cure for alcoholics, which consisted of purges and a half-hourly soaking with cold water—in some Gothic asylum.

Suppressing a sensation of vertigo, I drink. And then I smile.

Not at all bad, reminiscent of pastis, the licorice-flavored French aperitif, but with a slightly bitter undertone. Loosening up, I start trading anecdotes with my drinking companions about our worst debauches. The Belgian wins hands down—naturally—with his sad saga of three bottles of red wine, abrupt eviction from the restaurant where he'd consumed them and his subsequent awakening to a curious sound: the slick hiss of car tires whipping past his ear in the gutter he'd chosen for his bed. Mary looks at the rapidly dwindling level of my glass and says with some concern: "You might want to slow down. This is brain damage stuff." I, however, am eager to test Wilde's description of absinthe's effects: "After the first glass, you see things as you wish they were. After the second glass, you see things as they are not. Finally you see things as they really are, and that is the most horrible thing in the world."

In fact, as I finish my glass, the Bar Marsella is suddenly looking like the most wonderful place on God's earth. When I walked in, I had been pretty sure that I was surrounded by nothing more than particularly hip backpackers, but suddenly the people at the next table begin to look strangely fascinating. They must be artists, I think to myself. And, as I work on another glass, the second phase of Wilde's dictum begins to kick in: I start to see things as they aren't. Isn't that woman—the one with her arm around the red-headed guy with the goatee—staring at me through her half-lidded eyes?

My eyes, too, are playing tricks on me: when I focus on an ash-tray or a beer spigot, the center of my field of vision becomes un-usually clear, but the periphery looks watery, indistinct. Objects seem to be surrounded by yellowish haloes, as in a van Gogh painting (the Dutch artist was on an absinthe bender for much of his career, including the binge in which he ran at Paul Gauguin with a razor and then cut off the tip of his own ear). The overall effect is of wearing a pair of ill-fitting goggles in the bottom of a filthy—but surprisingly comfortable—aquarium.

Just as I'm beginning to think this bar would be a great place to live—like, for the next few decades—the owner starts to lower the metal curtains. In spite of this clear intimation of closing time, a couple of local roustabouts slip in and start insistently ordering wine. The bartender's repeated yelling of "*Tancat!*" seems to have no effect, and I consider getting up and helping to explain to these uncouth gentlemen that our host is employing the Catalan word for "closed." However, remembering my Canadian friends' warning about absinthe's tendency to lead to fistfights, and noticing that the woman at the next table has somehow vaporized, I instead suggest to Mary and Henri that we take our custom elsewhere.

Henri begs off, the combined effects of hard liquor and two days of driving with the French having taken their toll, but Mary and I continue our crawl through the Barrio Chino. Most of the rest of the *madrugada* (not surprisingly, the Spanish have a single word for the early hours of the morning) is a blur. We wander past the Franco-era prostitutes of Carrer d'en Robador, anarchist cafes and the inevitable piles of street-corner refuse giving off fascinating, unidentifiable odors. We stop at a nightclub called El Cangrejo, where a transvestite of the stature of the late Divine is performing beneath a sheep dog-sized wig. We poke our heads into the Bar Pastís, a temple of Francophilia where the jukebox has been playing Edith Piaf since the '40s; the London Bar, where people come to worship swinging England; and finally the Bar Kentucky, which is what an American tavern might look like if Antonio Gaudí was hired as a decorator. A barman who calls himself Pinocchio—he explains his sobriquet with a gesture to his bent nose—serves us our last absinthes of the night, and Mary and I ferry our drinks to the end of the mobile home–length bar.

As taxi drivers and prostitutes squeeze past us, we clink glasses, toasting what's left of Barcelona's rapidly gentrifying Barrio Chino. On this night, I won't make it to Wilde's ultimate phase of absinthism (it would take at least five more glasses), the one in which one's surroundings reveal themselves in all their horror. In the Kentucky, on the contrary, the seediness continues to look glamorous. I remember all those who had succumbed to the allure of the Green Fairy: among them, Toulouse-Lautrec, who carried absinthe around Montmartre cabarets in a hollow cane, and Alfred

Jarry, the playwright who dyed his face and hands green, toted pistols on his absinthe binges and died at the age of 34. With the opaline, nerve-damaging muse in hand, I drink to squandered talent and beautiful corpses. But I'm really drinking to danger—and to the grateful realization that, in this world in which people are increasingly protected from themselves, there are still places left where we are free to choose our own poison.

Taras Grescoe has written for numerous publications, including Wired, Islands, Saveur, *the* Independent, *and the* Times *of London.* *He lives in Montreal.*

ROBERT L. STRAUSS

360 Days a Year

It's a tough way to earn a living.

COMPETITION IS VICIOUS. MARGINS ARE SMALL. WORKING
conditions are hot and close-quartered. And the hours are long, incredibly long. Running a neighborhood restaurant in Vietnam is
not the easiest or quickest way to cash in on the country's economic boom.

The Phuong Anh restaurant, on Mai Hac De Street just
around the corner from To Hien Thanh Street in Hanoi, isn't
much to look at. From the curb, it's hardly different from the
hundreds or thousands of small eating places that line the roads
all over Asia. But over several days my wife and I had eaten lunch
at Phuong Anh and each day the food had been marvelous. There
were five or six different pork dishes. The same number of
poultry and fish plates. There were a dozen delicious vegetable
selections. There was no menu. We didn't know the names of
anything. We simply pointed to dishes that looked tasty and
ample servings piled onto small plates were brought to our table.
With prices for everything in Hanoi shooting up, we were astonished each time we had a wonderful five- or six-course lunch for
two—never for more than $3.

"How does she make any money?" my wife asked. "How does

she get everything ready?" was what I wondered. The restaurant itself was tiny, no more than a ten-by-twelve-foot room. At lunchtime it was jammed with up to twenty customers. The staff sidestepped in and around diners as Nguyen Thi Bich, the 36-year-old owner, served up portions from an equally packed alcove at the front of the restaurant. One second she was serving, the next adding up a bill and making change, the next asking one of her ten workers for something. Every second she was on the go.

"Oh geez," Nina said, putting down her chopsticks. "Look at that." I followed her gaze to a corner of the room. An older, white-haired man was slowly climbing down through a small hole in the ceiling. From one metal rung embedded in the concrete walls to the next, he carefully lowered himself down, just above the customers' heads. Only Nina and I acted as though this was unusual behavior for a restaurant. The old man squeezed onto a wooden couch that was already crowded with four customers and lit up a smoke. "We've got to find out more about this place," Nina said.

I often work as a small business consultant. Nina is a wonderful cook. Yet both of us, watching the frenzy of activity in the tiny restaurant, were absolutely bewildered. With the help of a translator, I explained to Bich that I wanted to find out more about what it took to run a small cook shop like hers.

She told me that the secret of her success rested on three key factors: fresh food, low prices, and good service. If we wanted, we could follow her around for a day and she'd show us what was involved.

That day began the following morning at 6:00 A.M. Perhaps three-quarters of Bich's supplies come from bicycle-peddling vendors who roll up to the restaurant all day long with rice, salt, vegetables, roasted poultry, and frozen fish. But for the key ingredients, Bich goes to the market herself. She bicycled there. We trailed alongside on a motorcycle.

"She's so slim," Nina remarked as we followed Bich through the empty streets of early morning Hanoi. Bich had the trim figure of an athlete. One would never know she was the mother of two teenage children.

At 6:30 the small market was surprisingly empty. We'd visited markets throughout Asia and the one common denominator shared by all was the overpowering, dank smell of animal blood and rotting vegetables stewing underfoot in the hot tropical weather. But at six in the morning, the meat and produce were still fresh. There was no smell but that of the cool morning. There were very few customers. Only restaurant and cook shop owners. They picked through the offerings like fur traders trying to select the best pelts. The variety of food before them was astonishing.

Live eels swam in basins next to still quivering, freshly skinned frogs. Thousands of small sand crabs tried to climb out of the metal basins that held them. Dozens of market women shaved the hair off the hides of slaughtered pigs and the skin of plucked chickens with double-edged razor blades held gingerly between thumb and index finger.

There were vegetables we had never seen before and the intestines of animals we wished we hadn't seen. Meanwhile Bich was selecting fresh meat and fish.

"Can you believe this?" Nina said as she watched Bich. "She's cutting her own meat." With the dexterity of a master butcher, Bich took a cleaver and pared the cuts she wanted from several large slabs of beef and pork. At stall after stall she selected just what she wanted. She trimmed away the bone and fat and paid only for the choice cuts she had made. "Try doing that at Safeway," Nina said.

When we returned to the restaurant at 7:30 A.M., the place was already buzzing. Bich's mother, father, aunt, and a variety of young relatives were all at work. The older women, also with razor blades, were slicing hundreds of scallions into what seemed to be thousands of thin green ribbons. They did this while squatting on the sidewalk, just inches from the street, where the earlier quiet of Hanoi had been drowned out by the continuous flow of cars, trucks, bicycles, motorcycles, and cyclos. Across the street, construction on a new office building had begun. In and around the restaurant, Bich's employees quickly and methodically went about the dozens of tasks needed in a country where prepared foods have yet to hit the shelves.

In an alley alongside the restaurant, several girls tended two woks and several pots boiling with eggs and greens. An older woman squatted further down the sidewalk. She was washing dishes. For the next fifteen hours that is all she would do.

Bich's elderly parents had been at work since early morning. I asked Bich where they lived, wondering if they had to come from far away. She pointed to the space above the restaurant and the hole in the ceiling where we had seen the old man appear the day before. Turns out he is her father and the three-year-old restaurant is actually the parents' home. The dining area is their former living room. Their bedroom is the loft just above where we had eaten each day.

"How old is your father?" I asked.

"Eighty-three," she answered with a show of fingers.

"How many 83-year-old American men do you think are climbing up walls to get to their bedrooms?" Nina asked.

I pointed to Bich's mother, who was squatting in the middle of the room slicing tree ear mushrooms paper thin, and asked how old she was. Bich held up seven, then six fingers. Not too likely she'd be working a twelve-hour shift at Denny's in the States.

Soon after Bich's return from the market, all activity became centered in the middle of the living room. To be precise, on the floor. Twenty bowls and basins filled with meat, poultry, fish, mushrooms, spices, oils, fish sauce, and molasses sat in the center of a circle formed by Bich, her mother, her aunt, and a teenage relative. For the next three hours they hardly moved from their squatting position. I told Nina to try squatting with her knees tucked up in her shoulders the way the women were. She lasted less than a minute and then hobbled around for several more complaining she'd been crippled for life.

Basins of greens and boiled meats and fish came in from outside. The women quickly diced, sliced, mixed, kneaded, and rolled these together with other ingredients and spices. Bich's mother measured out molasses in the palm of her hand. Bich's fingers were the scoop used to measure sugar, salt and pepper. Everything was measured by hand. No one sampled a thing. As quickly as the staff brought new items in, so went the now-seasoned dish back outside for steaming, boiling or deep-frying. It was an assembly line where there was little talk. Everything was done with the precision of a Japanese manufacturing plant. Except that it was all happening on the floor, in a tiny space, with only the light of two dim bulbs.

Watching the fluidity with which everything was happening, I asked if Bich made the same things every day. "No," she said. "It depends on what is fresh in the market." But I never saw her tell anyone that today they would be making this dish or that. Everyone just seemed to know.

Slowly, almost by sleight of hand, finished dishes began to gather on the tables that had been pushed to the side of the small room. The place itself wasn't much on decor. Nothing more than a few outdated calendars and beer posters. Along one wall was the parents' large, mirrored wardrobe. High in a corner was a traditional altar, framed by Bich's two dead brothers, one killed in Hue in 1975, the other dead after an unsuccessful operation. The room was now a restaurant, but still had the soul of a Vietnamese living room.

Nina and I watched as tray after tray of complicated dishes of fried fish, steamed vegetables, boiled pork, and barbecued meats took shape. "The work they do, it's just amazing," Nina said as we watched the women working into their second and third hour of chopping, boiling, stirring, turning, flipping, and steaming, almost never rising from their crouches just inches from the floor.

Bich's fluency as a chef was very clear as she began making *van may* (cloud in the sky), a Vietnamese dish that is something like a stuffed crepe. Earlier, one of the younger workers had made dozens of yellow and white crepes from separated duck eggs. Now, Bich, with a cleaver in each hand, began mincing together the pork, garlic, and other ingredients that she would roll inside the crepes before steaming them. For an hour, the small room reverberated with the rapid pace of a drum roll as Bich minced ingredients using only the two cleavers and a small chopping board that was nothing more than a round section cut from a tree.

"Do you know how fast you could do this with a Cuisinart?" Nina whispered to me. The only time Bich stopped work was when she quickly sharpened her knives and cleavers by dashing them back and forth against the bottom of a plate with the same practiced indifference as a barber sharpening a straight razor against a leather strap. She did this every few minutes.

"How often do we sharpen our knives?" I asked Nina.

"About once a year," she told me. "But we should do it more often."

"We'll have to buy some plates," I told her.

I asked Bich if she had ever tried using a machine to mince the stuffing for the *van may*. She said she had but the machine couldn't produce the fine blend she wanted and it quickly broke from wear and tear. She went back to the basics even though she wears out her cutting knives in a month's time and her cleavers in six.

After four hours of tossing, mixing, shaking, kneading, chopping, hacking, slicing, and cooking, it was time to move outside. Twenty different platters were ready for the lunchtime crowd. Spring rolls, shish kabobs, and eight other entrees were still waiting their chance in the wok or over the brazier. Bich still hadn't taken a break, hadn't eaten, hadn't stopped moving since before sunrise. "I'm exhausted," Nina said to me. "And I haven't done a thing."

We asked Bich how many hours she worked every day. "From six in the morning to ten or eleven at night," she said. How many days a year? "Three hundred sixty," she told us. She takes five days off during the Tet holiday when she mainly stays at home and tries not to think about food or cooking. She doesn't go out to other restaurants except to learn what they are doing. She told us she doesn't need to taste the food to know how it will turn out. She has the chef's equivalent of a musician's sense of perfect pitch.

As we chatted, the place was quickly swept clean. Tables were set out as were a dozen of the tiny stools the Vietnamese use for chairs. The thirty different dishes were stacked atop one another on the outside counter.

There were sea fish and river fish. Three different types of chicken. Six different types of pork. There was a shrimp dish and a squid plate. There were several varieties of small, broiled birds. She had salads of green beans, bean sprouts, pickled eggplant, and spinach. There was a fried tofu dish, something like a frittata. There were spring rolls and shish kabob. For the refined diner, there was a platter of butterfly larva.

Five hours earlier, when we met Bich outside her neighborhood home, nothing had been done, nothing had been prepped. Her brimming counter was a tour de force of Vietnamese cooking. Bich's mother lit a handful of joss sticks and placed them at the front edge of the counter. Perhaps this was to ward off evil spirits. Certainly it wasn't to cover up any unappetizing smells as everything Bich had made that morning was fresh, clean and wonderfully spiced.

The sign above the entrance to the Phuong Anh restaurant, which is named for Bich's daughter, says *Cac Mon An* and *Com Binh Dan,* which translates to something like "All kinds of food" and "Everyday home cooking." Evidently, Bich needn't say anything more because soon after she had laid out the dishes, lunchtime customers began to gather at the front of Phuong Anh. For the next two hours, the small space was jammed with regulars. Bich stood at the doorway, now playing the roles of maitre d', cashier, hostess and server. In the alley, the staff continued cooking, replenishing the most popular dishes.

Nina and I squeezed into a corner, my back jammed between the small refrigerator and the large wooden wardrobe. We had pointed to shish kabob, the *van may* cloud, freshwater fish, a green bean salad, and a deep-fried, minced squid dish that looked more like a potato pancake than seafood. Our drinks came to us warm. We fished hunks of ice from a bucket. Earlier we had watched Bich's mother as she hacked a large block of ice into the cubes we dropped in our glasses.

Everything was delicious. Bich had no time to attend to us as she was completely occupied making change, filling plates, adding up bills, squeezing in new customers, directing her staff, and laughing at jokes.

I took a break from eating to take in the incredibly crowded space. The walls were painted in what might be called a "distressed Jackson Pollack" style. A locked door had the weathered look of the faux finishing that is now the rage in the States. It was weathered from wear—not from the hand of an artist. A ceiling fan wobbled above the lunchtime crowd and provided a soft breeze but little cooling. A bunch of young men at one table took turns flirting with a table of young women. Like in every other small Vietnamese restaurant, bones and napkins were idly dropped on the floor to be swept into the street later on.

Outside, Bich continued serving up new portions. In place of a serving spoon or fork she used a large tailor's shears to pick up the food and cut it into smaller portions. Our five-course lunch had filled us completely. It was so much better than meals we had eaten at many of Hanoi's more established and widely reviewed restaurants. When we got up to go, Bich quickly totalled up our bill. She tapped her pen on the figure: 33,000 dong. About $3 for lunch for two—including drinks.

By 1:00 P.M., lunchtime business was thinning. Bich stopped moving for the first time in seven hours. She leaned against a wall and lit up a "555." From two until five, the restaurant was closed—although several workers continued cooking. Another rush of diners filled Phuong Anh from 6:00 till 8:30 P.M. That's when we came back for dinner. Bich had set out two small tables on the sidewalk to handle the overflow crowd.

I went back to the restaurant around 11:00 P.M. The tables had been put away. The food was all eaten. The restaurant was again a living room. The father said goodnight and climbed up the iron rungs on the wall to the bedroom. Bich, her husband and children watched television. I don't know how long they stayed up. I never did get around to asking Bich if she makes any money. If she does, she certainly deserves it. For me, it was time for sleep. I had had a long day.

The next morning at 6:00 A.M., I went out for a run. Bich's mother was already slicing onions on the sidewalk in front of the restaurant. As I jogged past the market, I saw Bich haggling with the meat sellers. She didn't have time to waste. Lunch was only six hours away.

Robert L. Strauss also contributed "The Ceremony of One Chip" in Part Two.

TOM BENTLEY

⋆ ⋆ ⋆

In a Bad Bean Funk

*As Abraham Lincoln once said, "If this is coffee,
please bring me some tea; if this is tea,
please bring me some coffee."*

I JUST CAME BACK FROM 30 DAYS ON THE ROAD, DRIVING 10,000 miles across America and back, and the first thing I did when I arrived home was kiss my Krups. I've got some strong advice to any coffee lover who's considering the same: Don't go—I was lucky to survive. I'm not saying that a cup of coffee is grace, joy, and love—you know, the Sistine-Chapel-in-the-mouth kind of thing—but there's been more than one morning when, if I had a choice between a steaming cup of caffeine and the keys to a 911 Porsche, I'd have to do my accelerating internally—junk the wheels, give me the juice.

In a world that's often so downbeat, there's something like optimism in that cup; it's one of the few things that can be relied upon. Of course, it's got to be good coffee, stuff with weight and a slight edge of menace. A morning cup should be both stimulating and bracing, sweet-tongued succubus and brawny drill instructor, the lady and the tiger.

I never realized just how heavy a hold the daily grind has on me until a few days into my trip, when the deep psychic injuries I suffered from the watery cruelty served up at roadside diners began to take its toll. Long before the eastward blur of the plains I was jonesing hard for a fix.

Here in San Francisco, coffee snobbery is a matter of course; the Peet Squad squaring off against the jousting cups of Team Trieste—it's easy to get spoiled. Hell, we've got businesspeople with espresso machines built into their briefcases, street people cadging for lattes.

No more will this man take that pot of liquid gold for granted.

There I was, as free as I pleased to go on whatever road that beckoned, reduced to a narrow obsession with finding a good cup of joe. Can you fault me, though? Devil caffeine is such a righteous high, it's cheap, and incredibly enough, legal.

Sure, there's caffeine in those roadside pots—drink enough and you can get that ice-grinder stomach howling like a screaming Coltrane solo. But getting to the caffeine in that woeful coffee, saints protect me.

To compound the trouble with its taste, roadside coffee rarely has any staying power. I found that only an hour or two after dosing up at some joint with some of that wobbly brew, my mind became a kind of crock pot, gently snurfling a soggy head of cabbage around in a tepid broth.

So I had to start playing on-the-road wake-up games: sticking my face out the window, hoping that a mug full of high plains wind would stir me, or craning my head completely sideways, parallel to the dashboard, which created a curious and wonderfully warped perspective that made the road appear to be driving itself into my face, a situation that would have become literal had I persisted. I even tried listening to Rush Limbaugh's vitriol stab out of the radio. But these are only surface substitutes for what you want in your blood—good coffee works from the inside out.

Even the heraldic lineup of signs for Wall Drug, which begin hundreds of miles from its holy grounds in South Dakota, couldn't regale me out of my bad bean funk. Wall Drug and its renowned five-cent coffee became a mantra of sorts, until I arrived, 500 signs later, drained a cup, and felt like telling them it was overpriced.

So I calmed down and got practical. I began planning my trip around sure things: college towns like Madison, Wisconsin, where students, connoisseurs of cheap highs, can be relied upon to produce a buyer's market. Bang down a couple of triple espressos and hope that the residuals would last until the next caffeine oasis. But sometimes the road just stretched on forever, the Avron B. Fogleman Expressways leading to the Elroy Sparta Highways, past the Tank and Tummy Truck-stops, the El Cheapo gas stations, towns like Arkadelphia, Teutopolis, Palestine, Baghdad, with all manner of inns and cafés, those kind with the old, boxy movie-house bubbling vats of orange juice, the Formica counters, tables topped with Sweet 'n' Low, and coffee, coffee everywhere, but not a drop that's drinkable.

I found so many things: that if you can eat a 72-ounce steak (approximately the size of a cocker spaniel) in one hour in a certain Texas roadhouse, it's on the house; that music spills like sonic sugar out of every café and bar in New Orleans; that there are fields of placid-eyed camels just off the highways in Florida; that there are eye-popping carpets of van Gogh wildflowers along the interstate in Oklahoma; that the residential streets of Taos are perfumed with the intoxicating scent of a thousand lilac bushes; that in the space of seven seconds duration of passing and gaping at an attractive stranger at the wheel you enter a timeless world in which you are beckoned over to the roadside for the grand passion of a lifetime.

I found a thousand and one caresses and cuffings from the highways of this vast land; how come I couldn't get a decent cup of coffee?

Maybe it was just a language thing; maybe my neutral vowels and cautious California consonants caused my request for coffee to be heard by all those patient Mildreds and Mavises as a request for something else, for that exhausted hot brown water I was given at both roadhouse and restaurant. After a while the prospect of drinking that dejected brew was completely disheartening, but I couldn't quit.

On my way back west, I stopped at the Grand Canyon, that rather picturesque hole you've probably heard about. A sight it is, but a short while after I sat on its rim in boggled contemplation, all I could think of was how nice it would be if the mighty Colorado were a rushing river of fresh-brewed coffee.

You know, when I wrote earlier that maybe a cup of coffee isn't the end-all, be-all of existence, that was a bit of a stretcher. I lied. It is. A good cup, as all we honorary Agent Coopers of the world know, is it, the Zen distillate, the first thing the grunting beasts reached for in Plato's Cave, the glue of civilization, your first kiss, ever-renewed. Don't leave home without it.

Tom Bentley likes his coffee stirred, not shaken. And no matter what it does to his typing, he is grateful to be quiveringly close to the kitchen pot, a benefit of being a freelance writer. He lives in Watsonville, California.

DAVID LANSING

* * *

Confessions of a
Cheese Smuggler

What's that in your baggage, sir?

ELAINE HAS DONE ME A FAVOR. A HUGE FAVOR. AS THE PUBLIC
relations account executive for a major European hotel chain, she's
managed to arrange several nights accommodation for my wife
and me at a very swanky establishment in Paris, the Hôtel Lutétia.
During the high season, mind you. "Darling"—that's Elaine talking, not my wife; Elaine is very continental and always calls me
darling—"Darling, you're a very lucky man. The Lutétia is *très
chic*." Elaine is from Los Angeles but she can get away with nonsense like this because she's married to a Parisian, though I doubt
if her husband has ever said, "*très chic*" in his life.

Anyway, I'm indebted. "Sweetheart," I say to her (these silly en-
dearments are a game we play), "What can I bring you back from
the City of Light? Foie gras from Fauchon? A lacquered tray from
Pallidio? Tell me, *mon petit écureuil*, what do you desire?"

Elaine does a little trilling laugh over the phone that she knows
drives me crazy. "*Rien, rien, rien,*" she says. And then she pauses.
"Unless…."

Ah hah! I think. Payback time. "Yes?"

"No, nothing. It would be an inconvenience."

"Tell me, my little ferret. What do you desire?"

198

"Well, I was just thinking.... Perhaps some cheese?" she replies, phrasing it as a question.

That's it? I'm going to Paris and she wants a wedge of *fromage*? Meaning to be generous, I suggest something special. "Pepper roll, perhaps? Cranberry-flavored Neufchâtel?"

"*Epoisses,*" she growls. Of course, this is before I know what it is, so to me it sounds like she's just said "I pass" with a Brooklyn accent.

I ask her to repeat herself. "*Ay-pwoss,*" she cries, and I have to admit it is the sexiest thing I've ever heard her say.

"But of course," I say, having no idea what she's just asked for, "A little *ay-pwoss.*"

Two weeks later, my wife, Jan, is sitting in a bathtub drinking Veuve Clicquot. She is in total heaven. She loves the antique stores around Carré Rive Gauche, the wild strawberry sorbet at Berthillon, and the silk underwear at Sabbia Rosa, but mostly she loves lounging in the oversize tub in our hotel room sipping champagne and admiring the Eiffel Tower, which juts up into the cloudy sky just blocks away.

I am sitting shirtless and shoeless on a green couch in the Hôtel Lutétia's Opera Suite, eating a nougat bar, wedge by wedge, speaking on the phone with Diane Mincel, an extraordinarily beautiful and charming (aren't all French women?) *jeune femme* from the hotel's marketing department who, during our three-day stay, has done everything but walk our dog—and I'm sure she would have done that if we'd had one. I have waited until the last minute to secure Elaine's cheese, but we are leaving tomorrow, early, so I have asked Diane where, *s'il vois plaît*, I might find a little "*ay pwoss.*"

Diane makes that peculiarly French blowing noise, like giving the raspberry without sticking your tongue out, which, loosely translated, means either "Your guess is as good as mine" or "What a silly question."

"Perhaps I can find out for you," she says. The French always qualify everything by saying "perhaps." This way they always look like heroes when they actually do something. "I will call you back immediately."

★

So now I am sitting in the Opera Suite, with its black-and-white photos of famous people I have never heard of—all French, no doubt—eating chocolate and waiting for Diane to call and tell me where I can pick up some cheese.

After half an hour, she rings me up. She is very excited. "I have found a place for you. Marie-Anne Cantin. It is not far."

I tell Jan I'm off to get le cheese. She doesn't care. She has half a bottle of the Veuve Clicquot left and the bathwater is still hot. So, with Diane's meticulous but complicated directions in hand, I head off in the general direction of the golden cupola heralding Napoleon's tomb, which, evidently, is near the cheese shop.

Let's pause right here while I'm getting a bit lost wandering up and down streets that, for some reason, all seem to end at the Parc du Champ de Mars. I want to give you some information that, at this point in our story, I'm unaware of but I'm about to discover. It's about this cheese. *Epoisses. Epoisses de Bourgogne,* as it is officially called. Here's what I'm about to learn: in France, where they make over 500 different cheeses, and a good brie is as easy to find as a baguette, this particular cheese is rare and expensive. But in the United States it is more than rare. It is unavailable. It is unavailable because it is as illegal as Cuban cigars. You see, this unassuming little round orange bundle, which weighs about nine ounces and has something of a barnyard aroma to it, is made from unpasteurized milk. And in the good ol' US of A, raw-milk cheeses are absolutely, positively forbidden unless they have been aged for at least 60 days, which would sort of be like saying you couldn't sell fresh fish in a grocery store until it had been aged for at least two months.

There is a very good reason for this decree from the U.S. Food and Drug Administration. Bacteria that can cause diseases can be transmitted in raw milk. Nearly a century and a half ago, French microbiologist Louis Pasteur figured out a process to eliminate bacteria in wine by heating it. Later the process was applied to milk and came to be called, as every schoolkid knows, "pasteurization." Before Pasteur's process was applied, all cheese was made from raw milk. In France today only about half still is. But modern pasteurization, in which the milk is heated to 161 degrees Fahrenheit for fifteen seconds, can give milk a "cooked" flavor. And the whole point of having a fresh, raw-milk cheese, like *Epoisses de Bourgogne,* is so you taste the distinctive flavors that come from ripened, soft cheeses that have not had their rather pronounced (substitute smelly here if you want) aromas "cooked" away by pasteurization.

In fact, in France, many of these cheeses have a season. What the French call "*la meilleure époque*"—the best time to eat them. What determines the best time to eat a particular fresh cheese? It depends on two things: The pasturage of the animal that is providing the milk to make the cheese and the ideal amount of time necessary to age the cheese. Take a nice artisanal goat cheese like Pourly. These goats graze on grass from the limestone plateaus of Bourgogne. The most abundant, flavorful grass is the new growth in the spring. And the cheese takes only two to four weeks to properly age. So the best time to eat Pourly is late spring to early summer. And if you are a true French cheese-geek, that is when you would buy it from your local *fromager.*

But I do not know any of this yet because I have not met Marie-Anne Cantin who, in a moment, is going to tell me everything I don't know about cheese before she allows me out of her shop with $40 worth of *epoisses.* Let's meet her now, shall we?

Marie Anne Cantin's *fromagerie* is inconspicuously tucked into a narrow little side street midway between the Eiffel Tower and Napoleon's tomb. She is sharp, perky, greatly opinionated, and reminds me just a bit of Debbie Reynolds. She is a second-generation *fromager,* having taken over the business from her father. I ask her if she has any *ay-pwoss,* blowing out the second syllable as if getting rid of something nasty in my mouth, and she makes that same little raspberry noise that Diane made and leads me to one of her stunning little cheese displays where we stare, together, at four little creamy rounds that look like pumpkin-colored CDs "*Voilà!*" says Madame Cantin, as if she had just produced photos of her grandchildren.

She carefully lifts one up to my face. I smile and sniff. It is…odoriferous. Seeing my reaction, Madame Cantin gives me my first lesson in French cheese appreciation: "The worse the cheese smells," she tells me, "the better it tastes." Then she shrugs and adds, "This is a hard thing for Americans to understand."

Since I'm not eating it, I don't care. I tell her it is a gift for a friend in California and ask if she can wrap one up. She asks when I am leaving. Tomorrow, I tell her. "Then I will deliver it to your hotel. What time do you leave?" When I ask her why I can't just take it with me, she sighs, looks at me sadly, and says it is simply not possible. That is when she delivers the bombshell: "You know, of course, this cheese is illegal in your country," she says. No, I tell her. I did not know.

And then she sees the problem: I am a dupe. A rube. A cheese mule, as it were. I have been asked to carry nine ounces of an illegal substance, something I know nothing about. So her mission is clear. If I am to go through with this, first I must learn what I'm dealing with. Before she will sell me the *epoisses,* she insists on giving me a crash course in French cheesemaking (most of which I have already revealed to you).

Madame Cantin puts on a smart laboratory smock and leads me down some dark stairs at the rear of her shop to the cellar. Here she has two dark rooms full of stinky raw-milk cheeses. One room for goat cheese, another room for cow cheese. We enter the goat cheese room. There are hundreds—no, thousands—of little white slabs of cheese on trays stacked from floor to ceiling being aged to perfection. The Fort Knox of chèvre. For the next hour or so, I learn everything there is to know about curds and whey. I learn about rennet and mold and brine. I learn about washed-rind cheeses, like *epoisses,* which, as they ripen, are brushed with *mare,* a French alcohol. But mostly I learn about the joys of making cheese from unpasteurized milk.

Madame Cantin is a high priestess in the religion of raw-milk cheeses, and she works hard to convert me, putting out a large tray of different raw cow and goat-milk cheeses, any one of which would be illegal to sell in the United States. Seeing my trepidation, she says, "How can you be afraid to eat my cheese but not be afraid to eat a McDonald's hamburger?"

It is a question for which I have no answer.

I sample her cheeses. They are magnificent. She sees the look in my eyes and knows: I am a believer. Praise the lowly goat! Now she will sell me the *epoisses*.

The next morning, as we are checking out of the Hôtel Lutétia, a messenger arrives from Madame Cantin's *fromagerie*. He has a very large bundle for me. Two vacuum-packed parcels wrapped in tissue paper. About twenty pounds of unpasteurized cheeses, including all four rounds of the *epoisses* Madame Cantin had in her shop. I also have Camembert de Normandie, Langres, Vacherin Mont d'Or, and a dozen different fresh chèvres, some covered in ash, others rippling with a pale blue mold, all completely and totally illegal to bring back to the States.

My wife looks at me with alarm. "What's that smell?" she says as I hand her the packages and ask her to carry them for me.

"It's nothing," I tell her. "Just a little cheese."

"Is it okay to bring back?"

I do my little French snort. "Of course," I lie, "It's nothing. *Rien, rien, rien*." And then, as the taxi pulls away from the hotel, the precious bundles of cheese sitting prettily on her lap, I give her a kiss on the cheek. "Trust me, darling."

David Lansing is a columnist for the Los Angeles Times. *His travel stories and essays appear regularly in* National Geographic Traveler, Sunset, House Beautiful, *and other magazines. He lives in Newport Beach, California.*

Phnom Penh Pepper

Her kundalini *is tickled by candlelight.*

WHAT DOES ONE WEAR TO A NEPALESE DINNER PARTY? I wondered. As it was my first, I wanted to be careful. I'd arrived in Phnom Penh, Cambodia on Tuesday and now, on Friday, I stood before my closet, contemplating the dress code for my first social event in Asia. Still jetlagged, I was as grumpy as an overtired baby, numb from sensory overload. The crowds of Phnom Penh, so fast-moving, so energetic, so determined to catch up with the rest of the Asian tiger, left me frazzled. And with my first outing—a walk across the street to buy some bread—came the realization that living in this city would mean getting acclimated to life in a sauna. What's more, I was reminded of something I'd learned on other overseas stints: if you cannot handle being gawked at, if you're not willing to be made to feel like an American Indian brought to England to entertain the Queen's court for the winter season, you don't belong in the developing world.

My boyfriend Chris's arrival in Phnom Penh had preceded mine by three months. During that time, he had become fast friends with a Nepalese co-worker by the name of Nabendrah and his wife, Lilah. They lived about five minutes from us, and they would hear no excuses, dinner was tonight, at 7:00. No matter that the party was going to be about the 16th new experience I'd had in three days. No matter that I'd have preferred a night on the rattan sofa we'd just bought, maybe watching CNN and humming "The Battle Hymn of the Republic" while drinking Budweiser. But fatigue and snappishness notwithstanding, I wanted to make friends. So I stood at the closet door and agonized about what to wear. Most of my things were being shipped—be careful of the Limoges!—so the clothing I had to choose from was rather limited. Chris came to the bedroom door and said, "Casual." I glanced back at the clothes and grabbed some jeans and a white t-shirt. After all, I figured, I'm an American, so I'll go in native costume.

While we were walking to the Nepalese Dinner Party, the lights in the city went out. This is not unusual in Phnom Penh. There are frequent brownouts during the day, and nightly blackouts—unannounced, to keep things interesting—are routine. No one knows why, exactly. Businesses and the wealthy get along with generators. Everyone else can find their candles in the dark faster than you can say, "Not again!"

Because of this, I never did actually *see* the inside of Nabendrah and Lilah's apartment that night. While we felt our way up three flights of steep concrete stairs, Nabendrah, who had spied us from the balcony, stood with other guests and shouted encouragement. "Come on. We are high atop the mountain," he called out.

When we reached the top, we were joyously greeted—as if in fact we had made it to the peak of Everest—by about ten Nepalese adults and at least as many children. My first thought was that Nabendrah and Lilah were running some sort of a high-altitude daycare center out of their home. Every adult woman had a baby on her hip. I was waiting to be assigned mine, but it never happened, which was a bit of good luck for me in that I'd already begun sweating.

I never thought of myself as someone with cleavage, and yet I discovered it in Cambodia, because it was there that the sweat slid down my neck and rushed through the ravine between my breasts before making its ticklish way down to my abdomen. Chris said, "This is Rosemary," and I began shaking hands, sure that everyone there figured that "Rosemary" loosely translated meant "tall sweaty woman." Before the introductions were finished, my shirt and jeans were plastered to my body. They felt exactly like they did that time I'd fallen through the ice while skating on Chandlers Pond, except hotter, much hotter.

Chris had said that Nabendrah's English was pretty good, though somewhat slow and formal. "How formal?" I had asked. "Well, like today, instead of saying someone was boasting, he said, 'He was loudly proclaiming his cleverness.'" So when Nabendrah stumbled over my name, I didn't correct him. In fact, given that the dozen or so Nepalese names I was hearing didn't exactly trip off my tongue, I wanted to promote an atmosphere that was forgiving of pronunciation slip-ups.

I was polite about the children, grabbing their little fists and saying, "Aren't you cute!" They looked back at me, the ghost woman, and then turned away or looked at the woman holding them as if to say, "What's up with this one? She's all wet. Did she think she was coming to a wet t-shirt contest?"

The candles dominated the conversation at first. A breeze came in from the open sliding glass doors, ineffectual but enough to extinguish the candles with one especially energetic gust. We all laughed nervously, strangers in the dark, while Nabendrah relit them. In the meantime, Lilah and several women carried tray after tray of food to a table set up in a corner of the room. Food wasn't what I was longing for at that point. I'd have preferred air conditioning, or at least a fan. Yes, that was it. I wanted to lie on a bed with a fan blowing my hair around, *Cosmo* magazine style, and I wanted to sip a drink clinking with ice, not the warm beer that Nabendrah handed me saying, "I hope you do not have a problem with warm beer, Roseann. This is the Third World, and you will find that Frigidaires are reserved for the elites."

"Oh, no," I assured him, still not correcting him about my name. "Warm beer is fine with me. Really, I love warm beer." To myself I thought that it was unlikely we'd be having ice cream for dessert.

Dinner was finally served. It was to be buffet style. Lilah stood at the corner of the little table and watched each guest ladle out their dinner, then she doubled whatever amount one had taken. To me she said, "Oh, Rosebud, you are so thin. You must eat more of the—" then I lost the word, something like Buddha's belly, and she plopped a scoop of it on top of my plate.

I made my way to a sofa and sat next to Chris.

"I know this is hard," Chris whispered.

"Hard? Oh, no, it's not hard. It's fun. You know how I love warm beer," I joked.

"Shouldn't you have an infant on your hip while you eat that," he asked.

Nabendrah came over then. It was impossible not to like Nabendrah, I'd already decided. He was ever-smiling, kindly, and genuine. "Please, you must eat. There is plenty more," he said. I wanted to say, "Nabendrah, there's a water slide between my breasts and my body is too busy producing sweat to digest anything," but I simply answered, "Oh, I've got plenty here to keep me busy." Then, as if to prove my point, I opened my mouth and stuck in a forkful of the food I had never laid eyes on.

It was then that the beast was unleashed. As I said, I never did see exactly what it was I was eating, so the fire that leapt onto my tongue came with the surprise of a shark attack. I've had hot foods before. In fact, I'd always prided myself on my ability to handle them. Bring on the jalapeños, let me add some gringo killer to my rice, make my hot wings nuclear, thank you. What a fool I had been, proclaiming my own cleverness about such things. I now had one of the fires of hell in my maw in the form of some Asian pepper that made all of those cocky South American habaneros seem like something that was fit to put on top of one's morning scone.

My instinct was to try to swallow, figuring that would be tantamount to suffocating a fire by throwing a blanket on it. Alas, that only made the blaze spread. I was now in the unique position of feeling the fireball work its way through my system while being stared at by a small child sitting on the floor nearby. My eyes were watering, the sweat on my chest sizzled, and though I was sure I was about to die, I worried that whatever it was passing through

my body must be illuminating my large or small intestine—
whichever came first—and that was sure to alarm the small one
watching me.

Like a swimmer who desperately thrashes about in a riptide
while people nearby obliviously frolic in the water, I waited for
someone to notice my dilemma. I tapped Chris's arm, but he was
engrossed in conversation with Nabendrah.

It was Lilah who finally spotted me. "Oh, look," she said. She
pointed, and all of the Nepalese men and women and children
turned their almond eyes on me. Then she said something like,
"Rosebud must have gotten the *kundalini* pepper."

Everyone gazed at me the way you'd look at someone choking
in a restaurant while Nabendrah sprang into action. He handed me
a glass of water and said, "Roseann, you must now drink as much
water as you possibly can."

While I slugged down glass after glass, Nabendrah said, "Such a
pepper is not meant to be consumed." Was it simply the deep pit
of paranoia that resides in all of us working on me, or was there really a note of reprimand in Nabendrah's voice? Had I been able to
speak, I'd have assured him that, just as I avoid playing Russian
roulette, jumping from airplanes without a parachute, and sticking
my tongue out at burly insane-looking men on subways, I certainly would never have intentionally taken that pepper into my
body.

Once it was clear that I was out of danger of spontaneously
combusting, my picking of the pepper became the joke of the
evening. A man named Krishna said, "Now we will never get
Rosemary to try yak butter." And Chris said, "I'm sure her voice
will come back soon." Then one of the children began playing
with the Velcro strap on my sandal while Lilah came over and
talked about helping me find a job. In other words, it began to feel
like a party at home.

And the legacy of the pepper didn't end there. In addition to
evacuating my entire system within the hour and burning the bar-
riers of polite conversation to the ground, the pepper contained
the seed of a friendship with Nabendrah and Lilah that sustained

me through the rest of my time in Cambodia. Nabendrah eventually learned my name, I stopped scaring the children, and I learned to ask, "What's in this?" before eating another morsel of food in their home.

Rosemary Berkeley was born and raised in Boston, Massachusetts. She met her husband Chris (the "boyfriend" when this story took place) in Gabon, Central Africa, where they served as Peace Corps volunteers. Upon hearing of their marriage, Nabendrah wrote, "In Nepal, traditionally, we wish a married couple a big family with plenty of sons to fill the hills of Nepal. I do not think you or Rosemary would want such blessing. So, have a fantastic life together!" They now live in Jacksonville, Florida.

JONATHAN RABAN

The Season of Squirrel

I'll have a Schlitz with that.

SLIDING BY THROUGH THE ISLANDS, I HEARD THE DRY SNAPPING OF rifle fire in the forest. I pulled out of the channel, ran under a dripping railroad bridge and rowed the boat up a weedy lagoon where little pickerel scattered in fright as I splashed past. An old man with a broad reptilian face was sitting up at Withey's Bar when I entered; he was wearing a grubby red cravat which was held in place with a pearl pin, and he rested one mottled hand on a silver-topped walking cane. He looked as if he'd been left behind fifty years ago or more by a touring Shakespearean stock company.

I asked him what the shooting was about.

"Shooting?" he said, cupping his free hand to his ear. "I hear no shooting. No bullets, praise the Lord, have yet come…ricocheting…into the precincts of this quiet tavern. To confess the truth, sir, I move little in this world. I stick to my bar stool, departing only to empty my bladder in the porcelain temple there. But if you assert that there is shooting, I will believe you, my friend; let there be shooting. The question, however, remains: what is to be shot? Women? Children? Dogs? Cats?"

"It's the first day of the Wisconsin squirrel season," said the bartender. The old man's style of speech had evidently ceased to amuse him; he appeared not to notice it, even.

"Ah," said the old man, "we are enlightened. The shaft of dawn breaks upon the mind. What's getting shot? Squirrels are getting shot. Out in the woods, squirrel blood is being drawn, in bucketfuls."

"People *eat* squirrels around here?" I said.

"*Eat squirrels?*" the old man shouted, banging his stick up and down on the bar floor. "We do not 'eat' squirrels, sir. We may regale ourselves upon them. We might be described, on occasion, as consuming them. We do our humble best to honor the noble squirrel. We make, at the very least, a repast of him."

"What do they taste like?"

"Good," said the bartender.

"The bartender, sir, is a man from whose lips words fall like rocks. He has no poetry in him. The precise savor of the flesh of your squirrel is a subject that only a brave poet would assay." He kissed the inside of his fingers and flourished them in the air. Then he closed his eyes, tilted his head back and affected the smile of a dead saint.

"Don't pay no attention to that old gasbag," the bartender said. "He's been going on that way ever since I can remember. They got a whole ward full of guys like him up at the county hospital. How come they ain't got you there yet, hey? Best place for you, I reckon."

"Sonabitch," said the old man, with his eyes still closed. "Put another Schlitz in that goddamn glass, will you?"

The bar was filling with the Saturday-morning hunters and their dogs and guns. The first squirrels of the season were skinned, split open and laid out on a grill tray. Cooked, they looked disconcertingly like black bats. I was made to try one.

"Back legs is the best," said the bartender.

The few scraps of meat I was able to disentangle from the bones were tough and tasted vaguely of overhung pheasant. I noticed that the old man dismissed the squirrel that was offered to him with a lordly wave.

Jonathan Raban is the author of Soft City, Arabia, Foreign Land, Coasting, For Love and Money, Hunting Mr. Heartbreak, *and the best-selling* Bad Land, *winner of the National Book Critics Circle Award. He won the W. H. Heinemann Award for Literature in the 1982 and the Thomas Cook Award in 1981 and 1991. He also edited* The Oxford Book of the Sea. *He lives in Seattle. This story was excerpted from his book,* Old Glory: A Voyage Down the Mississippi.

JEFF SALZ

✱ ✱ ✱

The Taco that Changed
My Life

A simple meal unlocks a simple truth.

THE TACO VENDOR THREW A FEW MORE ON THE GLOWING *COMAL*.
Patillas, the cab driver, handed him a greasy wad of 100 peso notes.
His poncho covered his bulging pot belly like a tarpaulin over a
monument not yet unveiled to the public. It was 3 A.M. in a back
street in Mexico City.

His arm was around me. When he spoke, I tried to be nonchalant, dodging the shreds of tortilla and meat, which came at me like
shrapnel. It was a sacred moment.

"You are American. I am Mexican. It does not matter. *La nobleza no se conoce fronteras*." Translated: Nobility knows no borders.

We ate the next round together, shoulder to shoulder, our
breath visible in the frosty white light of the vendor's shack, cele-
brating the camaraderie of men awake when anyone in their right
mind should be sleeping. We savored salsa that could double for
battery acid and the unspoken feeling that individuals on street
corners might yet save the world.

I've recently noticed, after nearly a quarter of a century of
climbing and escaping from Asia to Albania, Argentina to
Australia, the tales I most often tell are not about summits attained

or untracked wildernesses traversed. The memories I most cherish are instead about people.

My personal turning point came in Chile the night Stephen and I almost shot our horse.

It was to have been an equestrian/alpine Andean expedition. Maraquetta, our chestnut pack horse, had turned up lame, having sawed her rear hock to the bone with her tether rope during the night. Maraquetta also had the bad habit of rolling on the ground whenever our backs were turned, scattering food, cook pots, and climbing gear across the countryside. But instead of shooting her we decided to put her and whatever we could not fit on the back of our individual horses temporarily out to pasture. It meant giving up ice axes, crampons, and hardware. No climbing rope, just a halter rope. Our goal was to travel the length of the Chilean Andes, from Talca to Temuco, like nomadic *huasos*, Chilean cowboys, roaming free and living off the land. We knew we were out to discover something in this enormity of roadless wilderness. We knew not what.

For months, we found shelter in the humble, tumble-down homes along the way or pitched our tent in farmers' fields while our horses fattened on gifts of oats and alfalfa. In a land so poor that, in the handful of villages where a phone was to be found, they joked about having to put fertilizer around the poles before they could speak over the wires, we were received like visiting dignitaries. Loaves of bread were baked, sheep slaughtered, precious casks of wine were broken open. We were welcomed and feasted in every log shanty and sod cabin we visited for a thousand miles.

How were these simple folk, who were barely able to subsist on their own, able to afford such hospitality? As Woody Guthrie used to say, it is always those who have the least who seem to give the most.

My life was changed by that trip. I came to see that the experience of "ecstatic oneness" wasn't exclusively mountaintop stuff. Experience taught me that, despite costume and language, the differences of strangers gradually fade, replaced by the inevitable recognition of sameness. I found what, unbeknownst to myself, I had been looking for from the start: the kindness and generosity that had been hiding in my own heart.

Traveling to remote places offers the good fortune of meeting ourselves in other guises. There are an infinite number of permutations of the human expression. There remains but one human spirit. Ultimately, it is our own reflection we see in the wild eyes of the Tibetan tribesman dancing his slow and ancient step in the Himalayan night, or in the sad eyes of the Salvadoran *campesina* whose son has disappeared on his way home from work, or in the endlessly loving eyes of the turbaned old Uighur of Turkestan who cradles his only remaining granddaughter in his arms. By experiencing ourselves in the many forms of humanity, we travel lifetimes in the course of an instant.

Like the experience of the mountaintop, from such grandeur we feel smaller, almost inconsequential, in our tiny chosen lives. Yet at the same time we become immense. We are everything we see. There is no separation. In a distant land, we are home.

To experience the kindness of a stranger in a strange land is really not that uncommon, yet for me it has become the reason I travel. I don't know if I had stayed at home if I ever would have learned the secret whispered to me that night on the lamp lit streets of Mexico City. *La nobleza no se conoce fronteras.* The human heart knows no bounds.

One thing I do know: very often it takes a taco or two in the wrong end of town to find out what really matters.

Jeff Salz holds a Ph.D. in anthropology and is a mountain guide and a contributing editor for Escape, *the Global Guide for the Adventurous* Traveler. *Most recently he has spent more time on top of horses than mountains, riding with the gauchos of Patagonia, the Khazaks of Chinese Turkestan, and the nomads of Mongolia. He supports his exotic travel habit by speaking to corporate executives on the topic of adventure in everyday life.*

NICOLE ALPER

Baguette

It was quite a loaf,
she recalled.

BREAD. A MULTIFARIOUS MIXTURE, USUALLY CONSISTING OF flour, water, and yeast. Across the world, strangers engaging in the simple act of breaking bread are swiftly transformed into fast friends. A bread's shape and texture, such as Israel's braided challah or India's fluffy *nan*, help define a country's culinary and cultural traditions. And bread's cost and availability even reflects a country's economic status. That's a lot to ask from a bit of dough.

It was in Paris, home of the baguette as well as the epicenter of culinary wizardry, that I came to know just how truly evocative and instructive bread could be. But the lesson I learned was not of rolling the perfect pastry dough or shaping the flawless roll. It was instead a lesson about family and the power of laughter, and it had very much to do with an imaginary loaf of bread.

My relationship with France first began when I was ten years old. My parents, hoping to educate me in the ways of French culture, deposited me into what turned out to be a certifiably insane family living in the city of Auvergne. During the week I stayed in town with the great-grandmother, Mrs. Legrand, who had a curious habit of bursting into my room every morning, brandishing a newspaper that contained articles about some horrific murder of an unsuspecting foreigner, yelling "*Tu vois, tu vois ce qui se passe?*"

She insisted I be home every evening by 5:00 P.M. to avoid such evils, and forbade me from making any English-speaking friends (certainly, in the eyes of most French, an evil of equal import). But nothing compared to the morning she came marching into my room, this time holding a box of tampons, rather that a newspaper, and insisted on knowing if I was already, or soon to be, a "woman."

The weekend madness, when I went to stay with the rest of the family in their country house, was equally entertaining. Dinner conversation invariably involved discussing the personality of the animals we were eating. My parents, prompted by my tearful phone call ("I can't take these people anymore!") came to visit. Monsieur Legrand, a hairdresser who presented himself with the pomp and authority of a duke, refused to serve the ice cream and cake my parents had brought them for desert. When my parents came to know that bathing was an optional activity, they quickly decided to switch me into a less offensive, and by their own admission less "French," family.

When I was fourteen years old, my mother decided that she and I should visit her native city of Paris together. Undoubtedly, she hoped to provide me with a more favorable view of my heritage. We secured a small studio in the 17th *arrondissement* on the Avenue Villiers, which had a deck, equal to the size of our apartment back home, overlooking the variegated rooftops of Paris. We could just barely make out the Eiffel Tower, poking its nose through the distant fog.

We set our daily routine early in the trip: indulging in the pleasures of mutual laziness, we rose every morning at 11:00 A.M. By 11:30 we were ambling to the local boulangerie, where a beautiful brunette with glowing red lips sold us a variety of baked goods. After stopping at the market on our way home for Camembert and grapes, we happily installed ourselves on the deck, inhaling our typical French brunch.

My mother took this opportunity to teach me a few words of her native tongue:

"Ça, c'est une voiture. Et ça, la bas, c'est L'Arc de Triomphe. Et on mange des croissants."

I quickly began to associate Paris with that buttery smell of freshly baked croissants; a scent so suggestive that years later I set out to roll my own croissant dough at the California Culinary Academy in San Francisco. My mother, who didn't even know how to boil an egg when she married my father, had, over the years, become an exceptional cook. These moments together on the deck, eating what felt like a little bit of Paris, were among the happiest of my life. Bonding over baguettes, I had never felt so close to my mother.

Our days were filled with long arm-in-arm walks, some of them through the Luxembourg gardens. There were visits to the Louvre, and dinners at sidewalk bistros, watching an illuminated Paris unfold. But there was another, darker dimension to our trip, which never strayed far from my mind.

The year was 1940 and the Nazis had arrived in Paris. These were times of immeasurable desperation, and sometimes chilling intuition. My grandparents, attempting to protect my mother, placed her in a Jewish Center near Montmartre, not realizing that this was the residence for children on their way to Auschwitz. One night my grandmother awoke from a terrible nightmare. She promptly took the metro to the center where my mother was hiding and brought her back home. The following day the Nazis came and delivered all sixty doctors, nurses, and children to the gas chambers.

On my mother's seventh birthday she was again hidden, this time in Souesmes, an *école sanitaire*, $1\frac{1}{2}$ hours from Paris, where Church attendance was required. She did in fact survive the war, but many close members of her family were not so lucky. My mother's brother Maurice (age three), sister Françoise (age five), and parents were all killed in the concentration camps, leaving herself and three brothers and one sister, Yvette, to fend for themselves.

On a sunny Sunday afternoon, which also happened to be my fourteenth birthday, we decided to visit my aunt Yvette for lunch at her apartment in the 16th *arrondissement,* on the Rue de Siam. My mother's sister was an exceptional beauty, who once upon a time, had been offered a career as a film star. She chose marriage and children instead of a glamorous career, but to me she still represented everything that was dramatic and elegant about French women. Her voice undulated in a melodic wave, and despite her white hair, she was still irrefutably gorgeous.

As we reached the elevator in her building my mother suggested, "You take it Nicole. I'll use the stairs. I need the exercise." She pulled back the accordion-like door for me, and disappeared up the winding staircase as I fished for the correct floor number, and slowly started to ascend.

As I climbed higher my thoughts wandered to the year 1942, when my young mother still lived with her parents and six siblings in a building not unlike the one we were now in. It was in front of that building that she witnessed the local gendarmes take her father away. With a policeman fastened to each arm he screamed, "Who will take care of my family? I have six children! Who will take care of them?!" My mother, too young to know what was happening thought "Papa, don't scream. You're embarrassing me. Please, go quietly."

It seemed like a million years ago, that war. I could not imagine those horrors taking place during my own mother's lifetime. I knew, no matter how much she loved France and her sister, that coming here was always bittersweet. After all, it was the French police who ultimately turned in both my grandparents, and seeing her sister brought back all the memories of a once poor, but very happy, family.

My thoughts were abruptly interrupted by a man I could see through the open iron slats. He was standing on the first floor near the elevator and he was fiddling with something, I looked more closely. Could it be? Was he doing what I think he was doing? The elevator reached Yvette's floor and there was my mother, out of breath, waiting for me. "Mom," I cried, nervously looking down the winding staircase, "there is a...a...flasher! There's a man flashing me!"

"What are you talking about Nicole? You're confused. What do you mean a flasher? Don't be ridiculous."

Could I have been wrong? After all, I wasn't well versed in the ways of French men, or any men for that matter. I began to doubt what my own eyes had seen: a cylindrical object that the stranger had menacingly waved my way. I was both thrilled with the potential danger (as well as the opportunity to prove my mother wrong), and terrified that I was about to encounter something quite…unfamiliar.

Just at that moment, as Yvette was opening the front door, the man appeared at the top of the stairs with his fly undone, wearing little more than a deranged smile. My mother's face was wrapped in the bewildered gaze of a deer in headlights. My aunt, appalled by what was trying to trail us into her home, grabbed us both by the arm and threw us inside her apartment. She slammed the door with the force of a hurricane and locked all five deadbolts, accompanying French expletives with every one.

Breathless from her tirade, Yvette leaned against the closed door with a look of triumph. We surveyed one another, exchanging looks of horror and curiosity. Who was this strange man? If he was an "ordinary" flasher, why had he followed us up the stairs? My aunt suddenly recoiled from the weight of the man's body on the other side of the door. He was trying to push his way in.

My mother panicked. She quickly ran to the terrace, as I followed, and leaned over the railing, screaming "*Au secours!*" (help) to the people walking on the street below. In perfect Parisian detachment, the pedestrians barely acknowledged my mother's frenzy, except with an occasional condescending nod of the head.

Standing on the balcony, I was again transported back to my mother's childhood. She once told me how she, on her way home from school, would stop in the street underneath her apartment building and cry up to her mother, "*Mama! Donne-moi du pain!*" Her mother soon appeared at the small kitchen window and threw down a precious treat they could barely afford, bread wrapped around a tiny nugget of chocolate. As it turned out, bread was to be a recurrent theme.

Amidst the crowd below, my mother spotted my uncle Jules, making his way towards the apartment building. We were saved!

She yelled to him, "Jules, *il y a un homme avec la braguette ouverte!*" ("There is a man with his fly undone!"). Jules, an intellectual with a perpetual air of detachment, pricked his ear towards her with his hand. "*Comment?*"

"*Il y a un homme avec la braguette ouverte!!*" But to his distant ears it sounded very much like she was saying. "*Va chercher une baguette!*" ("Go fetch us some bread!").

"Baguette?" he shouted back.

"*Braguette!*" we screamed. Not quite understanding the urgency, my uncle shrugged his shoulders, turned 180 degrees, and headed for the nearest boulangerie.

Suddenly everything, the atrocities of the war, the deranged and possibly dangerous flasher, my mother's tragic loss, all dissolved at the sound of our own laughter. Between the evocative shape of the illusory baguette, and the ridiculousness of the situation, my aunt and mother were reduced to a couple of schoolgirls, gasping for air between hysterics. There we were, two generations, two nationalities, one family, all sharing memories of a historical incarnation of hell. And all it took to forget, even if only for a brief moment, was the simple misunderstanding about a baguette.

We suddenly heard a soft thud on the other side of the door. My aunt pressed her eye to the peephole and reported that she could see part of the man's right leg, twisted underneath his body. He had passed out. Twenty minutes later my uncle finally returned from the boulangerie. Finding the flasher out cold on his doorstep, he grabbed him by the lapel, while precariously balancing the baguette under his chin, and marched him down three flights of stairs in a military "one-two, one-two, old boy."

Meanwhile, sirens began to scream in the distance. The police were finally arriving. The car screeched to a halt in the middle of the street as five petite, silly-hatted officers spilled out of the vehicle. They looked utterly ridiculous in their blue uniforms, each wielding a small baton. The policemen sprinted towards the building just as my uncle was stumbling out, carrying the flasher over his shoulder. We again began to laugh.

We came to learn that the previously unidentified man was a

local liquor store employee who had spent his paycheck on more alcohol than he could handle. Inhibitions anesthetized, he had wandered down the street looking for someone to shock. The trauma of my being flashed was somewhat mitigated by the fact that for years my parents had been dragging me to "cultural" (i.e. French) films, that invariably turned out to be verging on the pornographic. Perhaps the French side of me was able to see the humor of it all, despite my exposure to such a protuberance.

When the police finally left, my mother, aunt, uncle, and I sat at the table talking as we partook of the comic loaf. Jules kept musing over his auditory lapse. "Baguette," slapping his knee, "*braguette!* Baguette," he leaned into my face, "*braguette!*"

Despite the man's actions, we decided, it was hard to resent him. After all, he turned out to be harmless, at least in our company, and he had accidentally provided us with something very meaningful: the reminder that in the face of fear and tragedy, a sense of humor is sometimes all we've got. As for the baguette, it disappeared, along with a just a few of my mother's painful memories.

After graduating from San Francisco's California Culinary Academy, Nicole Alper soon traded in her toque for a pen to author Wild Women in the Kitchen, *a top-selling cookbook. She writes about travel, style, and fashion for major U.S. and international publications and has found herself on many adventures: diving Australia's Great Barrier Reef, climbing pagodas in Burma, bicycling through the Loire Valley, hiking the Colorado Rockies, studying yoga in India. She is currently working on a series of stories about her travels and a second cookbook.*

HARRY ROLNICK

★ ★ ★

The Great Durian
Airline Odyssey

The fact is, it stinks.

EVER SINCE MY FIRST DURIAN IN ITS PRIMORDIAL HOMELAND,
Sarawak on Borneo's west coast, I have been madly in love with
this, the most fetid of all fruits. In musical terms, the mango has
the sweetness of Barry Manilow, the papaya has the joy of Mozart,
but the durian is Arnold Schöenberg: difficult, alien, almost re-
pulsive at first taste, but with a depth of flavor and penetration of
emotions far more profound than its spiky surface. On those rare
moments when one meets fellow durian devotees, talk and adventures are inevitable.

John Everingham is an Australian photographer who lived in
Laos for many years, was thrown out by the Communists, crept
back one midnight by swimming the Mekong River, then res-
cued his girlfriend and swam back with her to Thailand. Later, a
movie was made of his exploits, and while John liked the actor
who played his part, the late Michael Landon, he found the
whole film ridiculous.

"What happened was that the producer flew to the Mekong
River and found that it wasn't 'Lao' enough, so he took the
whole crew and actors to Jamaica or Bermuda, where it was
much prettier."

John and I share the same love of durian, but where I could indulge endlessly in Thailand, he was in durian-less Laos, so he took every opportunity to eat them. Getting durians in Malaysia was one of the main reasons he joined me to shoot a story about the breeding habits of leatherback turtles in East Malaysia.

If one must stay up all night on a beach waiting for half-ton female turtles to trundle up the sand to lay eggs, it's easiest with somebody else who relishes Southeast Asian food. And that was the enthusiastic John. Under the moon, we argued about which country has the hottest curries, the spiciest peppers, Lao food versus Thai food.

When the turtles made their perambulatory strolls, we stopped talking. He shot, I wrote. About 4 A.M., the show was over, and we prepared for a three-hour wait for the bus, without coffee or beds or food. So the talk naturally turned to durians.

At first, we were sensible. We spoke of the different kinds of durian, from the "gibbon" to the ethereal "Golden Pillow."

"It's like butter," described John. "Butter and sweet almonds." He looked like TV's Homer Simpson, eyes rolling over the thought of a great meal.

"Nah," I said. "You can't even taste 'Golden Pillow.' It's like a perfume, like a creamy perfume where you catch the essence, not the flavor."

Then we discussed the aroma, cursing those visiting writers who themselves cursed the smell as a combination of rotten onions, sewage, New York subways or dogs in heat.

"Those poor slobs," said John. "They look at the silkworm, not the silk. Shit, anybody can eat a mango or an orange. Durians are for the elite."

Sunrise over the South China Sea is so glorious that even we were silent watching it ascend. Then we began to tell durian stories.

I remembered an American music critic who used to live in Thailand, who, during the season, would go to a durian warehouse with a special "durian stick." He would pat each durian until he found the perfect resonance which signified the perfect durian.

Then there was the famous Durian Court Case, which John hadn't heard of.

"You don't know the story of the bar girl, the GI and the durian?" I asked I mock astonishment.

"Well, last year, a GI in a Patpong Road bar was complaining about the 'crappy' smell coming from behind the bar. So up from the floor came this hooker who was eating a durian. I guess she was a bit drunk too, and she took the husk with all those pointed spears and attacked the GI in the face.

"The poor guy looked like he'd been with Mike Tyson for ten rounds, with blood coming down his nose and his mouth. He needed emergency treatment. So he got after the girl and sued her for damages."

"She was found innocent, right?"

"Not exactly. The judge, a patriotic Thai durian-eater himself, found the attack not quite justified. He fined her 200 baht and then paid the bill himself."

Then we talked about great durian recipes. The ice cream, of course, and durian stuffed into bamboo tree trunks. But John remembered a Sri Lanka specialty.

"They take fresh buffalo curd, then they roll durian meat around until it's pliable, and they combine the two. It's heaven on earth."

For the next hour, we told durian tales, both scatological and juicy, which were continued on the bus into Songkhla in south Thailand. There, John was determined to buy two-dozen durian to transport to Laos.

The problem was that we were flying from Songkhla to Bangkok (and later Laos). No airline will allow durian on board. The aroma is supposed to annoy the passengers to distraction.

So that night, after we had procured two-dozen big fruit, each about the size of a football, we searched around for a way to hide it from nosy airline personnel.

First, we scraped together tin foil and plastic bags from a dumpster near the hotel and a tiny hardware shop. Then, under the sky on the beach, we took reams and reams of plastic, covered each durian carefully, and covered it with tin foil. To finish the operation, we put each fruit into the bags which John usually uses for sealing rolls of film in tropical climates.

To stay on the safe side, though, we took this bundle of plastic-ed, foil-ed, bagg-ed fruits and locked them in a big suitcase which we could store in the baggage compartment. To celebrate these labors of Hercules, we shared a durian, and prayed that these labors would not be in vain.

The next morning, we put the suitcase into the baggage compartment of Thai Airways and boarded. The plane was to leave at 10 A.M., but, as usual, it was running late, and at 11 A.M., we were still on the ground. Hardly serious, we thought.

That, though, was when the stewardess stood in front of the plane and simply asked for our full attention. Being Thai, she tried to speak loudly, but her voice came out in a whisper announcing a serious problem on board.

In the translation from Thai, she said, "Somebody on this plane is not polite. Even though we have rules. A passenger has brought many durians on board. And the aroma had reached the cockpit. And the pilots are very unhappy. They will not take off from the ground."

She was silent, thinking what next to say. Then she must have remembered her school days.

"Would the impolite people," she asked, "please raise their hands?"

We looked around to see if somebody else would take the blame. But John finally took the blame and reluctantly obeyed, raising his hands, looking like a schoolboy caught smoking. I raised my own hands, almost prepared to ask the teacher if I could make a wee-wee. Our stewardess looked embarrassed to see such nice foreigners feeling so guilty. She darted back to the cockpit, then came back.

"You will," she said in halting English, "please do something with the durian. Please go outside. The durian are also outside."

After a moment of silence, an elderly Thai general asked how many durian we had. We told him we had two dozen. The general stood up and announced to the passengers his plan. In military language, he announced that if it was all right with the *farang* (foreigners), everybody would disembark and share the durians together.

The stewardess darted back again to the cockpit, and the pilots agreed to this plan. The controls were discontrolled, the doors opened, and we all got off.

Our suitcase came out of the hold, bags were opened, storage container unglued, tin foil removed, plastic unwrapped, and one of the passenger (presumably a terrorist) took out a carving knife to cut open the fruit.

Thus, for the next hour, while the plane lolled on the runway, we sat on the tarmac and ate durian and told stories and laughed and became soppy with the fruits and our new friends: passengers, pilots, and of course our newest friend, the stewardess.

The sun was scorching us, but the durian cooled us, and the thought that we could recite yet another Homeric tale of durians cheered us and made us woozy with pleasure.

And when we finally boarded a mere two hours late at high noon, every breath we took over the next two hours back to Bangkok breathed out that delicate aroma of Limburger cheese, old socks and the sweet taste of heaven (albeit surrounded by the aromatic smoke of hell).

The community of durian-lovers together, as durable, acrid, and luscious as life itself.

Harry Rolnick is a Grand Prize winner of the Pacific Asia Travel Association and writer/contributor to fifteen books on the Far East. After two decades in Asia and later Eastern Europe, he has returned to New York, where his latest projects are The Veal of Turin: An Atheist Cookbook *and* Wagner's Bagels: Letters Written by Distinguished Composers to Their Pals.

Taste of Eros

It resonates in memory.

IT BOGGLES MY MIND TO THINK THAT I HAD BEEN SEXUALLY ACTIVE for seven years without the benefit of red wine, strong cheeses, and those jewels called fish. My first encounter with Greek food changed my life.

I was twenty-five years old, and had just completed my master's degree in Colorado. I was traveling through Europe on my way to India, and was glad to finally be in Greece, meeting up with a friend from my graduate program. My friend and her father collected me from the Xania airport on Kriti (Crete). She was five feet tall, as was he. His enormous belly swung before him. He drove us to an outdoor taverna for my first meal in Greece.

No-nonsense tables and chairs stood under shady trees, and the day's menu recited by the proprietor appeared substantially different from the typo-splattered tourist card. Greek, however, was Greek to me—my acquaintance with French and Italian, not to mention several Indian languages, didn't aid my comprehension in the least. The proclamation of my Indian origins resulted in full glasses of ouzo and the sudden appearance of gawking staff. My friend translated her father's numerous questions. He had never met anyone from India. Being a learned European, he of course knew about the *Kama Sutra,* and was horrified to discover that I had never read it.

Our meal arrived: slabs of grilled swordfish with lemon. I'd hardly tasted fresh fish before that day. In India, my family were vegetarian until I turned seven. We eventually graduated to chicken, mutton, even beef, but not fish. My mother had something of a fish phobia, able to smell it a mile away. I grew up in Bombay on the Arabian Sea, surrounded by delicious seafood, but only tasted Tandoori Pomfret once. Later, in the U.S., only battered, deep fried frozen fish graced our dining table.

After a long, relaxed meal, we set out for the beach house. Like many Greeks, Pop drove in darkness with the headlights off. This supposedly helped "save" on the car battery, but basically provided cheap thrills. The ouzo kept me detached, and my cultural exposure to reincarnation came in handy as we hurtled through near-misses on the winding road. Finally we entered the last village on the highway before descending to the beach house. My friend shouted greetings of reassurance up and down the road, receiving slightly hostile rumbles of recognition in exchange.

I awoke the next morning to the smell of coffee. The thick, Turkish-style brew was served unfiltered in small cups, accompanied by fruit, bread, butter, honey, and Mizitra, a wonderfully tangy cheese. My experience of cheese until then had been limited to hot pepper jack, cheddar, cream cheese, Swiss. Following instructions, I layered honey and Mizitra on thick chunks of bread, a previously incomprehensible combination for me. It was delicious. The family procured a variety of other cheeses: sharp, nutty Graviera and Kefalotiri, the standard feta and also sheep's milk yogurt, as thick and pungent as cheese.

The charm of any beach house is, of course, eating fresh seafood. Every afternoon Pop rendezvoused with the returning fishermen. He brought back thick purple octopus, monkfish, and Mediterranean lobster resembling armored tanks. The seafood was grilled, sautéed, steamed, or poached. No breading or deep frying. This first immersion into the essence of fish reminded me ecstatically of certain amorous encounters with humans.

As much as the Greeks disparage the Turks, the Islamic appetite for internal organs was strongly evident in this family, where everyone cleaned out their fish heads except me. Determining that I had indeed rejected my portion, my friend grabbed the head and sucked it clean. Similarly, every spindly leg of the lobster was lovingly cracked and consumed.

I surrendered my unwanted rejects, content to sip my red wine. Like the locals, this household cultivated grapes and pressed their own wine annually, adding to a glass vat that included distillations ten years old. Due to a combination of ignorance and low budget, American jug wines had defined the extent of my acquaintance thus far. This wine was exquisite: ruby red, dense, fruity, full-bodied. Pop warned me that it was rationed, part of a stock that had been aging for ten years or more, so I had to make do with one glass a day. Unrationed spirits included retzina: white wine spiked with pine pitch; raki: homemade 80 proof grape liquor; and the ubiquitous ouzo. I had no complaints.

My second restaurant meal was with a group of mainlanders all vacationing on Kriti. Twenty of us settled in at a taverna. Unbeknownst to me, my friend had a reputation as a woman with balls, and so, long before the main meal, she and I were each presented with a single sphere of dark meat. She popped this item nonchalantly into her mouth. What is it, I asked, probing with my fork. Eat! barked my friend's father, who watched me chew, then held up his ouzo in salute. Kidney? Liver? My friend revealed the mystery meat as a cock's testicle. I looked up with a start, causing the men to laugh appreciatively and regard me with renewed interest.

The Greeks had a hard time with me. The less educated never heard of India. The closest they understood was "West Indies." They couldn't fathom why I didn't live in my "own" country, even though my friend didn't live in "hers," being a student in the U.S. The educated Greeks knew of India, but none spoke any English. My friend tiredly translated the same questions about the *Kama Sutra,* Indira Gandhi, Sai Baba, Nehru.

In London, I had purchased a few ingredients for an impromptu

Indian meal on Crete. My friend's mother, a refined member of upper-class Alexandrian society, was thrilled that I wanted to cook for them. She set the date, cleared the kitchen, pulled out all the pots and pans. She hovered around, asking a steady stream of questions impossible for me to focus on, about Indian geography, Indian customs, Indian cuisine. My friend dutifully translated. Unaccustomed to cooking for others, the food took me all day to prepare. When the meal was finally ready, everyone was ravenous. I served lentils with garlic and yogurt, spicy potatoes, coconut-ginger green beans, cucumber *raita*, rice and *papadum*.

It was a terrible faux pas. Like other Europeans, Greeks make meat the centerpiece of their meal, and my concoctions were entirely vegetarian. Mom could not stop exclaiming at this pitiful version of nourishment. No wonder Indians were emaciated, she thundered. How could they possibly have energy for sex? And still there were eight hundred million of them!

The food was properly condemned, and Mom commenced cooking a "proper" meal. My friend's father was more sympathetic, tasting each dish and making loud appreciative sounds before abandoning the meal. The younger sister sampled only the potatoes. Only my friend ate with relish; in the U.S. she had turned vegetarian.

Pop was dying to show me around Kriti, and so we took long day trips, covering different parts of the island. When Greeks eat out, they eat only Greek food. Grilled lamb, salad, and fried potatoes were the unvarying combination at every destination. I was appalled at this culinary insularity, and refused everything but the potatoes. My friend, being vegetarian and health-conscious, refused everything but the salad. Finally, impressed by my stubbornness, Pop drove us out of our way for a special, more expensive meal. The restaurant was pleasantly decorated, with a grapevine arbor and rustic furniture. Crisp calamari proved welcoming, accompanied by retzina. Mussels cooked in wine, followed, along with prawns cooked with garlic, then clams. A squeeze of lemon was the only condiment necessary for the perfectly prepared plates.

As always, my friend sat next to me, with Pop seated across.

Soon it became clear that Pop was communing with someone. His face and hands twitched in a variety of odd signals. My friend swung fully around to stare at the person behind us. The back of my neck burned. I kept my head low, willing my friend to resume her meal. Eventually she did, laughingly informing me that Pop was flirting with a woman whose husband was blissfully unaware. Look at her! Go on, turn around, my friend urged loudly. No! I cried, embarrassed. It's all right, she soothed. They're only flirting.

The woman must have managed some elaborate communication, because suddenly Pop switched into high gear. He stood up, all puffed out. He had a clown's face, with sloping eyes, soft jowls and a bulbous nose. His low waist and short legs enhanced the comedy. He strutted alongside the table, first one way and then the other. My friend was standing now, enjoying herself thoroughly.

I contemplated how I might react to the sight of my own father flirting while eating dinner with me. The thought drew a complete blank. I couldn't even imagine it, let alone play it out. Such behavior was inconceivable. By now I was grumpy. My two hosts stood side by side, looking straight at the poor woman, commenting openly. The waiter brought the bill, the money was paid, and still they stood chatting animatedly. Shall we go? I inquired, and my friend shook her head. Soon, she promised. We're waiting for them to leave. My father wants to see her full body.

I felt anger slamming the back of my throat. This was outrageous. I glared at my friend with dagger eyes and she pointed out my red face to her father. He grinned and said in his heavily accented English, One minute, sorry! My friend gestured for silence. The couple stood up. Pop's target of desire was a heavyset, heavily made up blonde a head taller than him. She sashayed past us, tilting her chin in a clear sign. The husband veered off toward the bathroom, and the wife quickly exited the restaurant. My hosts rushed after her. I stayed put, keeping one eye on the toilets. A minute later father and daughter re-appeared.

Well, I snapped, did they get their quickie? My friend laughed and, much to my horror, immediately translated for her father, who also chuckled in delight. She was all over my dad, my friend giggled. Yeah, right! I snorted contemptuously. No really, back there, by her car, she grabbed his hand and put it on her thigh like this, bam! Can you imagine? She said to come back tomorrow, so I guess we will.

The following day I feigned sickness and we all stayed home. A personal connection between Greek food and enhanced sexual feeling was one thing, seeing it played out in public was quite another. Pop sensed my disapproval, and moped around in hurt silence.

Locals stopped by the house after lunch, inviting us to join them in diving for sea urchin eggs. My friend jumped at the chance, and I accompanied her. Sea urchin eggs are considered on a par with caviar, and I had tasted neither. The perfect bay was located, with crystal clear water. The divers needed unmuddied shallows to escape being punctured by the sea urchin spines. The operation of locating pregnant specimens was entirely hit-and-miss. But once the egg-loaded spheres were split open, they revealed their bounty in orange-red veins. By sunset, the treasure amounted to three tablespoons worth of clumped ova. Around us were littered the remains of dozens of spiny creatures. The precious booty was transported home, rinsed and garnished liberally with fresh lemon juice and a few drops of olive oil. Finally, we were ready for the tasting.

The first impact on the tongue was salty. But then, rolling and mashing the roe in my mouth, an irridescent rainbow of tastes shot out and blended into one another in breathtaking profusion: sweet crab, sour citrus, bitter liquor, meaty wild mushrooms, searing horseradish… it felt as though I had chewed through a kitchenful of food. The sticky essence lingered for an eternity, transforming, coaleascing, then mutating again all the way down the resonant tunnel of my throat. I was in shock. I felt drained, my body post-orgasmic in its stupor. I felt full to bursting. I could not bear the thought of any other food. I wanted to be alone. As I struggled to focus on the others, I realized there was silence at the table, a rare event for my voluble host family. I wasn't the only one transported by this magical food.

That night my friend and I walked through the village in a

heightened state, talking about sex. Cretan youth are shockingly beautiful, unlike their weathered elders. The locals were dead ringers for Calvin Klein models. The pre-pubescent boys eerily resembled the classical David, with curly hair, pouting mouths, and porcelain cheekbones. The girls looked like Aphrodite and Venus. My friend's family were darker, more Levantine, as were the faces I'd glimpsed in Athens. But on Kriti many of the natives are blond and light-eyed, a vivid reminder of their successful routing of the Turks, the one and only island able to keep the invaders at bay.

My friend pointed out the local "fishhooks": boys for hire who befriended solo women tourists. They had cocky good looks but vacant eyes. Any local male would have gladly bedded my friend, hungry to stain her blue-blooded Alexandrian ancestry. But her hot-blooded neighbors were a bad risk, since their good will was essential for her family's safe residence on the beach. Provincialism ruled, and people who owned beach houses were the clear outsiders.

We admired the effortless local beauty and pledged to hunt down more sea urchin eggs the next day. But clearly our luck had run out and I left Greece without tasting that wondrous food again. Once in a while, when satiated into a stupor, that rainbow of tastes re-ignites on my tongue, bringing my vivid initiation into Cretan pleasures rushing back, and I thank my stars for fate, chance, destiny, and the sacred talent of sensual enjoyment.

Bombay-born Ginu Kamani authored Junglee Girl, *a collection of stories exploring sexuality, sensuality, and power. Published in various anthologies, journals, and magazines, her essays and talks deal with gender, sexual self-knowledge, and hyphenated American identities. She is Visiting Writer in Fiction at Mills College, Oakland, California.*

HANNS EBENSTEN

* * *

A Caribbean Treat

A group of gay men enjoy the hidden cuisine
of the San Blas Islands off the
coast of Panama.

OUR HOST, CALIFORNIAN ROY STEWART, RAN HIS WHOLE ISLA DE Oro island establishment almost single-handed, with only three or four untrained Cuna Indian boys to assist him in an ineffective way. He organized the volleyball games and gave prizes, he arranged canoe excursions, crab races, sing-alongs, crossed to the mainland at least once each day to pick up the bottled water and beer and soft drinks that the planes from Panama City left for him at the edge of the airstrip, and, in the evenings, when we sat after dinner under an oil lamp swinging between two palm trees, kept us all enthralled with his stories about the Cuna Indians. He had studied everything that is known of their history, he knew their myths and their beliefs, he understood and admired and respected their way of life; and if he embellished his talks with his own inventions, he did so in a well-meaning effort to keep his audience dramatically entertained. He had cast himself in the role of the Cunas' protector and benefactor; and he held forth so eloquently about his Cuna Foundation (which existed only in his mind) that many of the tour members were quite carried away with enthusiasm and pressed cash contributions for it on him.

How convincingly he explained that he would send selected

Cuna youths to the Hotel El Panamá to be trained in the rudiments of operating a tourist resort—cooking, serving, cleaning; that he would purchase carpenter's and shipbuilding tools to enable the idle men of Aligandi to engage in useful work in which they could take pride and that would benefit the whole community; that he was taking a group of pretty Cuna maidens Stateside to give promotional performances of their traditional dances—and as he spoke of all this, he had every intention of doing it, but somehow none of it ever happened.

Meanwhile, no one knew better how to keep a group of men happy and content. He did all the cooking himself, in a small, dark space behind the dining room, and refused all offers of help.

We ate bananas from morning to night, and although this became a joke among the tour members, no one seemed to mind. For breakfast, Roy served bananas either whole or sliced in bowls of rich refreshing cream; for luncheon, we had fruit salads that consisted of sliced bananas with a few pieces of coconut and a raisin or two and lemon juice, accompanied by chilled chocolate or coffee-flavored milkshakes—"to build up you growing boys," quipped Roy. With drinks before dinner there were always platters of deep-fried crisp banana slices, more delicious than potato chips, very salty in order to encourage the guests to run up sizable tabs at the bar; and dinners always included more banana chips or bananas sliced lengthwise and fried in batter. Desserts were milky banana puddings or, as a special treat, bananas flambéed in local rum. And great bunches of bananas were hung daily from a tree outside the main hut, so that anyone who had not enjoyed enough bananas at meals could pick one for a snack.

The bananas came from the mainland, where Roy said he owned a plantation; but often, when the canoe returned that he sent there each day with two Cuna boys to cut down and bring the bananas, we heard angry voices and saw Cuna women on the mainland shore running to and fro waving their arms. It seemed that Roy's boys had raided their plantations.

Each afternoon, after his nap in what he called his "stateroom" aboard the derelict trimaran, Roy sequestered himself in his kitchen to prepare our gourmet meals—and truly splendid they always were, consisting of rice or spaghetti or beans with some pungent, tasty, richly spiced meat or fish sauce, topped with finely chopped onions or cheese. We ate like kings on the Isla do Oro and were always hungry after the day's swimming, snorkeling, volleyball games, hikes on the reef, and jungle excursions. There was always plenty of food, the hot coffee and cocoa that followed the dessert were excellent and creamy, and Roy was smug in accepting the many compliments on his catering and, on the tours' last evenings, the applause when we toasted him.

His most-acclaimed dish was what he called Chicken Supreme, a pilaf of rice with chopped peppers and onions and many spices, and chicken breasts cut into small, narrow strips, served under a creamy sauce. "Can we have Chicken Supreme again?" I would ask Roy.

"You all really go for that, don't you?" he said. "Sure, I'll fix it again for dinner tomorrow."

The tour members asked him where he bought the chickens. We saw none in Aligandi. Roy said that he bred them at a farm of his some miles up one of the rivers on the mainland; but I never saw a live chicken, or a dead one. "You don't really have a chicken farm, do you?" I asked him one day when he and I were alone.

He laughed. He was so proud of his deception that he could not resist confiding in me. "Don't tell any of the guys," he said. "Chicken Supreme is iguana, cut up so small that no one knows the difference. It tastes the same, with all those spices, but the guys wouldn't eat it if they knew."

I was amused. After all, the iguana meat was always fresh.

But then, toward the end of our fourth tour on the island, when I was looking for Roy and ventured into his kitchen and found it empty, in the semidarkness I saw some curious packages; I lifted a lid, and another, and a third, and I gasped with disbelief when I saw the contents: All those delectable meat and fish dinners we enjoyed so much were made of canned dog food and cat food; bowls of rich cream at breakfast, the milk shakes, the tasty sauces, and the puddings were all created with the powder from a large tin container labeled ANIMAL FEED ONLY: DILUTE WITH WATER; the "freshly ground Colombian mountain-grown coffee" and the "cocoa which my people pick in the hills" were dark liquids of industrial flavoring in two large bottles. Only the bananas were bananas.

I was truly appalled and ran to confront Roy in his "stateroom" aboard the *Tontine*. "Oh, take no notice of all that," he said, smiling happily. "I have it all labeled like that to avoid paying the high Panamanian import duty for bringing in gourmet foods from Stateside. I wouldn't dream of serving my guests pet food, would I?"

Not for a moment did his usual aplomb fail him; but he did not convince me. For two months, before the next tour to the Isla de Oro, I was deeply troubled every day by the thought of knowingly sending my tour members to a place where they would be fed animal food; but I knew that it would be useless to beg or order Roy to use anything else. He would simply adhere to his fairy tale of having gourmet foods hidden under spurious labels. And I assuaged my conscience with the thought that a total of 144 men on four tours had eaten offal and cattle feed with considerable relish and no ill effects.

As it turned out, I need not have worried about Roy's cooking ingredients. Fate intervened, and the members of the fifth (and, regrettably, last) tour to Panama did not eat canned pet food, did not stay on the Isla de Oro at all.

Hanns Ebensten has arranged and conducted tours, cruises, and expeditions to remote, unusually interesting, and adventurous places for forty years. His agency, Hanns Ebensten Travel, Inc., in Key West, Florida, was founded in 1972. He is a regular contributor to Christopher Street, Archaeology Magazine, The Advocate, *and the* Society for Hellenic Travel Review, *among other publications. This story was excerpted from his book,* Volleyball with Cuna Indians: And Other Gay Travel Adventures.

Goulash

Blend the spices carefully, and simmer long and slow.

MY LOVER INFURIATES ME. IN MANY WAYS, TOO MANY TO COUNT. He stays up half the night, he hugs other women, his pate glows greasy with hair tonic, he smothers his food in hot paprika, his political tirades border on fascism, he looses his emotions like a whirlwind over the smallest thing....

Even before he senses my anger, he has his excuse ready. Always the same, arrogant excuse: "But, my dear, I'm Hungarian!"

I am an American of sorts. And while I acknowledge that my national identity influences my behavior, never would it occur to me to use it as an excuse to dismiss my idiosyncrasies. "But, my dear, I'm American!"—so what? I reserve my passion for art, causes, and the pursuit of happiness.

My lover, however—let's call him Janos—feels passionately about being Hungarian. Like his bullied little country, he has known multiple losses—property, friends, family—and like Hungary, he has survived through a combination of astuteness, obstinacy, and the unique ability to laugh and cry at the same time. All qualities I find infuriating.

Our romance has the zing of a well-cooked goulash, highly spiced if hard to digest.

Janos has had many lovers but only one wife, Eva—a Hungarian, naturally. His choice of a mate was at once sentimental and culinary: no one but a good Hungarian wench can produce a true Hungarian goulash, he is convinced, as if his precious Eva carried the recipe in her bloodlines.

His craving for the stuff is epic. For no apparent reason he will suddenly recall a goulash he ate forty years ago in a Buda bistro, and, transported, his mouth will water, his eyes fill with tears. This hunger of his bypasses the stomach, it resides in his genes, his history, in his very essence.

Well-intentioned, I once tried my hand at a generic recipe—meat, potatoes, onions, carrots, paprika...nothing fancy. But there was a lesson for me in that hot pot, I knew, as I watched the ingredients sputter and fight one other, then gradually submit, and finally fuse in one pungent, viscous aggregate.

With what tender solicitation I placed a bowlful before my Magyar. I remember how he sniffed the crockery before inserting a fork into the steaming concoction. His nostrils flared, his lips curled—I took these to be good signs—and he ingested a big hearty mouthful that sent streams of gravy down his chin. For a moment his face looked as placid as a nursing baby's, then his nose puckered.

"Timid," he pronounced it, lacking that peppery *je ne sais quoi* only Eva and her tribe know how to give it.

My creation was mere stew; it could not evoke a single sunset over Lake Balaton nor the refrain of a half-forgotten rhapsody nor the aroma of his mother's kitchen. Defeated, I cleared away the dishes while he poured himself a water glass full of Tokay.

His words of consolation? "But my dear, I'm Hungarian!"

There is no rebuttal. After six months of fretting over his habits and quirks, customs and manias, I have ceased to look for one. Instead, I tell myself that like any good goulash, in time, our various ingredients will mingle, our flavors and spices coalesce. Janos will mellow, I will take on piquancy. What an exquisite meal love's alchemy will make of our differences!

But the process is slow and fraught with annoyances. Janos is determined to recover Transylvania, he dresses like a refugee, his breath smells perpetually of onions, he uses too much aftershave lotion, his jealousy follows me like a spy...And there's no use complaining. No. He has his retort ready: "But, my dear, I'm Hungarian!"

Itinerant writer Germaine W. Shames has written from five continents—soon to add a sixth—on topics ranging from Latin lovers to sex-crazed swamis. Her essays have appeared in such anthologies as Cupid's Wild Arrow *and* Travelers' Tales Mexico. *She was last spotted trailing a gypsy caravan through Transylvania, having celebrated her 40th birthday in questionable company at Dracula's Castle.*

JOSEPH DIEDRICH

The French Waiter

He means business, and his way
is not your way.

MY FRIEND WILSON, WHO LIVED TO EAT, WAS GOING TO PARIS FOR
the first time.

"You lived there for a while," he said. "Will I be able to get by in
the restaurants with my French?" He treated me to a demonstration.

"Frankly, I don't think so."

"Well," he said, taken aback, "most Parisians speak English anyway, don't they?"

"Most of the Parisians you will meet can speak some English
but they won't want to. Cabdrivers are particularly bad about not
speaking English but waiters are even worse. Any Parisian waiter
worth his salt will make an extra effort not to understand you."

"But why?"

"Two reasons: because they are Parisians and because they are
waiters. Waiters have gone to a lot of trouble learning how not to
look at a customer. He might want something if they did. It's even
better if they can't understand him as well in case he somehow
does get their attention."

I tried to explain it to him. No Frenchman likes to hear his language spoken poorly and Parisians are the Frenchest of the French.
They sniff at the accent of someone from the wrong part of town.

They disparage the French spoken in other parts of the country and they make nasty jokes about the French-speaking Belgians. When they hear the accent of an American, a mongrel race to which they feel great cultural superiority, Parisians simply refuse to acknowledge that what they are hearing is French at all. As for speaking English, *bien*, this is France and in France the language is French and someone who is unable to speak proper French probably isn't worth speaking to anyway.

Only under the most extreme provocation will a true Parisian's knowledge of English come to the surface, such as the evening in a Paris *brasserie* when a Good Ole Boy from Texas sat down at the table near to mine. After a while a waiter strolled over to take his order.

"I b'lieve I'll have a steak, well done, and some French fries," the Texan announced in a loud voice.

The waiter just looked at him.

"A steak. Well done. And French fries," he said again, louder.

The waiter regarded the Texan for a moment more, then turned away. Before he could escape a well dressed woman at the next table intervened.

"*Entrecote et pommes frites.*" She explained to the waiter. "*Et l'entrecote bien cuit.*" She made a little face.

The waiter looked at the Texan in amazement, then shrugged and went off towards the kitchen. Steaks in France are usually cut thin and do not tolerate being well done. Parisian *pommes frites* on the other hand are usually a quantum leap above the tasteless, brown, overcooked American French fries. This *brasserie* was particularly proud of its delicious *pommes frites*, which were a specialty of the house.

After a few minutes the waiter returned with a thin, overcooked steak and a heaping platter of golden French fries. The Texan stared at what had been put before him.

"Where's the ketchup?" he demanded.

Again the waiter just looked at him.

The Texan made motions of shaking a ketchup bottle over his plate. "Ketchup." He repeated angrily. "You cain't eat French fries without ketchup, can you?"

The waiter shook his head in disbelief and turned away. This time, I noticed, the well dressed Frenchwoman chose not to intervene, but the Texan was not to be denied.

"Garkon!" he shouted after the retreating waiter, "You damn well bring me some ketchup for these here French fries!"

The waiter stopped, turned, and walked slowly back to the Texan's table. All eyes in the room were on him. He looked at the beautiful platter of golden potatoes. Then he looked at the Texan.

"*No*," he said, and went away.

Joseph Diedrich is a retired Pan Am pilot who spends his time traveling, sailing, trekking, and "messing about." He and his wife live in Mallorca, Spain.

LISA KREMER

*　*　*

Tibetan Cravings

Hunger brings you closer
to the root of all things.

ASIANS EAT TO LIVE—NOT THE OTHER WAY AROUND. THIS philosophy is taken to the extreme in Tibet, where, unlike in most of Asia, cuisine never really developed into something one could describe as rich and varied, or even appetizing. For a traveler thumbing it through the high desert of the Tibetan Changtang, this fact, coupled with a simple dearth of supplies, brings the notion of eating to live, rather than living to eat, to the furthest extreme.

Wind whips through my hair, blown slack and dusty on an open-backed truck rumbling along the road to…well, actually, it seems to nowhere. At every rut in this road that is better described as a track, a direction across the terrain, I grab the sides of the truck to keep from being tossed overboard by its wild rocking. In fact this ride is about as comfortable as riding a bucking bronco across the plateau would be, and although we move a lot we do not seem to cover much distance. We sit piled high atop the truck's load. My seat on a sack of some kind of grain, most probably barley, is actually not so bad, although it is hard, and every time we hit an extra large bump, my backside cries out for mercy in the form of a cushion. But besides our hulking truck, I see no other vehicles on

this route, so there is no use in complaining. Since leaving the
Lhasa-Kathmandu "highway" I have been on the road for a week
now, sometimes on trucks, more often on the roadside, waiting for
a ride that will concede to stop for Western travelers. I am thankful for my present lift, as every day waiting translates into a less-
ening of the meager supplies I have been able to carry. Here, in
journeying through a landscape that in itself is a realization of the
depths of my imagination, I am also beginning a journey into the
depths of hunger. Not only is there practically nothing to eat, anything that is available is so unappetizing it is confusing: how do
the Tibetans of the plateau live?

Later I will a laugh upon seeing Tibetan restaurants in the
States. What could they be serving—blood sausage, dried un-
cooked meat, roasted barley, butter tea? Don't get me wrong, I am
actually quite a fan of butter tea. Off the beaten path in Tibet, facing high altitude and cold weather, its fat and salt are particularly
welcome. But in New York? I suppose people frequent those
restaurants to rack up on some good karma helping the refugees—
a valid enough reason. But what Tibetans do to accumulate good
karma is a bit more extreme. They set off on pilgrimages to holy
sites scattered across the great wilderness that is their homeland.
Besides monasteries built by the human hand, many of these sites
are natural temples, a lake here, a mountain there.

Most of my comrades on this truck are Khampas from East
Tibet, en route to Mount Kailash, the holiest mountain for
Buddhists in all Asia. Khampas resemble cowboys, with similar
hats and a comparably rugged nature. Hats carefully balance on
their long hair, which is braided with red fabric and wrapped
around the top of their heads; great robe-like coats called *chubas*
swathe their tall frames; a long sword is tied around their waists;
and turquoise stones dangle from their ears. I happen to be with
them because Mount Kailash has become for me the latest in a series of travel goals that included simply crossing the border from
Nepal to Tibet, to visiting Lhasa, to this journey now, which has
taken on the weight of a pilgrimage. If I am a pilgrim, then I am
among friends here—Tibet being the perfect land to undertake a

pilgrimage of this difficulty. Hearty walkers, who do not think it strange to set off on year-long journeys, circumambulate Mount Kailash, as I plan to do, walking the 35-mile trail that encircles the mountain. Or perhaps they prostrate—hands together in prayer position high above the head, down to touch the forehead, the chest, then diving to the ground, splayed out on rocks, snow, ice, whatever is in their path, turning two days of walking around the mountain into two weeks.

Tibet inspires travelers, and with this inspiration comes a sort of nonchalant boldness that ushers one, almost unawares, into the realm of adventure. That is why when warned by a kind, fellow-vegetarian traveler that his journey to Kailash the previous year met with a span of malnutrition that almost left him dead in his tracks, I hardly heard him, let alone heeded his warning. He advised that I eat meat once on the plateau, because the food situation was dismal. But for me there was no question—I would find a way to remain a vegetarian; I would not eat meat just because I was a bit hungry. What I did not realize back then, trading tales in the courtyard of our Lhasa guest house, was just how hungry one could get.

Perhaps just as much as eating meat, a jeep tour organized by the Chinese government tourist agency went against my grain. That would have been the simplest way to solve the problem of a lack of transportation, as well as the dearth of food, as I could have carried enough supplies from Lhasa for the journey. But I reveled in the freedom afforded by forging my own way, and I certainly did not want a Chinese government guide as a fellow journeyman through Tibet. Why my traveling companion and I could catch a ride on a pilgrim truck to Kailash, couldn't we? What was the ruckus? But before one has traveled across the Tibetan Changtang, as this malnourished chap was attempting to explain, one does not understand wilderness, and one's concepts of food, or the lack thereof, are irrelevant.

Sometimes I feel as if my insides are shaking too much—jolted to and fro, how can my organs remain in place with all this moving about? But the feel of the clean air against my face and the view of tiny frosted peaks dotting the distant Nepali–Tibetan border throw my worries to the wind. The landscape is so different than that of Nepal. In fact, on my overland journey from there I have traveled up and up, above the mountains, to reach a land whose lowest valleys are found in the realm of high altitude. I actually have a package of granola in my bag, which represents the last of the outback food I purchased in Nepal before coming on this journey. I lugged this granola from Kathmandu, only to have my bag get soaked with kerosene on my last ride, but I carry it anyway, because I am starting to realize the roughness of the situation in which I find myself. This is no place to throw away food.

Like my trucking partners, Tibetans who see this journey as a must in this lifetime in preparation for the next, I also carry a sack of *tsampa*, roasted barley flour that is the staple here. This is the meal that most Tibetans eat, morning, noon, and night, their entire lives. For a New Yorker who grew up eating exotic food in restaurants, partaking of the same meal every day seems a life sentence, a concept difficult to digest. The *tsampa* itself is not much easier.

We slowly approach a rectangular mud structure, a roadside inn in a place that so defines the concept of the middle of nowhere that there is not even an outhouse. Here we stop for a round of butter tea, served from a large Chinese thermos painted with dragons, called a *chatham*. Enamel mugs and small sacks of *tsampa* are pulled from pockets. The cups are filled and *tsampa* is mixed in with a kneading motion of the hand to form a wet, buttery, salty dough. I have not quite gotten the gist of the ratio between *tsampa* and tea. While eating the *tsampa* more tea is poured, and so I fill more *tsampa* and it seems to never end and then all of a sudden it does, as the driver, who is all powerful, starts the truck. People run, because they know that the driver could very easily leave them if he so desired and when would they find another ride, when just one truck passes here on a lucky day?

Just as practiced Tibetan fingers formed balls of *tsampa*, the *tsampa* now forms itself into a ball in my stomach. Only a few minutes ago I was warmed by the hearty tea about which most tourists love to complain, but already I am cold in the afternoon wind. It is true, the tea is salty, the butter is strong and rancid, but distaste quickly turns to appreciation when exposed to the elements. I have already grown to love it as one should love and honor anything that offers warmth on the 15,000-foot-high plateau, where the only constant besides flatness is chill wind. And the saltiness hits the spot, as high altitude dehydrates the body. For those not facing such physical extremes, simply addressing the tea as soup should be all it takes to foster appreciation. The tea represents life, for without it you cannot eat *tsampa*. Although *tsampa* is the staple, even Tibetan nomads do not consider it a meal when only mixed with water. Mind you, it is digestible—I was forced to rely on it, traveling like the innocent idiot I was, stove-less across the Changtang.

Another foodstuff in my bag is ramen noodles. They are a good thing, because no matter where you stop in Tibet you will find a *chatham* filled with boiling water; then you whip out your cup from your pocket and you have a meal. Or if you are really hungry you can just munch on them raw. How I wish I had brought more packages along. What was I thinking?

Every few hours we pass a herd of yaks who flee at the sight of our truck barreling across the expanse. You would never think an animal so big could be so graceful, but indeed they are as they gallop, long hair easing on the wind. The yak, or actually the female *dzo*, is a life-force on this land: a fount of milk, which is churned to butter; a pack animal; a source of hair woven into the coarse brown wool of which nomad homes are fashioned; eventually giving its life for meat. Far, far in the distance I see a tremendous yak, the biggest yak I have ever seen. I watch for what seems an hour, then we are upon it and it turns out to be a yak hair tent.

Two men wearing caps, Chinese army jackets, and blue Mao trousers, stand outside the tent, in the center of the vast wilderness. As they climb aboard I see they are not Tibetan, but Uigur, Muslims of Xinjiang province north of Tibet. Perhaps they are brothers as their faces are similar, with squinty eyes, the semi-collapsed nose of a boxer who has seen too many bouts, and a crooked mouth—looks that prompt my traveling companion to say, "Here are the butchers." Our laughter is muffled by the coughing of the engine as we begin our vibrating crawl into the distance.

The sun hanging low at the edges of the plateau, we stop in a pasture, a sheltered nook among buttery rises that have folded up in the middle of the flats. There are nomads here with herds of goat and yak. The Tibetans laugh as my companion and I join them in collecting yak dung, contributing to the group effort to make tea. Cooking is an active experience in Tibet—to boil water, you need to keep your eyes pealed for yak dung, the organic, bacteria-free fuel of this arid land. It is a bit difficult to light, but if you have a pocket bellows, leather stretched on a mouth-like frame, you are set. As long as the bellows are pumped, the fire will crackle, water will boil, and you can get a little nourishment. Food has regressed to fill its primary task of providing nourishment, nothing more. Eating is not a hobby, nor an experience, but a routine of *tsampa* and tea, tea and *tsampa*. Besides the bellows a pilgrim pulls out another wonderfully Tibetan travel gadget—a miniature butter churn used to make authentic butter tea.

In another group effort a large tent is erected, and I realize that part of the gear on the truck is a yak hair tent, like the one we passed on the lonely plain a few miles and hours back. Traveling is a slow venture in Tibet, every mile sucking energy you never thought you would need just to rock on the back of a truck. Exhausted, I fall to sleep in the corner of the tent, waking to find that my partner and I are the only ones who have slept inside, the rest of our fellow journeyers preferring to sleep under the marquee of the night sky alit with stars. Boarding the truck my companion and I share a laugh as we realize that the Uigurs are indeed butchers, peripatetic butchers; now a slaughtered goat lies on his back, yet another addition to our crowded truck. He will roast in the high altitude sun and dry in the arid air so rapidly that as early as this afternoon the travelers will partake of his meat.

Upon first hearing that Tibetan Buddhists eat meat, I was

shocked. It just did not seem congruous with Buddhism. But upon seeing the way of life out here, I can understand why it has to be that way. Nothing grows but fragrant patches of sage and juniper. The nomads herd goats and yaks, and, conducting business with passing trucks, trade the animals, their skins, dried meat, and any dairy products they can spare, such as butter and dried cheese. Like native peoples the world over, they utilize every part of the animal: skins are stitched into fifteen-pound *chubas* worn against the wind and slept under at night; the stomach is used to wrap butter; the blood is used to make blood sausage, one of Tibet's few delicacies. In return they get *tsampa*, the grain that is synonymous with life on the Changtang.

Since Buddhists should not kill, slaughtering animals becomes quite complicated for nomads of the high plateau. Those who are forced to slaughter perform a ceremony in which they pray for a better rebirth for the soul of the animal. But, if they can, Buddhists generally prefer to hire Muslim butchers. So the Tibetans eat *halal* meat and the Muslims are employed. My companion partakes of the now dried meat and actually purchases a limb of sorts, which he eats off the bone using the sword he purchased in the Barkor, the lively market area encircling the Jokhang, Lhasa's holiest monastery. This sword acts as a bridge between him and the other Tibetan men, who also carry swords. In fact a rousing conversation is devoted to checking out the Westerners' sword, having him examine theirs, answering the question of how much was paid, and if he would be willing to make a trade. All the while meat is sawed off and passed about.

We huddle together as we travel into the night, the temperature rapidly dropping. I wonder just how much longer we will drive against the frigid wind when our truck veers towards a tent where, as the token Westerners, we are invited in for tea and *palay*, Tibetan barley bread. Chewing on something as substantial as bread has, in just a few weeks, become a novel experience. My hands resting on my stomach, I lie down to sleep in the bed of the truck. The sky, crowded with brilliant stars, resembles a phosphorescent sea over the plateau, which itself was once a sea. We awake to the expanse, now empty of the tent that inhabited it, and which brought an inexplicable sense of relief to this stretch. It has been folded, and next to it stand a few trunks. Onto this truck, already completely laden with people and cargo, the gear is loaded, and the oldest sister climbs aboard. Her hair is braided with turquoise and beads as is the way of the Drog-pa, Tibetan nomads, and she wears an embroidered visor and a heavy coral necklace. She waves goodbye to her family, who, unburdened by their belongings will slowly drive their herd to the next grazing area. And so I become party to a Tibetan nomad moving truck. The girl taps on the cab of the truck. In the distance a group of shanties on a hill of sand come into focus. We stop in front of one of them, and she jumps off to unlock what turns out to be a small storehouse, equipped with sacks of rice and barley—a pantry in the middle of the wilderness. The driver helps the girl load a few sacks, and the truck that did not seem as if it could hold any more, indeed does.

The colors of the plain are a rich mélange of turquoise, mauve, ochre—any color but brown. Indeed the landscape seems a canvas oozing the brilliant colors of the minerals that make up its earth. Ice blue rivers braid across this land, rivers whose sources freeze in the night, disappearing, and by late afternoon, with the warming of the sun, again roar through their channels. The girl and I share a smile. I wonder if she recognizes the beauty of her land, or perhaps she does not know that her place is unique and wild. I wonder if she has suffered hunger.

After hours of driving across the flat open plain, the truck driver suddenly turns off the main valley into a relatively narrow side valley. We cross one small river, the truck rocking a bit wildly, and then over another smaller one. With the noise of the truck, which carries over the blustering of the wind, an old woman and two younger ones emerge from a tent. Here the nomad family's belongings are unloaded. The nomad girl and an old woman share an embrace that involves touching foreheads. A young boy walks hand in hand with a tiny girl. Eyes suddenly wide, they stop and stare. Perhaps we are the first Westerners these pint-sized nomads have ever seen.

Bending, the driver disappears into the flaps of the yak hair tent. Smoke curls out of the hole in the roof that acts as a vacuum, sucking the smoke of the yak dung fire out the tent and keeping the hearth burning all day. We climb down from the truck and sit in a circle out of the reaches of its shadow, granting the high-altitude sun a chance to heat us, to give us joy from warmth as does butter tea. We are a truckload of folks so I know that we are not about to get fed, but apparently yogurt from the morning milking is ready and a young woman lugs over a large plastic jug, generously filling each of our cups. At this point any food other than *tsampa* would have been a welcome surprise, but this is almost too much! It is delicious, the best yogurt I have ever tasted. Slowly drinking it down, I experience pure joy. I reinvent the experience of savoring. I concentrate on its movement and texture, feeling the yogurt in my mouth, its fresh taste, its pleasant tang, its smoothness. I follow its flow down my esophagus into my waiting stomach. All I can wish for is more.

On this grazing land, remoter than remote, the wide-eyed boy and girl form lovely figures. They gravitate towards us, hovering about, fascinated by our looks, our gear. We attempt to communicate. I show them some pictures I carry among my things and the boy opens his lips,

"Dah." I quickly put my finger to my lips and he is silent. I have read his mind—he wants a Dali Lama picture, which we have in our bags as presents, and which somehow everyone seems to suspect we have, as I guess it is the Western traveler's gift of choice. But my partner has tired of people begging for Dalai Lama photos, and I know he will not want to give a picture if the boy asks for one. For the next couple of hours, I am on the alert for an untimely, "*Dahl,*" ready with my finger to my lips. The boy heeds me, not understanding why. Later my companion indeed hands the young boy a Dali Lama picture and his face lights up and we share a smile. As for the little girl I give her the greatest gift, a few of which I purchased in the Barkor before setting out on the journey. It is a clear plastic heart pendant, in it a tiny picture of the Dalai Lama and behind it, in a bubble in the plastic, a grain of *tsampa*, symbolizing an offering to the Dalai Lama himself.

In this country of paucity the *tsampa* grain takes on religious significance: Tibetans bring *tsampa* to monasteries; altars are always graced with overflowing bowls of the grain; and the quai note offerings they leave for the monastery are inevitably stuck into these small mountains of kernels. Also decking the altars are traditional brass lamps, lit by flickering wicks that float in glistening liquefied butter. It is not strange to see a pilgrim in a cowboy hat carrying a bag of butter and a large spoon. His offering to the monastery is one of light: he fuels the lamps, eyes concentrated as he scoops the butter with a large spoon, his lips in constant motion mouthing the mantra, *ohm mani padme hum.*

We sit around long enough for the driver to stumble out of the tent, relieve himself, stumble back in, and then out again to take the wheel, sufficiently sobered (I hope). He has been drinking *chang*, the Tibetan brewed barley moonshine that tastes like sour malt and sits in one's stomach like a hearty meal, which is perhaps why the Tibetans so value it. With *chang's* sneak-up-on-you brand of drunkenness, it has been known to catch many a traveler unaware. But even if the driver is similar to travelers when it comes to holding his *chang*, do we have a choice?—we are now even off the "road" that cuts through the wilderness.

We say goodbye to the children, who enter a tent only to come racing back to us with a tin of special white butter and a tiny square of cheese, real hard cheese, in their small brown hands. So touched by this gesture, I think about it for a long time, realizing later that here in this land devoid of sustenance, we—my traveling companion and I, and the children—have in turn given each other gifts of sustenance, religious and tangible. The girl sticks her tiny finger in the butter and smoothes it on her lips, showing me that it will soothe my lips, so dry and chapped. I smile into her eyes, drinking her sweetness in, and transfer the goods to another container so she can take the tin, waving as I board the truck.

A Tibetan ancient who has decided to join our transport struggles to climb aboard. I reach out to lend him my hand, but he is a jokester, and rather than taking my hand, he waves to me, grabs the side of the truck, swings his legs over, and is in. A grandpa with treats in his pocket, he hands me *chura*, another dried foodstuff that carries the Tibetans through the seasons. It is basically a yogurt cheese squeezed into finger-length pieces that are then dried in the sun. I have actually purchased a kilo or two in the Lhasa market, but the pebble-like bits in my bag do not compare to his *chura*, which is dried, but not too much, retaining the taste of fresh yogurt. I hope that grandpa will come up with another handful, but for naught. I can hardly stomach my *chura* anymore as I have gotten down to bits that seem filled with some kind of fuzz that makes me gag. Later I will come across a nomad camp where *chura* lies drying on a yak wool rug—it is then I realize the origins of the hair.

We set off again, laughing as we hold on tight to the sides of the truck again crossing the rivers that have risen with the midday sun. One part of me is in wonderland, looking out on the sky; the other is in dreamland, the dreamland of yogurt and *chura*—satisfying food.

For I have discovered that hunger is not anything like what most of us call being hungry in the West. Hunger is a constant. Hunger is something that does not go away after one has finished a meal and even become "full." But my situation is, to a great degree, my own creation, and in that respect I felt exceedingly lucky. In feeling hunger, I can actually relate to the feelings of such a sadly significant percentage of the world population, yet know that hunger is not part of the forecast for my life. I can play a bit with hunger because I know that I have money in my pocket and I will eventually make it to Lhasa where food is available for purchase.

My stomach rumbles, almost as if having been awakened after glimpsing some decent food. I find myself looking out on the sky as it suddenly echoes my stomach, and within minutes turns a threatening shade of charcoal gray. As if projected by the gods, light filters magically through the thick clouds. The wind picks up and the truck stops. We sit underneath it as a rainstorm blows past. In twenty minutes we can see the precipitation over the distant rises that mark the periphery of this valley. And with the storm come and gone a great rainbow arches above. A full rainbow. The emptiness, the silence after the storm, the light, all fill me as food never could.

With all the wonder of the landscape and the richness of faith and spirituality, combined with the hardship of producing the very food they eat and knowing that the food needs to last through the seasons, food holds a different significance for Tibetans than for Westerners. On this journey, especially as a vegetarian and a Westerner unused to the food, I am catching a glimpse of the place it occupies. Its significance in survival is all important, and enjoyment is derived out of a certain thankfulness; on the other hand food as a source of delicacy seems unknown. Perhaps having so little, Tibetans never had a chance to get attached to food or to regard elaborate dishes with undue importance. Food is surely the greatest example of the Buddhist concept of impermanence and transformation—after all, what else in life transforms so immediately and obviously?

Thus Tibetans have taken their understanding of impermanence and transformation and the fact that a human body is flesh and blood, to the limits. Just as the meat of animals feed humans, human flesh can feed the animals. That is where "sky burial"—the Tibetan manner of interring the dead—takes shape. The human body is chopped and mixed with *tsampa*, becoming food for the birds. From a practical point of view, this means of disposal makes sense. In a land where the ground is frozen most of the year, a land burial would not work, for how would graves be dug? In a land with no trees, it is not practical to burn bodies, and, in an area which is landlocked, a body cannot be set out for burial at sea. Sky burial, which fits so perfectly with Buddhist philosophy, is actually the most pragmatic way of disposing of remains. So in Tibet, where food is scarce, even human bodies participate in the feeding of its inhabitants. To me it is a poignant concept that so completely and utterly expresses the belief that the body is just a vessel, and once the contents—the soul—has gone on its way, the vessel is worth nothing but the materials of which it is fashioned.

The white peaks along the border seem farther away now, but

with their distance a row of small brown hills have grown up to the east. Suddenly the truck jolts to a stop and we alight to prostrate and marvel, for among these knolls we catch our first glimpse of a mountain that stands out markedly on the plain—massive, snow-covered, pyramid-shaped—Mount Kailash. Somewhere within, deeper than my stomach, I am starting to realize why I took this journey. I am seeing firsthand how this mountain has captured the imagination of Asian believers the world over. Kailash means home of the gods, and for Hindus, Kailash in Tibet represents the main home of the Lord Shiva's four Himalayan abodes. For Tibetans the Mountain is Gang Rinpoche, Jewel of Snow, and indeed the mountain is a glittering gem, where the Buddhist saint Milarepa meditated and won the Tibetan nation over to the pure path of Buddhism. We make it to Darchen, the tent city at the base of the mountain, where colorful Buddhist prayer flags flap on the wind. I go from tent to tent trying my luck. *Tsampa* is in my pocket, but since I do not supplement it with meat I can not keep the meat on my bones. I look for noodles, something, anything...

After five weeks on the road I have returned to Lhasa. Lines of dust have penetrated every pore so that it takes three boiling showers to really become clean. In the shower I am shocked at my body, skinny as I was before puberty.

I embrace Lhasa with open arms, feeling one with the pilgrims I see. Maybe I can never understand the depth of their faith, but I do understand the inspiration of a mountain and the hardship of pilgrimage. I embrace the restaurants and street stalls of Lhasa with an insatiable hunger—true hunger—the long term stay at high altitude revving up my metabolism to new speeds. In my wanderings through the holy city, every meal is eaten with the discovery of breaking a fast.

The first restaurant I visit is called The Followers Restaurant, perhaps a bad translation of "the pilgrims." It is a Chinese restaurant frequented by Tibetans and travelers alike, with a lazy Susan on the table that spins with all the amazing vegetable and tofu dishes you can order. The menu is written in Chinese and English and you point to the English and the waitress jots down the order in Chinese. It is generally an efficient system, although there are a couple of dishes that don't correspond, which makes for some surprises and a few good laughs. It is here that I celebrate my 24th birthday, inviting some travelers from my guest house out for a meal and beers on me. The fragrant Chinese food offers a taste of bliss, of satisfaction, of knowing that perhaps it is possible to fill the bottomless pit that has become your sunken stomach. But if you've got a Tibetan craving and you want to go local, you can still take a seat at a tea shop in the Barkor, order a piping hot *chatham* of butter tea, pull out your sack of *tsampa*, and reminisce about the times when you ate to live and not the other way around.

Lisa Kremer is a traveler with an Asian obsession, who writes, photographs, and practices yoga. Having trekked over a thousand miles in the Himalayas, one might call her an adventure traveler, and in kind she enjoys writing about adventure travel. Her travel photography is represented by Tony Stone Images, and she has published articles and photographs in the Israeli geographic publication, Masa Acher. *For Lisa, Tibet is a place close to her heart, where she met the love of her life, who led her to Tel Aviv, Israel, where she now resides. In addition to travel writing and photography, she is a freelance Web writer and designer.*

PART FOUR

IN THE SHADOWS

JEFFREY TAYLER

Sausage Wars

You make the best of it.

NOT LONG AGO, IN THE TOWN OF OZYORY, ABOUT A HUNDRED miles south of Moscow, I wandered into the state-run Produkty ("Groceries") store off the central square to buy some sausage. Meat of all varieties is usually available outside the capital these days, but the number of stores selling it—or anything else—has not grown as quickly as one might expect, owing to punishing tax laws, the spread of state corruption, and the prevalence of organized crime. As a result, one of the banes of Soviet life—standing in line—has not disappeared from Russia. Nor has the hostility that lines incvitably provoke among the long-suffering Russian people.

Inside the store I took my place behind ten or twelve rubber-booted babushki by the meat counter. A minute later the rotund woman I was standing behind addressed me.

"*Muzhchina* (man)! Will you hold my place in line? I want to go to the fish counter."

I agreed. She wobbled away.

Seconds later the door opened and a fierce-eyed, halt old codger with a cane—the prototypical ornery Soviet-era survivor—limped into the store. He shoved me aside and pried his cane between the babushki. Because of his age I pardoned him, but the woman ahead of me, herself in her sixties, didn't.

"Get to the back of the line, old goat!" she shouted.

"I'm a second-class invalid and a war veteran! I don't have to wait in line—look at that sign!" (The state divides the disabled into classes according to the severity of their disability and the benefits they receive.)

Indeed, the sign above read VETERANS OF THE GREAT PATRIOTIC WAR AND FIRST/SECOND CLASS INVALIDS SERVED OUT OF LINE.

"I'm a second-class invalid myself!" she shouted. "You don't see me crashing lines. No one pays attention to those signs these days!"

The woman whose place I was holding returned swinging a two-foot-long dried herring like a truncheon. She hollered at the invader.

"Get behind this young man! That's my place you're in!"

He muttered but obeyed.

The line progressed. Two women in white smocks and tall white paper hats stood behind the counter. One was quite pretty, with limpid blue eyes and flaxen hair; the other, the butcher, resembled a pug-nosed prize fighter. Both looked exceedingly put-upon, as if customers were unexpected intruders in their private idyll of sausages and beef shanks.

"What do you want?" the butcher barked at a woman ahead of me.

"I'll take a kilo of that red sausage there."

"Which red sausage? Make up your mind!"

"I can't see the label. That one, you know—"

"It's not up to me to read your mind!"

The woman behind me interceded.

"She wants some of that Kazanskaya brand."

The butcher yanked a hank of sausage out of the moldy display case, whacked at it with her cleaver, hurled it onto her scale, and barked, "Five thousand rubles. To the cashier." She shoved a chit at the woman, who scurried mincingly off to the cashier. The woman paid, then scurried back, handed in the chit, and the butcher slammed her sausage down in front of her.

My turn came, but as I stepped up to the counter the butcher charged off.

I waited. The other employee averted her eyes. The crowd began grumbling.

"Uncultured apes! Always the same!"

"These people don't know how to work!"

"I would file a complaint, but who listens nowadays!"

As they continued their litany of rancor I drifted in thought back to the trip I made around the U.S.S.R. in 1985. In those days the situation was markedly worse: outside Moscow and Leningrad few towns had stores with meat, and in some even butter was a rarity. The lines were the same, with the same angry characters, the same verbiage uttered in the same belligerent tones. Twelve years on so little has changed outside the capital. This was all truly saddening, and I felt myself giving in to the hopelessness that afflicts so many Russians now.

The butcher finally stomped back to her place. I got my sausage and left as another altercation erupted in line. Outside, a pair of militiamen were dragging a hapless trader out of his kiosk, demanding to see his license; three hearty peasant women with smiles of gold teeth were lugging sacks of beets down the lane to the market nearby. They were laughing—and making the best of it.

Jeffrey Tayler is a freelance writer based in Moscow. He has written on Transylvania, Siberia, and Zaire for The Atlantic Monthly, *and contributes regularly to* Atlantic Unbound.

Foie Gras Dreams

When ignorance is bliss, 'tis folly to be wise.

IT IS 45 MINUTES TO DINNER. MY HUSBAND, ARNOLD, AND I ARE standing ankle deep in French muck—beige and runny like potter's slip-glaze, but startlingly acrid to our noses—confronting a moral dilemma. Our host, Madame Etchegoyan, has just removed her feeding funnel from duck No. 13. She is persuading her flock to turn their brown, normal livers into pale, engorged, exquisite-tasting giants—the very same ambrosial, melt-in-the-mouth foie gras that we had sampled at her dinner table the evening before.

That's when we had arrived, unannounced, at 6 P.M. looking for lodgings outside the dot-sized Basque town of Arhansus. Unruffled, she showed us a room on the first floor, at the back of her large farmhouse, then asked us not whether we wanted dinner, but at what time. We liked her at once; here was a woman who understood from our ravenous but droopy appearance that we needed large quantities of good food but didn't want to go searching to find it. She wanted only to verify our foreign palates: Foie gras? *Garbure*? Confit? A *oui* to each segued into a nationalities guessing game: Were we *Anglais*? *Allemands*? *Irlandais*? Her teenage son offered *Australians*? Then they ran out of countries. Americans had never visited this remote spot in the

Pyrenees before. Astonished but delighted, she welcomed us into her home.

At the family dinner, we were launched into food lover's heaven on the first sublime morsel of fattened duck liver. It was difficult, even with faltering French and full mouth, to curtail our praise. Monsieur Etchegoyan beamed and boasted, *"Maison fait!"*—made right there, by Madame. We quit raving about the foie gras only long enough to devour the rest of the meal: rich regional vegetable soup, preserved duck with tiny fried potatoes, baby garden salad, farm cheese, crêpes—everything *"maison fait,"* everything delicious. While we stuffed ourselves, we fielded questions about hamburgers and handguns and interrogated them on foie gras making. How was it done? How could anything as common as a duck's liver taste this exalted? Their vague responses succeeded only in conjuring up visions of Madame E. endlessly dipping into her apron and tossing zillions of handfuls of corn to exceptionally hungry, exceedingly lucky ducks.

Dinner done at midnight, with bellies bursting, we were unconscious within moments in our room facing the chicken coops. But the fowl noises and smells must have contaminated some echoing snippets of our mealtime conversation, producing for me a vivid and unsettling dream. I saw my own mother—her Bronx accent eerily French—metamorphosed into a Basque harridan who nudged and crammed her skinny ducklings with more than they could possibly hold. She began softly, with encouraging coaxing, clucking noises. When that failed, she cried out—how often I'd heard this—"Babies are starving all over the world and you do not like my cooking?" This guilt trip worked magic on the dream ducks, just as it used to on me: willingly, they ate and they ate until their little livers puffed and ballooned and began to explode, like dried corn in a hot pan, in front of my closed eyes. I opened them—smiling with relief when I heard only the chickens clucking and pecking outside our windows.

The following morning, Monsieur E., his teenage son, and his farmer brother joined us at the breakfast table. Innocently, we opted for the same meal the men were served daily—an option that has since replaced the word "continental" with "monumental" whenever I think of French breakfasts. We each ate a fried farm egg, house-made Bayonne ham (rubbed with local peppers from nearby Espelette), house-cured bacon and an entire baguette (which the Basques held against their chests to slice). A carafe of strong coffee was placed between my husband and me, alongside a juice pitcher of boiled raw milk. The men also had large pitchers in front of them, but these contained red wine, which they polished off, one juice glass at a time.

Madame E. took only tea. Finished with her morning chores, she sat with us and talked foie gras. We learned she fed 60 ducks at a time during a two-week fattening process. The feed, 100 kilos (220 pounds) of corn and one cup of salt, was pressure-cooked, by her—*maison fait* again!—every morning. Methodically, the daily feedings were increased: ten ounces, morning and evening, on Day 1; three and a third pounds, morning and evening, by Day 14.

What appetites these birds had! Curiosity overpowering us, we finally asked to watch how this sublime delicacy was achieved. Madame, to our surprise, looked reluctant, but Monsieur beamed once more and complemented me on my use of precisely the right word. He said it was the delicacy of her touch in feeding the ducks that made them eat much more than others—himself included— could persuade them to. (I surveyed our breakfast plates and worried for our own livers; were we incubating two more sitting ducks for Madame E.'s rich foods and delicate insistence?) Arrangements were made to observe that evening's feeding.

We arrive in the duck barn promptly at 7 P.M. There is a waist-high open platform divided into two back-to-back rows of 30 individual wire cages from which 60 duck heads protrude. On the floor, under each animal, is a mountain of putty-like guano almost reaching the cage wires. The smell is revolting. Madame E., garbed in a large plastic apron, has just begun but is already splattered— face, arms, apron—with streaks of this putty. An overhead track runs the length of the platform; attached to it, dangling from a bungee-like cord, is a feeding funnel with an 18-inch shaft. Madame E. grabs a head and deftly inserts the tube into the open

beak in one double-quick move. The end of the spout is somewhere deep inside the bird. She plops a huge amount of feed—it
is almost Day 14—into the cone, then hits a switch. The funnel
vibrates noisily as the food is mechanically pushed through it, into
the gut of the duck. The tube is removed; the animal is dazed,
immobilized, barely alive. I think, "What nasty business I'm watching." My face must reflect this. Madame looks up and quietly
echoes my thought. "*C'est méchant, non?*" Then she moves delicately down the line.

A duck is four months old at the end of this frenzy. Madame E.
inserts a kitchen knife into the beak and slits the roof of the
mouth. She removes the liver, keeps it and the bird on ice, hoses
and disinfects the barn and personally delivers her product. The
grossly enlarged, creamy-yellow liver weighs between one and two
pounds and will grace some of the region's finest menus.

Foie gras is the supreme fruit of gastronomy and Madame E.
produces the choicest fruit on the vine. She keeps only 10 livers,
but as many as 60 ducks a year for family eating. The livers are too
dear to withhold more; their tasty incubators are more affordable.
The following day she ushers 60 new birds into her barn.

In the fantasies of a foolish, squeamish American, foie gras making was a Walt Disney production with folksy overtones. The
reality is harsh. But delicate Madame E. understands her business
very well; a farmer's life just doesn't happen to be a dream.

She moves down the line. We leave the barn to prepare for
dinner.

Melinda Bergman Burgener is a writer who lives in San Francisco.

DEREK PECK

High on the Mountain

It all depends on what you've ingested.

FIRST THERE IS A MOUNTAIN, THEN THERE IS NO MOUNTAIN. WE have been driving upward all day and have just penetrated a thick white layer of clouds, sealing off the rest of the world below, when suddenly the words from the 1968 Donovan song make sense to me. At first there was a mountain, and now there is just Huautla, a Mazatec Indian village on steep lush slopes, dampened by mist and rain, and isolated not just by distance, but by natural powers of concealment.

Given what I know of the strange and magical history of the place, it seems perfectly right to me, and as we continue into the town itself, I am filled with a sense of occult expectation. But when we get off the bus, my Australian travel companion Carlos and I are greeted only by a jovial Indian man in his mid-30s, wearing dirty pants and scruffy leather sandals and smiling optimistically, who offers to lead us to a room. Eduardo, as he introduces himself, brings out our good humor more than our mystical awe. But then, as we're trudging up inclined alleyways and steep, winding dirt trails, he suddenly turns and asks, "So you are here to eat the sacred *hongos?*"

I tell him we haven't decided yet, and he nods understandingly, then adds: "Anyway, I will bring you to a shaman."

Eduardo leads us inside a small compound of houses. There is an old woman who he says is the shaman, or *currandera*. Two of her teenage grandchildren greet us and immediately start pattering about mushrooms and a nice place to sleep—a package deal for a good price. It seems a number of Mazatec families have gotten into the business of hosting pseudo *veladas*, as the mushroom-taking ceremonies are known, in order to make a few extra bucks off the occasional gringo seeker before he can locate a real shaman. Politely, we look at the room, then say we'd prefer to be in the center of town. Though he has missed the chance to make a commission, Eduardo is gracious enough to walk us to a hotel. Along the way I ask him if he ever takes mushrooms himself. He says, "Yes, but only when I'm sick. So I can go to the other side and heal myself."

Carlos and I look at each other quizzically. Such a strange idea: tripping when you're sick. In our culture you trip when you're well, to feel even better. The idea of taking hallucinogenic mushrooms when you've got a high fever makes us laugh, though it is precisely this approach that put Huautla on the map.

That history began in the mid-1950s, when Huautla was still about as remote as a place can be. Located high in Mexico's Sierra Madre del Sur, about 250 miles southeast of Mexico City, it took ten hours just to make the 38-mile journey from the bottom of the mountain to the top. Nevertheless, two Westerners made their way to the village. They were R. Gordon Wasson and Allan Richardson. Wasson was vice president of J. P. Morgan Co., the huge banking firm, and Richardson was a New York fashion photographer. The two men wanted to know more about Mazatec spiritual and curative practices, which were said to center on ingesting sacred, vision producing mushrooms, called *teonanacatl* ("flesh of the gods") by the Indians. Succeeding in their quest, Wasson and Richardson participated in an all-night ceremony led by María Sabina, the local *currandera* who subsequently became a cult figure; they were the first outsiders ever to experience the sacred *teonanacatl*.

Subsequently Wasson returned with his wife and the Swiss

chemist Dr. Albert Hoffman, the inventor of LSD, to record a sacred *velada*. Hoffman had isolated the active alkaloids in the mushrooms, psilocybin and psilobin, and wanted to see how synthetic
capsules would stack up against the mushrooms. After the ceremony, Sabina declared that they contained the same spirit. Wasson
also published an account of his experiences in *Life* magazine in
1957. Today, that article is considered by many as the catalyst that
kicked off the Psychedelic Revolution, giving Huautla a key—if
unwitting—influence on 1960s and '70s pop culture.

In the years that followed, Sabina received a long procession of
the era's most important rock 'n' roll musicians, writers, poets and
counterculture personalities, including Donovan, Bob Dylan,
Timothy Leary, the Rolling Stones, Peter Townshend and, most fa-
mously, the Beatles. John, Paul, George, and Ringo are said to have
arrived by helicopter in 1968 as part of Ringo's birthday celebration. They took part in a sacred night ceremony with Sabina, at her
home in El Fortín, at the top of the mountain just outside of town.
Legend has it that during the *velada* Sabina warned John that she
saw a vision of a gun pointed at him.

By 1969, hundreds of hippies had swarmed into the small mountain village, crowding the square and open spaces with makeshift
encampments. Locals who remember say that the hippies often be-
haved badly, tripping freely in public—disrespecting the age-old
ritual of the *teonanacatl*—not only on mushrooms but on LSD, and
also defecating and fornicating with apparently no reserve.

It didn't take long for the Mazatecan and Mexican authorities
to grow weary of what they saw as a grotesque display of
American youth immorality, and by the early '70s the military had
driven the hippies out and set up checkpoints at the foot of the
mountain, thus ending the Magical Mushroom Tour.

Today, Huautla is still relatively unknown to the travelers who
visit Mexico's southern state of Oaxaca. In recent years the town
has prospered and grown substantially through coffee cultivation,
yet it is still picturesque, with winding streets and crooked net-
works of stairs that connect it vertically, and breath-stopping views
of lushly foliated hills and mist-shrouded mountaintops.

On our first night in town, Carlos and I step out to the corner *comedor* for dinner and end up watching Game Four of the NBA Championships—remote as Huautla is, satellite receivers still point skyward from numerous tin rooftops. Later, as we return to our hotel across the town square-cum-outdoor basketball court—the same town square that once housed throngs of hippies—we're challenged to a game of one-on-two by a young Mazatec. The court is dark, except for some light that shifts in from a nearby building and a generous moon. And although we are much taller and change every few points so we can catch our breath in this altitude, the kid's jumps defy gravity and he apparently has infrared vision, too; he beats us handily, 10-2, and sends us home sucking air.

The next day we get up early and hike to El Fortín. It's a long hike that mostly follows the course of a winding road past the outskirts of town and myriad scenes of rural Mexican life. There are dirty children playing alongside the dusty road; men butchering a freshly slaughtered steer; women carrying heavy loads on their heads, or sitting in front of their shack-like houses with a basket of mangoes to sell and their breasts given out to hungry mouths.

The higher we walk, the more spectacular—almost aerial—views we get of Huautla, seemingly floating in mist, and the deep ravine that drops off to its side. On the last stretch to El Fortín, we cut through a coffee grove and follow a crooked dirt trail to the top. There we meet with Filogonio Garcia, the grandson of María Sabina and current practitioner of the family tradition. In fact, according to local belief, he's the direct inheritor of her formidable mystical gifts.

When he enters the hut where Carlos and I are waiting, I'm immediately held by his dark, lucent stare. Although he's in his 50s, he doesn't look a day over 35, with shiny coffee-brown skin and black, short-cropped hair. He takes a seat facing us and smiles.

First I tell him that I've come to learn about the sacred mushrooms and his grandmother, and he kindly allows me to peruse his own archive, which contains old books and photographs. In one book I glimpse the quote: "The sacred mushroom ceremony brings about a direct confrontation with the sacred world that obliges us to reevaluate all our concepts of the universe and of man." Hmm. This is definitely not just for fun.

Later, after answering more of my questions, Filogonio says: "But if you want to know the mushrooms, you have to eat the mushrooms."

I look to Carlos, who gives a slight, affirmative nod. So I ask Filogonio if a ceremony is possible. For a price, of course, it is. (Charging for a ceremony is one way in which the tradition has changed due to contact with outsiders.) Then he tells us we should abstain from smoking, drinking, and sex, and come to see him again the following night, just before midnight, with reverence in our hearts.

The history of the mushroom tradition, of course, goes back much further than María Sabina, at least to about 1000 B.C., according to archaeologists. This date is based on pre-Columbian stone artifacts that have been discovered in the Mayan highland zone, stretching from the grassy highlands of western Guatemala to the piney mountains of Mexico, in southern Chiapas state. Roughly hewn and generally measuring about a foot high, the stones, which resemble mushrooms and have been dubbed "the mushroom stones" by archaeologists, are thought to be linked to religious mushroom cults that were found in Mexico at the time of the Spanish conquest.

Sixteenth-century chroniclers wrote extensively of the Aztecs' religious practices, which included sacred mushroom-taking for the purposes of divination, receiving visions, meeting the divine, and expelling evil spirits. The most important of these chroniclers was the Franciscan friar Bernardino de Sahagun, whose famous codex, "A General History of the Things of New Spain," written between 1529 and 1590, contains this description: "And they ate mushrooms with honey…There was dancing, there was weeping. Some saw in a vision that they would die in war. Some saw…that they would be devoured by wild beasts. Some saw in a vision that they would become rich…buy slaves…Some saw…that they would perish in the water. Some saw...that they would pass to tranquillity in death...All such things they saw."

Of course, this posed a problem for the Catholic Church, for there were remarkable parallels between the Indians' *teonanacatl* and the Christian sacrament of Holy Communion. Both the mushrooms and the Eucharist were believed to be the symbolic body of God. But whereas in the Catholic tradition one's communion with God is largely a matter of faith and affiliation with the established religious order, for the Indians who ate *teonanacatl* it was a real, immediate, and direct communication with God. Accordingly, every measure was taken to extinguish the cult.

To a large degree these measures were successful—but in pockets the *teonanacatl* practice did survive, due mainly to the remoteness of the regions where it was practiced, the blending of Christian beliefs into the cult, and the efforts of some practitioners to make the rites secret.

Sabina was the woman who finally revealed those rites. It's said she saw in a vision that outsiders would come to her asking about the mushrooms and that she was to share their sacrament with them. But she paid for this: her family home of several generations was burned to the ground and she was banished from the town.

Relocating to El Fortín—which would become nearly synonymous with Huautla and Sabina herself; as Donovan sang in his song "Mellow Yellow," "I'm just mad about Fortín. Fortín's mad about me"—Sabina finished her life redeemed in the village's eyes. Today she is regarded as something of a saint, and in home shrines throughout the town, I saw photographs of her simultaneously dark and luminous face hanging alongside that of the Holy Virgin.

Sabina began her relationship with the sacred mushrooms at the age of twelve. Her father, grandfather and great-grandfather were all shamans, yet she was considered by the Mazatecs to possess extraordinary powers even beyond her favorable pedigree. She once explained her gift in these words: "There is a world beyond ours, and that is where God lives...a world where everything has already happened and everything is known. That world talks. It has a language of its own. I report what it says. The sacred mushroom takes me by the hands and brings me to the world where everything is known."

The next night we arrive at El Fortín about ten minutes before the witching hour. Filogonio greets us and asks, "Your hearts are open?" After we tell him they are, he takes us inside the temple, a small adobe room set back behind his house, containing a prominent altar with bountiful images of Jesus and the Virgin and alight with burning candles. The room is filled with the scent of sweet copal incense. We take off our shoes and sit down on two straw mats that have been laid on the smooth, patted clay floor.

Filogonio now stands at the altar, which is also adorned with statuettes of pre-Columbian gods and bouquets of fresh flowers, and recites a prayer blessing the mushrooms, which I see are arranged on banana leaves. Then he turns and walks toward us, putting down two small clay bowls on each mat. One is filled with the fresh mushrooms, the other half-filled with honey. He blesses us, blowing copal from the coals over our faces and bodies, and encourages us to eat.

I dip the mushrooms in the honey and plop them into my mouth. I'm pleased by the sweetness of the honey, which mellows the natural bitterness of the mushrooms.

Filogonio, who has blown out all the candles except for one that he sets now on the floor, sits cross-legged facing us and begins eating his portion, which looks about twice the size of ours. Carlos looks at me as if to say, Oh, man, we're definitely not in Kansas anymore. It's the last sober communication between us for the next six hours.

Once we've all finished eating, Filogonio blows out the last candle, leaving us in complete darkness. He instructs us to lie down on our backs, then starts chanting and singing, brushing our faces with an eagle feather and flowers. The chants are beautiful and eerie; I'm not lulled by them, and am honest-to-God wondering at this point if it's still not too late to run.

But the effects of the mushrooms soon begin, and I'm washed over by an intense euphoria that makes me lose the concept that there's any other place than here. Next I'm overcome by extreme giddiness and laugh uncontrollably. Carlos is too. I can hear him, but can't see him in the dark. Perhaps because of the serious spiritual atmosphere, that stage passes quickly and next I feel enclosed in a complex labyrinth of colorful, geometrically shaped patterns. I marvel at their intricacy and beauty and think for a moment that I must be brilliant. Then I pass through this and find myself in an ancient city, a place that feels familiar. I realize that I've visited this place often in my dreams and have never been able to hold onto it—and now here I am walking freely amid the classical architecture, huge pillars and arches and pink marble corridors. I have the distinct impression that I'm traveling, going through layers of— what? consciousness? memory? reality? And even more astounding, Filogonio is right there, leading me.

By now I'm completely inert, but traveling faster than I ever imagined possible. Fabulous scene after fabulous scene appears before me, one melting into the other like the patterns of a kaleidoscope that form and transform from the same raw material. At times I'm aware of Filogonio's singing (and when I am it seems like I can understand it), though mostly I just soar inward through these various magical worlds.

Later, once we have started to descend, we get up and dance around the room together as Filogonio still chants, Carlos and I seemingly inhabited by Mazatec spirits. To end the ceremony we all sit in a circle holding hands in silence. Then Filogonio tells us what he saw, about our life, our character, our future, our past.

As we leave, Filogonio shakes our hands and says, "We are all now brothers of God as known through *teonanacatl*." Holding onto his hand, I look into his eyes, dark and lucent still. The corners of his mouth crack in smile, and I feel he is looking through me, with more wisdom than I will ever know.

First there was a mountain, then there was no mountain. Soft gray clouds fill the valley once again and we are silent, walking down the trail in purple morning light.

The next day, back on earth, I'm sitting in the Cafeteria María Sabina, a small *comedor* located next door to the Hotel Olympico above the market. The proprietor, an old Mazatec woman named

Josephina Diaz, after serving Carlos and me, sits down at the long banquet-style table with us. She moves slowly, like a woman who has spent too much time on her feet, for too many years. But although she looks physically tired, there is a certain lively sparkle in her eyes and I can tell that she's enjoying this opportunity to sit and chat with a couple of travelers from far away. After telling her where we're from, the conversation turns to mushrooms.

I try to follow her with my rough Spanish, Spanish that I'd believed myself fluent in the night before, as she meanders on, zigzagging like the road that runs down these mountains.

Carlos leans back lazily with his beer, only asking for occasional translations. I tell him bits as I can fit them in, because the words keep flowing from her mouth even as I talk to him, in a steady, unexcitable flow. I imagine that I'm listening to Gabriel García Márquez's grandmother tell the most fabulous stories without ever changing her voice.

She describes men going into the earth, flying down through it on wings. And speaks of shamans so powerful they can sit down comfortably with the gods, as if they were chatting over coffee.

She says that Sabina was the most powerful shaman Huautla has had in many generations, and that no one is her equal today—not even Filogonio.

Carlos wants to know if she thinks there is anyone in Mexico, not just Huautla, who might be as powerful as Sabina once was. It's an unanswerable question, I know, but I assume he wants to ask it just to see her response, and so I translate. She shrugs her shoulders and then, without changing her voice, answers me with unassailable logic: "If there is," she says, "they know who they are."

Derek Peck is currently living in San Cristobal de las Casas, Mexico, where he is working on a novel.

★ ★ ★

Hearts Get Broken

Eat your sorrows.

PEOPLE'S HEARTS GET BROKEN EVERY DAY, DON'T THEY? HOW many times have I listened to other people's tears; me with all the answers? I stop to pick up stray bits of Kleenex from the floor, wash dirty dishes, try to feel organized, try not to agonize. An effort to put the brain in neutral, to carry on through regular activities as if nothing is wrong. I eat the same thing for breakfast that I had for dinner the night before, except now it's cold. Cold pizza, day old. The funny thing is that it doesn't make any difference, I've reached my saturation point, where I'm impervious to everything. Numb. Frozen hands, dry eyes. Here's when I become truly dangerous, when I begin to be past caring. It's amazing how much abuse the human heart can take and still keep beating, still keep pumping that vital fluid to all those organs to keep this organism alive. Yes, keep breathing. Right now I feel as if: why bother?

It's Labor Day, and a friend and I decide to go outdoors to barbeque. Consoling ourselves with purchases: candles, matches, string. We've chosen meat for our meal and as I unwrap the steaks from their pristine white wrappers I feel a strange, bloody thrill. Before me they lie, awaiting my attentions. There's something utterly sexual about the texture and sound made as I slap them with the steak knife, patting the herbs and seasonings into their flesh. Exchanging smiles, my friend and I. Laughing a little too loudly. We pour red wine over them, baptizing and bloodying them further. More prodding, more tenderizing. Ah yes, they are a most lovely shade of red. The fire is ready; as I put them on the grill I realize this is a meal of vengeance. It's your flesh that I'm burning, our love I've seasoned so well and now commit to the fire, first one side and then the other. Me, the person who believed you were the one and only. Me, the woman who felt she had made the ultimate commitment. Closing my eyes, I inhale the smoke with anticipation. I realize my heart's pounding and this causes me to swallow…swallow back the saliva. Swallow back my vicious appetite. But I'm smiling now as I watch the meat blacken; as I smell it cooking I fantasize about it's flavor. How will it feel as I chew it, as I swallow the warm juices? It has become my feast of triumph: we toast ourselves. Our glasses clink with a clear, musical sound. I'm only mildly disappointed as I cut into my steak that it isn't as tender as I'd imagined it. For it's your heart's blood that I see before me, forming a pool on my plate as it runs down my chin.

Mishell Erickson is a native Californian who lives in the San Francisco Bay Area. She has written poetry and prose since she was a child and now focuses on reading it aloud in the cafés and saloons of San Francisco and Berkeley. Currently she is preparing a spicy collection of poems entitled "Kiss and Tell" and continuing her study of the romantic arts.

CLIO TARAZI

⋆ ⋆ ⋆

Alexandria Sweet

*Drama and ritual, and the tastes
of life and death.*

AMERICA IS A LIFETIME OF JOURNEYS FOR A FOREIGNER. A SERIES
of journeys that continually take you to the place you came from
and bring you to your destiny, right here in America. Journeys that
make you pine for a distant place and another time but once
America has you she will not release you to your past. I constantly
make these journeys; daily commonplace events, sensations and
emotions are subtle reminders of the two worlds that I live in, but
the big events such as birth, marriage, and death are jolting reminders of the contrasting worlds. While attending an American
funeral with my elderly mother, I had to try to explain the
American rituals that I did not understand.

I am a Greek from Alexandria, Egypt. Greeks and Egyptians
combined probably have had 10,000 years to perfect the symbols
and traditions of death. America's death traditions have pieces of
various cultures, but basically death does not have the prominence
it has for Greeks. Death in America is not nurtured in the same way
with specific tastes, traditions, and tales. Even the words American
people say to each other in death are not prescribed. They are individual and spontaneous, hence the feeling of awkwardness.
Traditions provide clarity for the mourners and the family of the

deceased, they tell you that you are doing the right thing. The lack of a common tradition creates a feeling of awkwardness and social clumsiness that is often articulated by avoiding funerals and memorials, or a common feeling of triteness with language.

The traditions of the Greeks, the words that are prescribed, the foods, the clothing all make you feel like you are doing the right thing and take away the awkwardness of death. The focus of much of the tradition around death among the Greeks, as you may have guessed, are around food. The food and traditions of death are vivid reminders of the cultural differences, the cultures of the past and the America of the future. Greek food for funerals is very special and full of symbolism. In Greek culture death must have its special tastes. In America the food is everyday, people gather to eat, but the food has no symbols, it is everyday fare. The focus is on the living and not the dead. Everyone admits the service and gathering are for the living in America, in Greece it's about doing the right thing on the dead person's behalf.

My first experience of American death was at the funeral of an elderly man in suburban San Francisco. I went to the funeral with my mother, the official carrier of all the traditions of life and death in our family. My mother had a comfort around the tragic and happy events. We knew it would be different but we did not expect all the differences we encountered. I was glad to be with her, she would know the right things. But what were the right things in America?

The service started out in a church, a Protestant church. People wearing pastel colors. Not the required all black clothing of a funeral. I certainly knew the historical and philosophical differences among the Protestants, Catholics, and the Orthodox Christians but physically being in a Protestant church was a shock. The bare walls and ceiling, the air smelled barren as well, no layers of incense from the years of services. A podium and not a nave. I am not religious—as a matter of fact my family has been anti-religion for generations—but how can you rebel against something that has no visuals? The minister wore street clothes with the most subtle of collars, no robes, no beard, no rings, no melodic chanting with cantors, no large evangelion (new testament) covered in gold, just a small regular size black covered bible.

The deceased was in the coffin, the coffin was closed. My mother asked why it was closed. I did not know why. She asked "Don't we go up and kiss the dead one good-bye?" Obviously not, he stays hidden in the box. So, my mother wanted to know, "How do we know he is in there?" Why should we not see him dead was her question as well as mine. How do you ask that of the family? How is even that an option? In a Greek service the coffin is open and the mourners line up and each one says their good-byes and everyone kisses the deceased good-bye. The service was short. The family's cries were muffled and restrained. The music was a Pete Seeger song, my mother and I looked at each other in surprise. There was no *kolyva*.

Kolyva is the most symbolic and sacred of foods. After the long Greek church service, the good-byes to the deceased, either at the church or the graveside the mourners are served *kolyva*. *Kolyva* is the sweet symbol of life served upon a death to the people who come to the funeral. Wheat is the main ingredient, whole wheat a symbol of the Resurrection: "Unless the grain of wheat falls into the earth and dies, it remains alone, but if it dies it bears much fruit." *John 12:24*. As children we share in the secret delight of the taste of *kolyva*.

Women, from ancient times, in Greece are responsible for all the death rituals. *Kolyva* is prepared by old women, grandmas or *thias* (aunts). In America, usually the contact with a *kolyva* maker is made through the church. In Greece or other places where Greeks live, adults seem to know who those women are and how they can be contacted. Once the order is placed on the day of the funeral the *kolyva* appears.

Kolyva is boiled whole wheat that is sweetened with raisins and sugar and spiced with cinnamon, cloves, and nutmeg. The wheat is boiled like rice until it is really soft and mixed with the sugar and spices. The mixture is placed on a silver platter in the shape of a mound. The mound is then covered with powdered sugar and decorated with silver Jordan almonds. Usually the silver Jordan

almonds are shaped into a cross. All during the funeral the anticipation is unbearable. The tears, the prayers, the incense all are
worth the small cup of *kolyva* that the priest gives everyone as they
leave. The *kolyva* takes away the awkwardness and the need to re-
define the ritual. Everyone knows and expects the *kolyva* to be part
of death. It sweetens the pain, it makes it part of life. As you take
the *kolyva* you say, "Life to the living, may God forgive the deceased soul and may his memory be eternal." You don't always say
all three things, I never knew when you say one or the other or all
three, I just followed my mother's cues.

The children at funerals eat the *kolyva* greedily and ask for more
and adults will give up their share with a wink and smile: children
are allowed greed in Greek families even at the time of death.
There were no children at the American funeral, they explained to
me that funerals are not appropriate for children. My mother and
I wondered how will the children learn how to act in a funeral,
how will they become adult mourners, when will their time come
that they just cannot come to funerals with the sole purpose of
eating *kolyva*. When will they learn how to say the right things?
"Life to the living" and "May God forgive the dead person's soul"
and cross yourself at all the right passages in the service, or at least
pick out the old man or woman to copy. But there were no specific things to say and there was no specific place to cross yourself
in the service. No one crossed themselves.

Forty days after the funeral *kolyva* is served again, and at each
anniversary, at all souls day, and if you hang out at graveyards you
can always get some. The only concern I have with talking about
kolyva to outsiders is that most likely a vegan cook could take it
and make it into a healthy dessert that will appear at a Berkeley
health food store, with a small sign describing how good it is for
you and a disconnection from its past and meaning. Touting the
whole grain benefits and the lack of dairy products. And I will be
responsible for giving away the secret of *kolyva*.

After the burial we went to the widow's house. Once again my
mother and I did not know what to expect. I tried to understand

the differences in my liberal way. My mother was outraged. We were both surprised. The house was cheerful, the pictures and mirrors were not covered with black cloth, the TV and music were playing. My mother crossed herself and muttered, "May Christ forgive them." I tried to argue with my mother that maybe mourning does not encompass all the sadness and self-denial that we Greeks impose on the living and maybe this is a better way to do things. She would have no part of it. I was once again torn by the sensations of the past and traditions and the total shedding of my known rules. I wished that I had not brought her, that the contrasts would not be so obvious. If I were alone I could just think of them and pretend to fit in. Now she who always made me comfortable, my mother, was making me uncomfortable.

A table was filled with potluck type foods that various people brought. A ham, macaroni salad, potato salad, carrot-and-raisin salad, fruit salad, and a gigantic green Jell-O mold. I think the Jell-O undid my mother. The fact that the Jell-O was so green, so cheerful and so disconnected from the past. She kept asking how come they eat Jell-O, that could not be a long standing tradition, Jell-O is new. The drink was punch, Hawaiian Punch, sweet and manufactured, no wine or cognac. No one cried, wailed, or laughed.

My mother and I remembered how on the day of the death the traditional foods begin and how the food is the responsibility of the family, not of others to produce. On the day of the death, the big pots come out and the search for the appropriate fish for soup starts. God forbid that the male who goes to procure the fish come back with the wrong fish. What the right fish is, or for that matter the right anything in a Greek family, is a secret of the mother never to be told or articulated. The father's job is to spend a lifetime searching to please the mother. The number of times my father was told the butcher or vegetable salesman cheated him I would not start to count. And why did he continue to go shopping and then get yelled at for his gullibility and or blindness? I cannot explain. While at home my mother would ponder what stupidity he would bring home today.

The fish arrives and is cleaned and made whole into a soup, more of a clear broth with only onions, carrots, and celery with some rice. Plain stuff. My mother violated the rules by taking the boiled fish meat and serving it with the most delicious homemade mayonnaise decorated with lots of fresh vegetables: carrots, beets, green onions, and of course capers. The house smells of fish soup. I cannot smell fish soup without thinking someone died. My mother always seemed to have this drive to make the soup, between her mourning and sadness, if the soup was not made, that somehow we were not doing right by the dead. This is part of the Greek tradition of making the women responsible for the death rituals. From preparing the body, to arranging the funeral, to making the food. In America, only the food preparation is left to the women.

At the house after the funeral the mourners arrive to eat fish, again, but the main thing is the *paximadia,* a Greek biscotti, with Mavrodafni, a sweet red wine or cognac. *Paximadia* again are made by those old ladies that make the *kolyva*. Mavrodafni you find in any Greek store. Mavrodafni is very sweet and very red, basically the Greek communion wine. The *paximadia* being dry and the wine sweet must be symbolic of the body of Christ, or if I know my ancestors, it's probably some pagan symbol sanitized for Christianity. Most Americans cringe at the taste of Mavrodafni. We like it, it's like gulping communion without having had to fast for a week. It's the Greek secret handshake.

The mourners cluster. The widow or main mourner is surrounded and greeted by everyone as they come in. Usually each new person brings a somber greeting, hugs and kisses. "Life to the living" again. As each person comes in, the widow's crying dissipates, then everyone starts remembering the funny things about the dead person. People find themselves going from belly laughs to wailing and crying. This can go on for hours. I remember one funeral as a child, where the widow would every so often wail: "The column of my house is gone, the temple will crumble." The man was about 120 pounds, 5'2". The mourners would each take turns exaggerating the man's stature and commenting on the crumbling condition of the temple. At my father's funeral, we the children and my mother could not stay very serious, each new mourner would remember my father's exploits and laugh along with the rest of us. As a new one came in we had to control ourselves, then we would let them into the laughter. But we kept the dead person in our midst with memories. My surprise was how everyone avoided talk of the deceased at the American funeral. How the gathering was like any other gathering in suburban America and how people did not kiss each other or mourn.

Each death reminds us that our turn is coming. But yet it feels like in America nobody wants it to be special, and they don't want to be reminded of our own mortality. Death is made an everyday thing. Simple and without drama. But death is drama and ritual. And through the drama and ritual we struggle to cope with it and to learn how to accept its inevitable nature.

America is driven by its own tradition and mythology. A tradition of control and individuality. Control of your life and destiny. Individuality in not having prescribed traditions to adhere to and give yourself some comfort. If you believe that you control your life how could you accept the inevitability of death. The mythology exists that somehow you will live forever and that death is not in your future. Hence, you leave death in a distant place and take away its special rites. Each culture that came to America brought its death traditions and slowly shed them for a new standard that does not focus on the death or the mourning. It is logical, cool and collected, controlled. No pagan rituals, no room for crying or laughter. No room for satire or for the sheer joy, of "Hey, we are still alive, that sucker is dead, who knows when we will go?"

So many of the mourners told me they felt awkward at funerals, not knowing what to say, or having the feeling that anything they said felt trite. I thought how terrible, instead of feeling the sadness of the death, each and every mourner had to contemplate his awkwardness. Worrying about being awkward instead of feeling the loss. Traditions give us the rules, take away the awkwardness, and allow us to grieve for the dead person instead of worrying about our situation. The rituals remind us that death is with us always. The lack of ritual makes death feel like it will not come for us, that there is no continuity in life and death. And each time we encounter it, it's a strange new experience.

Greeks seem to have a special food for each occasion, many of the connections for other occasions have been* lost through the years, but the food connected with death is still strongly connected to the collective Greek memory. At the American funeral the food was everyday food: potato salad, ham, Jell-O salads, and chocolate cake. It felt strange and antiseptic without symbols or traditions. How do we know that we are not angering those who control such things? As the years pass, I see Greeks in America shedding some of the traditions, except the food. The food of Greek death has a sacred connection that we seem to not want to shed. I just hope my children will have the right food at my death.

Clio Tarazi works for the creation and preservation of affordable housing. She lives in Berkeley, California, with her two children.

★ ★ ★

A Seat at the Table

Is it tongue in cheek?

I BECAME A CANNIBAL ABOUT THREE WEEKS AFTER LOSING MY JOB as an accordion player at the Casanova Nightclub in downtown Damascus.

The first time I mentioned this incident, my listener was astonished.

"How come they fired you? You're not a bad accordion player," he said.

He obviously hadn't heard the "C-word." "Cannibalism" sounds like a morbid flatulence. Cannibalism, in fact, is Death's skeleton in the closet.

Anyhow, my friend had known me as a kid, when I loathed the accordion, but still played okay. So to him it seemed unlikely I would be fired, especially not in Damascus. And after all, it had been a pretty cushy gig.

Briefly, the job entailed playing each night from 9 P.M. to 1 A.M., with an illegal double-bass player from Somalia who was usually stoned on *qat,* but since he never learned how to actually tune his instrument, the drug was superfluous. Sometimes a drummer would turn up. He had learned his trade while studying dishwashing at the American Congregationalist school in Aleppo.

I would lead them in traditional wedding and bar mitzvah stuff, sometimes segueing into some Rossini overtures, Lawrence Welk polkas, and, if requested, the equivalent of a pop Arab tune from Oum Khaltoun, the Rosemary Clooney of the Arab world.

Whatever made the rich Arabs and their girlfriends or their rouged, kohl-eyed boyfriends jump up and dance was kosher in Damascus.

Anyhow, I wasn't really fired. I was "relieved" for vaguely political and religious reasons. Probably I would be there to this day if I hadn't been informed by Aram, my loveable fat Armenian boss, that I would die if I continued playing.

One afternoon, Aram came to my rented room in the *souk,* where I was feeling really good. A poet friend had won an award in Beirut, and he was showering those beautiful Syrian roses on all his friends, so I was adding some flowers to the basically bare quarters. I wasn't expecting visitors, but Aram was such a genial man that he was certainly welcome.

I guess he had puffed his way from the Casanova, and he was sweating and nervous. But since Aram had come to save my life, I gave him some orange juice and some *arak* and six glowing pink roses for his wife, and sat him down on one of the wicker chairs, and he gulped the juice and pushed the *arak* to the side, and came to the point.

"Harry, you know I don't give care about a person's religion," said Aram. I nodded.

"And I also know that you don't believe in God anyhow. But these damned people in the market, they do. They are religious. And the word going around the market is that you're…you're not the right religion. To be frank, they think you are Jewish."

"The People of the Book," I told him, "along with Muslims and Nazarenes."

"They think Jews are the people of the account book," he said. "Whether you are Jewish or not, it's not my business. To them, a Jewish accordion player is equivalent to an Israeli spy."

He continued quickly.

"So may I humbly suggest that you do not play your accordion any more in the Casanova? I hope you don't think that I'm taking sides with those…those soldiers and street people…."

Vaguely, I tried to picture Aram playing Bogart as Rick in *Casablanca*. The non-committal ideology was right, but the likeness was absurd. I couldn't even imagine myself as the movie's Sam. It was obvious when it came to accordions, I wouldn't be able to play it…to play it again.

I knew—and Aram knew—that in Damascus, I had squeezed my last box.

He made it even more clear. "Do you have a visa for Jordan?" he asked. "If not, I could arrange it."

I told him that I always had a Jordanian visa, that I would pack my rucksack (the squeezebox belonged to the nightclub), and that I would take a bus to the border.

"No," said this ever-generous man. "My driver will take you to the border. In case of any problems."

Aram also gave me about $30 in Jordanian money. "Thank you," I said. "Now I don't have to guess who's coming for dinar. It's me."

He looked sad, but it wasn't because of the pun. He felt almost ashamed.

"It isn't that I have any real fear," he said "But you never can tell.

I never saw Aram after that, and thought it prudent not to write to him. His driver picked me up on a dusty Toyota, and we made the dusty trip along what had been the Overland Desert Mail Service Route to the border, arriving about 11 P.M., when the usual Customs people were sleeping.

They were nice enough in a drowsy way, but one was curious about my origins. My hair, it seemed, looked…well, Semitic. But my name was hardly Middle Eastern.

"Oh, my father was Polish," I told him (thus the name), but my mother was Spanish (thus the kinky hair). I wanted to give that old chestnut about my sister never sure whether she was Carmen or Cohen, but decided against it. Especially since he embraced me and kissed me on both cheeks.

"You are Spanish. We also once had Spain. We are brothers."

He also wanted me to spend the night at the Customs post, since the desert area had wolves and "uncivilized Bedu people." But I wanted to get on. Anyhow, I enjoyed sleeping in the desert. The bedroll was warm, the evenings were freezing, and you could find stars never even imagined in any urban area.

A three-mile walk in that landscape was a mere jump away. And when I saw out in the fields, about a half-mile from the road, the greyish tents of the "uncivilized" Bedouin, I had no choice in those early days but to introduce myself.

The visit lasted three weeks, since one of the tribal leaders wanted to speak English. He also spoke Italian and some Hebrew, but was out of practice, so I was adopted and walked or camped with the Bedu.

The whole group consisted of about 70 families, the richer ones with camels, most of the others with mangy dogs and mangy sheep. The Rudolf Valentino picture of Bedouin life was romantic nonsense, of course. You get up in the morning, put coffee on the stove, giggle with the children, sit around, roll cigarettes from tobacco made of gunpowder, and walk around. Once we went to a town to sell some wool, but mainly it was camping for a few days, then walking a few miles.

The food was terrible. Essentially, it was weak coffee which became weaker as the week went on, since the Saturday beans were boiled up all week long until the following Friday. The other food consisted of Egyptian fava beans bought in the town, along with hard rice and bean sprouts. If lucky, a bit of yoghurt from camel milk, and some cumin and cardamom with the rice. Once in the two weeks, a piece of rabbit.

The one incident which altered life was the Incident of the Arab Thigh.

The Bedu had several minor chiefs, one of whom was Sheikh Abdulla. I hardly saw him, since he was in his tent most of the time, wheezing and coughing and lighting up his cigarette and wheezing and coughing again. He had one wife, a crone of about 45, I guess, and she would bring him in plates of rice. He would take a few bites, presumably, but a few minutes later, she would take out the platter and sit down with her kids and they would eat the rest.

One day, Sheikh Abdulla died. I knew that he had died, since the camels whinnied, the women feebly ululated, and the men sat around and moped in their coffee. I guess they were talking about him, but I didn't know what they had to say. Perhaps in his youth, he had been a great warrior, a magnificent stealer of sheep. But lately, he had been a nuisance.

Not having known the Sheikh, I went for a quiet walk in the hills. Perhaps I should have ruminated on the frailty of human existence, but I was cussing out the tribe, since they didn't even have any watery coffee.

Nonetheless, I put on a morbid face when returning, hoping they would think I was overcome with grief. Actually, nobody paid attention. The Sheikh's body was dumped in a makeshift wooden carton, and the tribe hoisted him up and walked him out to the hills. While I wondered whether to follow, I was obviously not "family," so stayed back with the women and camels, trying to find some coffee.

The men were out for about five hours, and I took it for granted they were offering prayers. After burying him, I guessed they would sit around, smoke, have some coffee (they had taken the beanbag with them), and then all would remain the same.

That night, instead of having dinner with my adopted clan, I was invited to sit with about fifteen clan leaders outside. A mat was set in front of all of us. Instead of the usual communal pot of beans and rice in the center, from which we would dip our fingers (no utensils were used), we were presented with plate-size pieces of cardboard, from the carton of fava beans which they had bought in Amman the month before.

On top of each "plate," used only on special occasions, was a dust-pale disc about the size of a large baby's fist.

Initially, I thought it might have been part of a jackal or a wolf or wild fox, which would have been a treat. But the shape was puzzling. I played innocent.

"Um…er…rabbit?" I asked my host. His English was learned with the British Army, and he was terse at the best of times.

"No," he said. "It is Abdulla. It is the Sheikh."

"Scuse??" I asked.

"It is Sheikh Abdulla. We take him inside us."

"Sorry?" I said, suspecting nothing. "I thought you had buried the Sheikh this morning."

"Yes, yes…" He was a bit impatient, but paused to give his explanation. "We have buried his body. But his…the piece behind…this we have carefully taken out. We have cut him *halal* style, so his blood ran out and the skin is pure. Then we cut it. And we give it to those in the tribe who we admire.

"And to you also, Harry. For we admire you."

I was trying to imagine what I could be admired for. Maybe one of the tribe had seen me playing accordion. Then I realized they simply liked me. It was quite a compliment.

"We take Sheikh Abdulla into our own bodies, so that his good qualities will become our good qualities."

I tried to remember what good qualities he had. Outside of rolling cigarettes pretty deftly, he wasn't so great. On the other hand, I was starting to panic inside. I really didn't feel like ingesting the cheek of the Sheikh, but tried to put it out of my mind.

And my mouth.

"You Christians should understand this," said my protector. "It was long ago. But I was told, when I was in your army, that in your religious service, you eat the flesh and blood of the man you consider the Son of God.

The others listened to this, not understanding his English but they looked at me like a child being educated. Which I was. And when my education came to an end, the moment of truth had arrived.

The others proceeded to pick up Sheikh Abdulla's ass in their hands and held it aloft.

My own thought was to say, "Just a moment here. The Bible thing is symbolic. I have no intention of…"

The next thought was that they were serious. And that, in a moment more emotional for them than I cared to admit, I would have to be serious as well. They wouldn't have harmed me if I hadn't eaten the Sheikh. But they had gone to all this trouble to cut up the fatty part of the man, to boil it for about 20 minutes to make it soft and malleable (the only time men would cook), and then to offer it to a supposed Nazarene like myself.

They would have been disappointed, though. So it was time, I realized almost with gratitude, time for dinner.

So we all held our piece of his ass in our hands, downed it, and had a gulp of water, water which probably was more disease-ridden than the old man. Abdulla's son said a few words in Arabic, probably from the Holy Koran, and the ceremony was over.

The ceremonial cardboard wafer-plates were removed, and the communal pot of fava beans and fire replaced them. After, I went to a surprisingly gentle sleep.

Today, friends ask how he "tasted." Well, I usually answer, the taste was okay, a bit bland, the presentation was without imagination. Perhaps his derriere might have rested in the middle of a salad, or wrapped in vine leaves like a Turkish *dolma*. A slice of cucumber might have done wonders.

Or sometimes I give that old culinary platitude that Sheikh Abdulla "tasted like chicken, only more gamey."

Usually, I tell the truth, that it was the opposite of Bill Clinton's description of pot: I inhaled but didn't taste.

No, Sheikh Abdulla's ass was boiled to a pulp, and it was conveniently throat-sized, so one did not have to chew, savor, or swirl in the mouth like a Cabernet Sauvignon. I simply swallowed.

Looking back, it is evident that just as one swallow does not make a summer, one bit of flesh does not make a cannibal. But it certainly was more than a symbolic ritual. I had pleased my hosts and pleased myself.

I left the tribe four days later for more Middle Eastern adventures, but of course always remembered them. They were good people, taking in a stranger like me. Then again (sometimes I think ghoulishly), I took in a stranger myself.

Harry Rolnick also contributed "The Great Durian Airline Odyssey" in Part Three.

SETH ZUCKERMAN

Whales

Getting beyond bumper-sticker chic.

TWO MORNINGS AFTER THE MAKAH INDIANS KILLED THEIR FIRST whale in more that 70 years, I lie on my stomach in a tidepool near my home on the California coast. Groping far under a ledge, I find what I am looking for: a hefty abalone, more than a handspan in length.

I work my pry bar under the mollusk and pop it from the rock. It is my third of the day, leaving one more before I'd reach the legal limit, but I decide I've had enough—one for myself and one each for two neighbors.

Like the Makah with respect to their whale, I would probably survive without this abalone, but it connects me with the wild in the ecosystem that is my home. For people tied to a particular place—as the Makah are, as I have chosen to be—it is a relationship that enriches and anchors our lives.

This connection invites inhabitants to restrain their consumption so that the gifts of nature might perpetuate themselves. In fact, the Makah ceased their pursuit of gray whales in the 1920s; a quarter-century before industrial nations stopped hunting them as well.

Since the Makah took their whale off the Washington Coast, their culture has come under intense scrutiny. Observers note the modern ways adopted by the Makah—using a gun to dispatch the whale, giving chase in a motorboat, washing down chunks of blubber with Coca-Cola.

Rather than deconstructing Makah culture, we would do well to inspect our own. Most of the Makahs' critics would have us believe that whales are for viewing, not eating. They suggest the tribe forgo whale hunting in favor of other pursuits, including a whale-watching business.

On one level, theirs is an understandable reaction to the view that treats nature as a commodity, recognizing no limits and converting nature into profit as quickly as possible. This value system pushed whales to the brink of extinction and gave us clearcut forests and the Exxon *Valdez* oil spill.

The look-but-don't-touch position, however, is perilous. It's powerful to encounter whales in their element, but to define watching them as the only legitimate interaction leads to a slippery slope. What else in the wild is just for watching—deer, chanterelle mushrooms, blackberries? Each is as beautiful and sacred as a whale. Humans draw sustenance from other organisms and have an impact on the wild if only by dedicating land and water to agriculture.

Partisans of the for-eyes-only view separate themselves from the biosphere that supports us all. They treat nature as a peep show, not a drama in which they play a role. Even now that gray whale populations have rebounded and the mammals have been removed from the endangered species list, "Save the Whales" adheres to their minds the way old bumper stickers cling to cars.

The Makahs' hunt symbolizes a third way: nature as our very context for being. The gray whale is one of several edible creatures at the tip of the Olympic Peninsula that together make possible a way of life. The Makah can take one for food, knowing their action does not threaten the whales and the web of marine life to which they belong. They might agree with the deep ecologists' credo that all living things are connected, but they don't exclude themselves.

Humans too, are part of the great chain of being, whether we

are predators on the ocean, or prey in grizzly country, or inadvertently nourishing a mosquito in the woods. The fact that we
are sentient beings does not exempt us, any more than it exempts
the whales.

Back home, I sauté the abalone in butter and garlic. With each
bite I am reminded that Homo sapiens continues to be welcome
on this planet. To accept that welcome, we must embrace our role
as respectful participants in nature, not as its masters nor as couch
potatoes tuned to Mutual of Omaha's *Wild Kingdom*.

Seth Zuckerman covers the Pacific Northwest for the Tidepool *online news
service. He lives in Petrolia, California where he is active in watershed
restoration.*

PART FIVE

THE LAST WORD

MEGAN MCNAMER

* * *

Soup of the Day

It's been simmering for years.

RECENTLY I SHARED A TABLE AT A CROWDED RESTAURANT IN
Taipei with a silk-suited Taiwanese businessman. We exchanged
pleasant smiles but no more as he put away his wet umbrella. I pe-
rused the pictorial menu and pointed my request to the matter-of-
fact waitress.

As I did so, I was remembering a diner I used to go to twenty
years before. I was on my first foreign adventure then, just out of
college. The diner was next to the old Taipei train station—since
replaced by a grand temple-like structure that reduces the station
of my memory to a country stop.

There's nothing like that diner anymore. Nothing on the face
of the earth. That's how you feel when you return to a place you
haven't seen for so long: crack the lid on the details of your memories, and you set in motion a kind of mortality for them. I could
remember that diner perfectly until I tried to revisit it.

It was full of many wobbly wooden tables, each with a centerpiece of worn chopsticks clustered in a glass that shuddered with
the passing of the trains. It smelled of garlic and incense and pork
and seemed to be half-outdoors, the pound and hiss of winter
rain mixing with waves of shouted discussion, crackling oil, and

continuous laughter. It was a restaurant for families and friends to gather in, but it had that diner feel: basic provisions, no fuss, tasty and cheap, *now.*

"*Swaaaahn, lah, taaaaahng!*" The waiter would raise his eyebrows high and call to the faraway kitchen my carefully conveyed order for hot and sour soup, his voice rising and swooping like a shrike, his delivery carrying the authority of the most important general of the Peking opera. He made me feel that I had arrived, after a long deliberation, at the only perfect choice.

The diner was a good place to be generally mute and mysterious as a *yi ge rén*—a "one person"—the definition I proffered to the girl who would find me a spot at the tables she cleared. I felt well situated there, a rare feeling for me during that disoriented time. I was happy to be alone but not *all* alone—the exact condition required for nursing the huge wound of homesickness.

I had come to Taiwan to learn Chinese, penetrate Otherness, and become an Asia expert. Instead, I was spending a lot of time reading mystery novels, writing exiled thoughts, and penning tortured epistles home on those crinkly, pre-E-mail aerograms. I would hunker down with my books, papers, and a bowl of comfort food and try to ignore the giggling schoolboys with shaved heads who shoved each other into my view. They seemed to be everywhere, wanting to practice their English conversation. I felt that I already spent too many hours enacting frivolous encounters in American slang at the many teaching jobs I'd patched together to pay the rent. ("Hi, Mary, what's happening? Do you want to boogie? Far out.") Off duty, I wouldn't cooperate.

"I'm Romanian. I don't speak English," I sometimes said to the boys who actually approached. Then I'd scowl at their shaved heads, like those that had rubbed my upper arm raw on the crowded buses all through the sauna-hot summer, disrupting my alienation.

Twenty years later, while unwrapping my paper-encased chopsticks, I looked again at my sleek, silk-suited tablemate. Could he have been one of those grinning boys with the sandpaper hair? He was about the right age. If so, he had a new agenda. I watched him anxiously try to answer his ringing leather purse. When he forgot to turn on the cell phone he'd clicked open, he laughed—for the benefit of the crowd in general. I was neither here nor there to him, neither now nor then. Which was only fair, I knew, as I sat there pondering what words I myself might say to practice my Chinese. ("Hello, Harry. Can you tell me the way to the train station? No problem.")

I didn't come up with anything, and it didn't matter. I'm, O.K. now with not being an Asia expert. I had returned to Taiwan simply for a short-term, painless vacation. And I was meshing fine with the lunchtime crowd.

But I missed that old diner, the feeling of dreaming in the din. Alienation is sweet when you're 23. I missed my old homesick self. I missed my exchanges with the waiter. I missed the soup. There's no soup like that anymore. Nowhere in the world.

Travel at its best is like theater, just as theater is its own kind of trip. Both create boundaries around a heightened life. A simple order for food can become a weighty matter of urgent necessity, summoning joy. That long-ago waiter's performance made me feel vividly placed, at the exact moment, within a sure proscenium. Such was the immediacy in his ordering of hot-and-sour soup on a raw winter evening, his voice ringing with conviction.

Megan McNamer and her husband John Carter live in Missoula, Montana. They have two sons, who some day will set out in search of soup.

Recommended Reading

Ackerman, Diane. *A Natural History of the Senses*. New York: Vintage Books, 1990.

Brillat-Savarin, Jean Anthelme. M.F.K. Fisher, trans. *The Physiology of Taste*. New York: Harvest/HBJ, 1959.

Davidson, James N. *Courtesans and Fishcakes: The Consuming Passions of Classical Athens*. New York: Thomas Dunne Book, 1998.

Dumas, Alexandre. Louis Coleman, trans. *Alexandre Dumas' Dictionary of Cuisine*. New York: Avon Books, 1958.

Ebensten, Hanns. *Volleyball with the Cuna Indians: And Other Gay Travel Adventures*. New York: Penguin, 1994.

Gough, Laurie. *Kite Strings of the Southern Cross: A Woman's Travel Odyssey*. San Francisco: Travelers' Tales, 1999; Toronto: Turnstone Press, 1998.

Jenkins, Emily. *Tongue First: Adventures in Physical Culture*. New York: An Owl Book, 1998.

Krich, John. *Won Ton Lust: Adventures in Search of the World's Best Chinese Restaurant*. New York: Kodansha International, 1997.

Kumin, Maxine. *Women, Animals and Vegetables: Essays and Stories*. New York: W.W. Norton and Company, 1994.

Mayes, Frances. *Under the Tuscan Sun: At Home in Italy*. New York: Broadway Books, 1996.

Olsen, W. Scott, and Scott Cairns, eds. *The Sacred Place: Witnessing the Holy in the Physical World*. Salt Lake City: University of Utah Press, 1996.

Raban, Jonathan. *Old Glory: A Voyage Down the Mississippi*. New York: Vintage Departures, 1981.

Read, Jan, and Maite Manjon. *Catalonia: Traditions, Places, Wine and Food*. London: The Herbert Press Ltd., 1992.

Read, Piers Paul. *Alive: The Story of the Andes Survivors*. New York: Avon Books, 1975.

Robbins, Maria Polushkin. *A Cook's Alphabet of Quotations*. New York: A Dutton Book, 1991.

Steingarten, Jeffrey. *The Man Who Ate Everything: And Other Gastronomic Feats, Disputes, and Pleasurable Pursuits*. New York: Borzoi Books, 1997.

Urrea, Luis Alberto. *By the Lake of Sleeping Children: The Secret Life of the Mexican Border*. New York: Anchor Books, 1996.

Wilson, Darryl Babe. *The Morning the Sun Went Down*. Berkeley: Heyday Books, 1998.

Yeadon, David. *The Back of Beyond: Travels to the Wild Places of the Earth*. New York: HarperCollins, 1991.

Index

Acknowledgements

First, I want to thank Susan Brady, because if I don't, she will punish me. And she might punish me anyway! (Susan is the one who keeps the machinery of production humming at Travelers' Tales.) Thanks to the ever-awake Sean O'Reilly for colluding and conspiring with me in sussing out the best material possible, and for being as ready with an opinion as a cavalier is with a sword. Thanks also to the rest of the Travelers' Tales team who had a hand in this book including Lisa Bach, Deborah Greco, Cynthia Lamb, Jennifer Leo, Natanya Pearlman, and Tara Weaver. And thanks to James O'Reilly and Larry Habegger who, after our last literary feast, said, "Ah. That was good, Richard. Let's do it again."

Frontispiece from "Of Rain Forests and Rivers" by Holly St. John Bergon reprinted from the Summer 1998 issue of *Terra Nova: Nature & Culture.* Copyright © 1998 by Holly St. John Bergon. Reprinted by permission of the author.

"Breakfast in Fiji" by Laurie Gough excerpted from *Kite Strings of the Southern Cross: A Woman's Travel Odyssey* by Laurie Gough. Copyright © 1998, 1999 by Laurie Gough. Reprinted by permission of Travelers' Tales, Inc. and Turnstone Press.

"Seduction à la Carte" by Thom Elkjer published with permission from the author. Copyright © 1999 by Thom Elkjer.

"Cat Fight *Cachapas*" by Lara Naaman published with permission from the author. Copyright © 1999 by Lara Naaman.

"The First Supper" by David Robinson published with permission from the author. Copyright © 1999 by David Robinson.

"Pizza Love" by Fredda Rosen published with permission from the author. Copyright © 1999 by Fredda Rosen.

"Doing Rumours" by Kelly Simon published with permission from the author. Copyright © 1999 by Kelly Simon.

"Eat, Drink, Man, Woman" by Heather Corinna published with permission from the author. Copyright © 1999 by Heather Corinna.

"The Last Meal" by Michael Paterniti reprinted from the May 1998 issue of *Esquire.* Copyright © 1998 by Michael Paterniti. Reprinted by permission of International Creative Management, Inc.

About the Editor

Richard Sterling is the travel editor of *Fiery Foods Magazine* and the editor of the best-selling *Travelers' Tales Food: A Taste of the Road,* winner of the Lowell Thomas Silver Award for Best Travel Book. He is the author of *The Fearless Diner: Travel Tips and Wisdom for Eating Around the World* (Travelers' Tales 1998), and co-author of *The Unofficial Guide to San Francisco* (Macmillan 1998). He is at work on the first two (Vietnam and Spain) of a series of culinary guides for Lonely Planet called *World Food* to be released in 2000. He lives in Berkeley, California where he is very often politically incorrect.

TRAVELERS' TALES GUIDES
LOOK FOR THESE TITLES IN THE SERIES

FOOTSTEPS: THE SOUL OF TRAVEL
A NEW IMPRINT FROM TRAVELERS' TALES GUIDES

An imprint of Travelers' Tales Guides, the Footsteps series unveils new works by first-time authors, established writers, and reprints of works whose time has come…again. Each book will fire your imagination, disturb your sleep, and feed your soul.

KITE STRINGS OF THE SOUTHERN CROSS
A Woman's Travel Odyssey
By Laurie Gough
ISBN 1-885211-30-9
400 pages, $24.00, Hardcover

THE SWORD OF HEAVEN
A Five Continent Odyssey to Save the World
By Mikkel Aaland
ISBN 1-885211-44-9
350 pages, $24.00, Hardcover

SPECIAL INTEREST

THE FEARLESS SHOPPER
How to Get the Best Deals on the Planet
By Kathy Borrus
ISBN 1-885211-39-2, 200 pages, $12.95

Check with your local bookstore for these titles
or visit our web site at www.travelerstales.com.

$\mathscr{S}$PECIAL INTEREST

THE GIFT OF BIRDS:
True Encounters with Avian Spirits
Edited by Larry Habegger & Amy Greimann Carlson
ISBN 1-885211-41-4, 275 pages, $17.95

TESTOSTERONE PLANET:
True Stories from a Man's World
Edited by Sean O'Reilly, Larry Habegger & James O'Reilly
ISBN 1-885211-43-0, 300 pages, $17.95

THE PENNY PINCHER'S PASSPORT TO LUXURY TRAVEL
The Art of Cultivating Preferred Customer Status
By Joel L. Widzer
ISBN 1-885211-31-7, 253 pages, $12.95

DANGER!
Ttue Stories of Trouble and Survival
Edited by James O'Reilly, Larry Habegger & Sean O'Reilly
ISBN 1-885211-32-5, 336 pages, $17.95

FAMILY TRAVEL:
The Farther You Go, the Closer You Get
Edited by Laura Manske
ISBN 1-885211-33-3, 368 pages, $17.95

✒PECIAL INTEREST

THE GIFT OF TRAVEL:
The Best of Travelers' Tales
Edited by Larry Habegger, James O'Reilly & Sean O'Reilly
ISBN 1-885211-25-2, 240 pages, $14.95

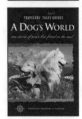

THERE'S NO TOILET PAPER...ON THE ROAD LESS TRAVELED:
The Best of Travel Humor and Misadventure
Edited by Doug Lansky
ISBN 1-885211-27-9, 207 pages, $12.95

A DOG'S WORLD:
True Stories of Man's Best Friend on the Road
Edited by Christine Hunsicker
ISBN 1-885211-23-6, 257 pages, $12.95

✑OMEN'S TRAVEL

A WOMAN'S PASSION FOR TRAVEL
More True Stories from A Woman's World
Edited by Marybeth Bond & Pamela Michael
ISBN 1-885211-36-8, 375 pages, $17.95

SAFETY AND SECURITY FOR WOMEN WHO TRAVEL
By Sheila Swan & Peter Laufer
ISBN 1-885211-29-5, 159 pages, $12.95

$\mathcal{W}$OMEN'S TRAVEL

WOMEN IN THE WILD:
True Stories of Adventure and Connection
Edited by Lucy McCauley
ISBN 1-885211-21-X, 307 pages, $17.95

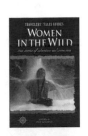

A MOTHER'S WORLD:
Journeys of the Heart
Edited by Marybeth Bond & Pamela Michael
ISBN 1-885211-26-0, 233 pages, $14.95

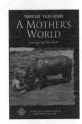

A WOMAN'S WORLD:
True Stories of Life on the Road

——— ★ ✱ ★ ———
Winner of the Lowell
Thomas Award for Best
Travel Book—Society of
American Travel Writers

Edited by Marybeth Bond
Introduction by Dervla Murphy
ISBN 1-885211-06-6
475 pages, $17.95

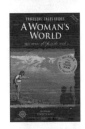

GUTSY WOMEN:
Travel Tips and Wisdom for the Road
By Marybeth Bond
ISBN 1-885211-15-5, 123 pages, $7.95

GUTSY MAMAS:
**Travel Tips and Wisdom for
Mothers on the Road**
By Marybeth Bond
ISBN 1-885211-20-1, 139 pages, $7.95

ℬODY & SOUL

THE ADVENTURE OF FOOD:
True Stories of Eating Everything
Edited by Richard Sterling
ISBN 1-885211-37-6, 375 pages, $17.95

THE ROAD WITHIN:
**True Stories of Transformation
and the Soul**
*Edited by Sean O'Reilly, James O'Reilly
& Tim O'Reilly*
ISBN 1-885211-19-8, 459 pages, $17.95

*Small Press Book
Award Winner and
Benjamin Franklin
Award Finalist*

LOVE & ROMANCE:
True Stories of Passion on the Road
Edited by Judith Babcock Wylie
ISBN 1-885211-18-X, 319 pages, $17.95

FOOD:
A Taste of the Road
Edited by Richard Sterling
Introduction by Margo True
ISBN 1-885211-09-0
467 pages, $17.95

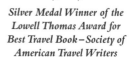

*Silver Medal Winner of the
Lowell Thomas Award for
Best Travel Book – Society of
American Travel Writers*

THE FEARLESS DINER:
**Travel Tips and Wisdom for Eating
around the World**
By Richard Sterling
ISBN 1-885211-22-8, 139 pages, $7.95

COUNTRY GUIDES

AUSTRALIA
True Stories of Life Down Under
Edited by Larry Habegger & Amy Greimann Carlson
ISBN 1-885211-40-6, 375 pages, $17.95

AMERICA
Edited by Fred Setterberg
ISBN 1-885211-28-7, 550 pages, $19.95

JAPAN
Edited by Donald W. George
& Amy Greimann Carlson
ISBN 1-885211-04-X, 437 pages, $17.95

ITALY
Edited by Anne Calcagno
Introduction by Jan Morris
ISBN 1-885211-16-3, 463 pages, $17.95

INDIA
Edited by James O'Reilly & Larry Habegger
ISBN 1-885211-01-5, 538 pages, $17.95

$\mathscr{C}$OUNTRY GUIDES

FRANCE
Edited by James O'Reilly, Larry Habegger
& Sean O'Reilly
ISBN 1-885211-02-3, 517 pages, $17.95

MEXICO
Edited by James O'Reilly & Larry Habegger
ISBN 1-885211-00-7, 463 pages, $17.95

THAILAND
Edited by James O'Reilly
& Larry Habegger
ISBN 1-885211-05-8
483 pages, $17.95

**Winner of the Lowell
Thomas Award for Best
Travel Book – Society of
American Travel Writers**

SPAIN
Edited by Lucy McCauley
ISBN 1-885211-07-4, 495 pages, $17.95

NEPAL
Edited by Rajendra S. Khadka
ISBN 1-885211-14-7, 423 pages, $17.95

COUNTRY GUIDES

BRAZIL

*Edited by Annette Haddad & Scott Doggett
Introduction by Alex Shoumatoff*
ISBN 1-885211-11-2
452 pages, $17.95

CITY GUIDES

HONG KONG

Edited by James O'Reilly, Larry Habegger & Sean O'Reilly
ISBN 1-885211-03-1, *439 pages, $17.95*

PARIS

Edited by James O'Reilly, Larry Habegger & Sean O'Reilly
ISBN 1-885211-10-4, *417 pages, $17.95*

SAN FRANCISCO

Edited by James O'Reilly, Larry Habegger & Sean O'Reilly
ISBN 1-885211-08-2, *491 pages, $17.95*

ᎡEGIONAL GUIDES

HAWAI'I
True Stories of the Island Spirit
Edited by Rick & Marcie Carroll
ISBN 1-885211-35-X, 416 pages, $17.95

GRAND CANYON
True Stories of Life Below the Rim
Edited by Sean O'Reilly,
James O'Reilly & Larry Habegger
ISBN 1-885211-34-1, 296 pages, $17.95

SUBMIT YOUR OWN TRAVEL TALE

Do you have a tale of your own that you would like to submit to
Travelers' Tales? We highly recommend that you first read one or more
of our books to get a feel for the kind of story we're looking for. For
submission guidelines and a list of titles in the works, send a SASE to:

Travelers' Tales Submission Guidelines
330 Townsend Street, Suite 208, San Francisco, CA 94107

or send email to *guidelines@travelerstales.com*
or visit our Web site at **www.travelerstales.com**

You can send your story to the address above or via email to
submit@travelerstales.com. On the outside of the envelope, *please indicate what country/topic your story is about*. If your story is selected for
one of our titles, we will contact you about rights and payment.

We hope to hear from you. In the meantime, enjoy the stories!